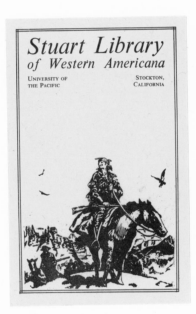

THE MINING FRONTIER
*Contemporary Accounts from the American West
in the Nineteenth Century*

TH

# MINING FRONTIER

CONTEMPORARY ACCOUNTS FROM THE

AMERICAN WEST IN THE NINETEENTH CENTURY

*Collected and Edited by Marvin Lewis*

UNIVERSITY OF OKLAHOMA PRESS  :  NORMAN

*Library of Congress Catalog Card Number: 67–15581*

Copyright 1967 by the University of Oklahoma Press, Publishing Division of the University. Composed and printed at Norman, Oklahoma, U.S.A., by the University of Oklahoma Press.

To my father, Isaac Lewis

# *Acknowledgments*

My friend and fellow researcher, Paul Ton of Denver, Colorado, assisted me in collecting and microfilming some of the materials that appear in this book. My thanks are extended to the Bancroft Library of the University of California, the Western History Department of the Denver Public Library, the Colorado Historical Society, the California State Library, the San Francisco Public Library, The Society of California Pioneers, the Huntington Library at San Marino, the University of Nevada Library, and Newton B. Drury for permission to quote from *An Editor on the Comstock Lode*, by Wells Drury.

# Introduction

This collection covers unexplored territory in the journalism of the Far West. The cultural environment in which men like Bret Harte, Mark Twain, and Joaquin Miller took root, grew, and matured is mirrored best in the work of the frontier press. Because the Far Western mining frontier was the scene of rapidly shifting events, the episodic and fleeting were paramount; most writing was merely grist for the print mills and was quickly lost in columns of newspaper print. But the files of the frontier press preserve a record of that writing which mirrored the confident and ebullient life of the times. The spell and traditions of frontier mining, evoked for participants and near contemporaries through the popular media, is represented in the pages of this book.

Journalism throve in the midst of movement and change. The discovery of gold in California opened a dramatic epoch in the colonization of the American continent. The mining booms peopled mountain fastnesses over thousands of miles. Wilderness and savage life gave way to an army of industry that was individualistic, enterprising, and freedom-loving. Those who had known the security of settled life became wild, free men. The mining population experienced epic adventure outside the well-trodden road of war; but frontier conditions exacted nevertheless a heavy toll of lives through accident, sickness, and homicide. Cities sprang up that brought the wares of the world's metropolises to the Pacific Coast. The mining frontier brought in its wake sporadic outbursts of prosperity, progress, and disorder.

The opening of the Far West progressed steadily after the discovery of gold in 1848. The California segment of the Pacific slope augmented its non-Indian population from about 14,000 in 1848 to 380,000 in 1860, gave birth to cities and a vigorous cultural life, and saw the multiplication of wealth. The Golden State within a decade provided men, materials, and money for the mining rushes to Fraser River, Idaho, Montana, and Nevada. Four years before the Union Pacific Railroad was authorized by Congress in 1862, the Pikes Peak rush was underway with untold consequences for the Plains Indians and the territorial future of Colorado. With the Pikes Peak rush the population of the area, known as Jefferson Territory, zoomed from almost nothing to the 34,277 figure of the 1860 census; but not until the 1870's, when Colorado began to realize her early mining promise, did the population show a second substantial increase. The Black Hills gold rush of 1875 culminated the push of the railroads and the farmers into Dakota Territory. There was hardly a territory that emerged in the Far West during the second half of the century that did not benefit in material growth from the impetus of mining booms.

The lures that made possible the rapid colonization of the Far West were real enough. The society of a new mining region was open, free, and independent; men reveled in dreams of opportunity and freedom of action. Each succeeding boom revived faded hopes and kept people optimistic and vital. In the first two or three years after the discovery of gold in California almost everyone shared in the prosperity of the diggings. Without doubt the work was hard, the privations were great, and there were those who quit mining in disgust. A government-sponsored survey published in 1867—the *Reports upon the Mineral Resources of the United States*—stated that, in California alone between July 1, 1849 and January 1, 1850, one-fifth of the immigration of about ninety thousand persons perished within six months after

x

arriving. Yet for those who survived, time was valuable, gold was everywhere, and, for the most part, work of every description was plentiful. Wages were at a peak of sixteen dollars a day in 1848 and the possibility of a rich strike bolstered courage and hope.

Between 1848 and 1853 mining provided a living, but by the end of 1853 the rich spots were few and wages had declined to five dollars a day, heralding the close of the peak period of prosperity for unskilled labor in California. With their simple implements the diggers had exhausted the streams and gravel beds. Partnerships of miners which formed pooled their energy and money in washing dirt from mountains and lifting rivers from their beds. As a parallel development miner-enterprisers began to work quartz rock along the slopes of the Sierra Nevada. Businessmen had proceeded with too much speed and confidence and by 1855 they had overextended themselves in loans and speculation at a time when the surface diggings were in decline and the shift to large scale quartz operations had merely begun. With the refinement and expansion of quartz mining operations in California, the discovery of placer gold in British Columbia, Idaho and Montana, and of gold and silver ore in Nevada, a new period of prosperity dawned for California.

What the Mother Lode had been to California, the Comstock Lode was to Nevada. Energy, labor, and intelligence were poured into the Comstock. The efforts of the ill-fated Grosch brothers, who were the first to initiate a systematic search for silver ore in the area and who lost their lives under tragic circumstances, were as typical of Comstock energy as Farmer Peel was of the riff-raff who made their homes in Virginia City. The engineering and mining genius of the Lode was combined with a rare degree of pluck and enterprise. Adolph Sutro, at the cost of $3,500,000 and nine years of innumerable difficulties, engineered the construction of a tunnel whose purpose was to drain water from the lower levels of the Lode. The laissez-faire economics of the Comstock, represented by William Sharon of the Bank of California and John W. Mackay, James G. Fair, James C. Flood, and William S. O'Brien of the Big Bonanza fame, evolved for over a decade a restless, vigorous, opportunistic, and independent population.

While California had served as a training school for miners during the fifties, Colorado did the same for those who arrived from the plains during the Pikes Peak rush. The panic of 1857, which caused widespread poverty and unemployment in the border states, promoted a large emigration to the Rocky Mountain mines. Many of the adventurers from the plains, not inured to mountain hardships and ignorant of mining, had to turn back. For those who remained, common hopes and aims forged strong bonds. But the placers were exhausted by the early 1860's, and except for experimentation with lode mining in Gilpin County, the mining outlook was bleak. Not until 1868, when a smelting plant was set up that could reduce Gilpin County ores, did mining show a future in Colorado. The discovery of silver-bearing ores in the late 1870's near the present site of Leadville set off a mining boom that catapulted Colorado into the ranks of the major metal-mining states.

Everywhere in an opening mining region the laboring man exhibited the energy and confidence born of great expectations. The scarcity of capital gave an impetus to labor and speculation. The placer diggings were called the "poor man's paradise." Pans, picks, and shovels, later the rocker and the tom, were the main working implements. When mining went underground, expenses mounted rapidly; money was needed for drilling and blasting, hoisting and pumping machinery, lighting, ventilation and hauling devices. In some places, after the initial discoveries, groups of skilled miners combined to work a mine. For the most part the scarcity of capital and the intensely speculative nature of mining encouraged reckless business practices. Thousands who had small amounts of money invested frantically in mines and were fleeced. The sound development of a mining area was often radically upset by the lack of adequate capital, the speculative bent of the people, and outright fraud.

xii

Work in a mining area opened a wide range of opportunities. Almost everyone possessed the flexibility and desire to try his hand at any number of occupations. One day a man might be a teamster or a prospector, and on another a justice of the peace, a correspondent for a newspaper, or a speculator in mines while opening a mine of his own. A rough equality, based on future hopes and prospects, prevailed in the mines. Rossiter Raymond, for many years the government commissioner of the mining survey studies, observed in the *Mineral Resources of the States and Territories*, published in 1869, that uncertainty of fortune gave rise to "mutual consideration, self-respect, and a spirit of independence."

The free, competitive, and speculative atmosphere of the prosperous mining areas fostered both socially destructive and socially constructive behavior. Violence and lawlessness offset the vitality, individuality, and generosity of frontier mining society. Many went to the devil in this environment. There were footpads, bunko artists, sporting women, scamps, bummers, and numerous fights over building lots and mining claims. Men fought with tongues and pens, brains and hands, pistols and daggers. Yet with all the social drawbacks, character was forged under the pressure of challenging circumstances; indeed there were those like the observant John D. Borthwick, author of *Three Years in California*, who felt that the majority of California-bound emigrants in need of improvement "got licked into shape, and polished." A recognizable type evolved, marked by a brash independence, a desire to make choices, and a willingness to live with self-imposed restraints.

The competitiveness of mining society created conflicts, not the least serious of which occurred between the dominant Anglo-Saxons and the French, Mexican, Chinese, Irish, and Indian minorities. The hatred of foreigners can be traced to economic causes. The French and the Mexicans were driven from good diggings to make room for the dominant Americans, and the Chinese were despised and mistreated because they undercut the price of labor. Humorous condescension was practiced by the Americans in their more amiable moments: the strange customs of the Chinese, the indolence and gawkery of the Indians, and the national mannerisms of the Irish, French, and Germans were the butt of satire and joke. The American conquest, though punctuated with individual and mob violence, and undermined by other civilized lapses, was nevertheless the stepchild of progress in its energy and sense of opportunity.

The work in the mines called for physical stamina, initiative, enterprise, and common sense, traits generally associated with the frontier. But the mining frontier had a cultural diversity not possessed by the cattlemen's and farmers' frontier; there was room in the mines and the trading centers for individuals who knew how to make a living by their wits. Journalism attracted this class of men to its ranks and gave them some sterling opportunities, the press having tremendous influence and support in the Far West.

The mining frontier was literate by the standards common to the second half of the nineteenth century. Eight years after the discovery of gold, according to the *Golden Era* of May 4, 1856, there was a population of three-hundred thousand in California, of which two-thirds read the English language at an expense of $1,134,000. The support for newspapers and journals was enthusiastic and scores of ambitious, short-lived ventures were spawned. In 1856, eighty-nine publications were printed in California and perhaps forty thousand weekly and semi-weekly papers were received from beyond the border with the arrival of every mail steamer. The great historian of the West, Hubert Howe Bancroft, asserted that California for years surpassed New York in the support its people gave to the press.

A printer with his press was not far behind the prospectors and the miners in every new mining development. These men of ink and type were the eyes and ears of the mining army; the newspapers ran the gamut of news and information, from the local mining area to the United States and the world beyond. Editors made place in their columns for mining matters, poetry, stories, tall tales, sensational news stories, philosophy, ethics, and morality: all jumbled together in a veritable deluge of print. With the prospectors and miners they rejoiced in success, commiserated in misfortune, provided mirth in all seasons, and succumbed to the speculative crazes, the perfervid optimism, and the immorality.

The press of California provided the journalistic leadership and innovation in the Far West. From the beginning with the publication of the *Alta California* in 1849, the *Golden Era* in 1852, the *Pioneer Magazine* in 1854, and *Hutchings' Illustrated California Magazine* in 1856, the aim was to cover the mining scene thoroughly and to provide fare that would inform and amuse the miners and ranchers of California. In later decades the *Overland Monthly* and the San Francisco *Argonaut* preserved the romance and realism of mining life. California's sister state, Nevada, had a vigorous press staffed by veteran Argonauts. The sagebrush school of journalism in the sixties and the seventies was known in newspaper offices everywhere for its original style; and men like Joseph T. Goodman, Denis McCarthy, Alf Doten, C. C. Goodwin, William Wright, Rollin Daggett, Samuel Clemens, Fred Hart, and William O. Forbes shared the same iconoclasm, realism, and love of fun in their writing. Most of the talents in this field whose copy appeared in the California and Nevada newspapers were quoted and emulated by editors in the other mining regions.

To turn the pages of the *Alta California*, the *Golden Era*, the *Territorial Enterprise*, or any number of other Far Western newspapers is to come face to face with the reality of the mining frontier. The work of the press provides a record encompassing the events, thoughts, and passions of an epoch. The chroniclers bring us to the heart of frontier existence in capturing the energy and confidence, the liberty and equality, the high-spirited jocosity and physical exuberance, attributes which are as much a part of the legend as the grisly violence.

Almost the entire press of the Far West speaks as one in

asserting the overall progressive character of frontier mining life. It was the age of the miner and the harping criticism of frontier society, coming from proper Bostonians armed with middle-class Victorian piety, irritated frontiersmen. Even though the missionaries and evangelists were enormously active in California from the opening gold rush decade, they failed to "make CALIFORNIA the MASSACHUSETTS of the PACIFIC." The mining frontier epoch was rowdy, bumptious, and irrepressible; successive gold and silver rushes kept the Far West stirred up and its people vigorously individualistic and irreverent.

The journalists and writers involved in the mainstream of mining life were liberal men who were little concerned with Eastern middle-class sensibilities. The petty sins and immoralities of the frontier brethern did not make them wince, and for the sake of individual freedom they were willing to tolerate along with everyone else a great deal of noisy exhibitionism. They knew that, even with all the faults mining society had, there were the redeeming virtues making life tolerable, even enjoyable. Vitality and high spirits softened the defeats, disappointments, and hardships of frontier life.

The mood is revealed most clearly by the conversational gusto of the journalists. There were some splendid talkers among them. William Wright, the "Dan De Quille" of the *Territorial Enterprise*, and Wells Drury, the Comstock editor, were tireless in recalling the vigor of their times. Mark Twain's *Roughing It* must have been talked out first in the Virginia City and the San Francisco saloons. The better saloon resounded with conversational high jinks; congenial company spouted poetry, concocted fantastic lies, and argued politics. Much of the fun found its way into the Far Western newspapers.

There was a sense of enjoyment and power for newspaper people in presiding over the rough and tumble public life of a mining community. Journalistic observations made on the character of men, society, and institutions were often caustic and to the point. Men engaged in public business were buried under an

xvi

avalanche of imprecations and epithets. Public censors prided themselves in the marked abruptness of their criticism. One of these iconoclasts, Dave F. Day, a peppery columnist and the owner of his own sheet, which was published in Ouray, a mining town in southwestern Colorado, defended in the August 2, 1877, issue of the *Solid Muldoon* a brand of journalism that reeked defiance: "The *Solid Muldoon* fights its political and party enemies in the broad, open light of day, and in language that permits of but one construction."

The love of a good fight was so genuinely enjoyed by participants and onlookers that a few contusions and broken bones were considered necessary sacrifices in the life of political, ethical, and social man. Passionate recrimination was often the product of this type of journalism, but there were those who argued with some justification that irreverence tended to make the people more skeptical and less willing to accept a naive and uninformed view of public life. Politicos and lawmakers were eloquently parodied; the lying clubs and the mock legislative meetings fused imagination and wit with realism. The members of the "Third House of Sovereigns," numbering the most articulate members of the community, made provocative and endless fun of fuzzy-minded and irresponsible politicos. The institution had an illustrious life in Mark Twain's Nevada and was attempted in Colorado.

The frontier mining press produced a highly realistic style of journalism, charged with diverting matters and conveyed with a baroque flourish and incisiveness. Plain humor and jest were unacceptable unless clothed with the conjurations of an extravagant imagination. Men outdid one another with the grand lie to test the calibre of wit possessed by the other fellow. Mark Twain and Dan De Quille were simply more successful than the many others in fathering hoaxes.

An air of youthfulness engulfs authentic work about the American mining frontier. Mark Twain grasped the zest of frontier life in Nevada and immortalized youth, his own and that of his time, in *Roughing It*. Those great histories of the West, planned by Hubert Howe Bancroft, are soaked in the frontier's youthful sense of achievement. Locked in the files of the press is the Argonaut's adventure in California's placer camps, the hard-rock bonanza areas of Nevada, Colorado, Montana, and the Comstock, the industrial behemoth rooted in the frontier. The flush, speculative epoch of mining reflected itself in the work of the popular press. To read the quaint, old fashioned writing today is to embark on a voyage of discovery into the singular world of the frontier mining population.

# Contents

Contents

# Illustrations

PART ONE

# *Placer Mining*

# Placer Camps

A CAMP OF 1849

Forceful leadership in protecting claim rights is depicted in this story about a camp of 1849. Toward the close of 1848 mining courts were organized by the first comers in many places to legalize the parceling out of claims. The second wave of arrivals had to find unclaimed ground, move on, or challenge the claims of the first comers. Compromises between original locators and jumpers were worked out, but when a showdown became inevitable the party with the most bravado often won out. ("Praying Abe Slocum," San Francisco *Argonaut*, November 17, 1877.)

There were eight of us in the mess; all from New England; all staid, quiet, well behaved, industrious young men. It was the year '49, and the average miner of that period was not the rough, vulgar, profane, and swaggering blackguard that Joaquin Miller, Bret Harte, and Mark Twain have idealized as the California miner. A more orderly, better educated, more industrious, and well behaved set of gentlemen were never gathered together than there went forth every morning with pick, shovel, and rocker to wash the auriferous gulches of Weaver Creek in El Dorado. We lived in a log cabin of comfortable construction, a broad fire-place built of stone and mud, the deep embrasure of which accommodated one bake-kettle, frying-pan, and coffee-pot. Eight spacious bunks, canvas-bottomed and well

3

blanketed, gave us beds of luxurious ease. Our meals were good. To the baked beans, slap-jacks, coffee, and bacon, we added a barrel of butter from Boston, potted meats, sardines, sauces, and an occasional deer as the result of a Sunday in the hills. The Sabbath was not ill-spent; the Bible was not unused. If we washed our weekly shirt in the morning, we wrote our home letters in the afternoon. Our cabin could always accommodate a guest, our board was ever ready to welcome the stranger in our diggings with an abundant meal. Honesty, industry, and quiet behavior was the rule; crime and violence was the exception. Later in the mines came the bully and the bravo. The gambling saloon was opened with its seductive allurements of lights, music, drinks, and games. Our claim was a rich one, and we were acquiring rapidly that fortune for which we had dared the peril of the voyage around the Horn, and were all looking forward to that happy time when we could follow our remittances back to our New England homes. The miner's law then allowed to each worker a claim upon the gulch sixteen feet in length, running back to the hill. The laws of mining claims were settled by a miners' meeting, and were accepted and recognized as binding upon all within the district. Finally there came to us the report that a party of desperadoes from the southern mines were going to jump our claim, and I felt not a little anxious, as it was of exceptional richness, and we had no fighting man in our camp. We had a praying man—his name was Abraham Slocum—a silent, self-restrained, quiet person, who read his Bible more frequently than the rest of us, who never washed his shirts on a Sabbath day, and of whom we suspected that his Sabbath morning stroll was in part for the purpose of asking God's blessing, and invoking the divine protection in prayer. Tall, spare, and sinewy was the frame of Abe Slocum. We repaired to our diggings early on Monday morning; a short time thereafter there came upon us some seven or eight of the roughest looking men I had ever seen in the mountains. Clad mostly in buckskin, long-haired, carrying rifles in an easy, lounging way, their waists girdled with the red sash of the

4

typical mountaineer, hats broad brimmed, trousers in their boots, bowie knives and revolvers in conspicuous display. To their waists was attached the prospector's tin pan, and each had shovel, pick, and crevice knife ready for work.

"Good morning, gentlemen," said Abe Slocum, "hunting diggins I 'spose." Abe seemed to have constituted himself the spokesman of our party.

"Reckon these are pretty good ones," said their leader, the longest-haired and most brigand-looking one of their band. "And if you haint no objection, old pard, we'll just pitch alongside."

Slocum laid down his pick-axe, and deliberately crawling from his hole, said:

"My pardners and myself are just eight; you can count us. The law of these diggins gives us sixteen feet apiece. I heard you was coming, and I brought along a tape line. So if you have no objection we will measure off our ground and show you our stakes."

Abe proceeded to measure off his ground.

"From that are rock to this ere tree is just one hundred and twenty-four feet, and you are welcome to pitch in above or below us."

The leading brigand, looking carelessly at the cock of his rifle, and shifting his revolver significantly in his belt, said:

"You infernal Yanks have jumped all the best claims in these diggins, and our fellers have concluded to divide this claim. You can give us half or git; we mean business."

In the meantime our party was upon the bank, and armed as all men were armed in those early days, and awaited events.

Slocum, deliberately winding up his tape measure, reached his hand around the rock and taking out his rifle said, in a deliberate tone:

"I am a God-fearing and peaceful man, I am. I seek no quarrel with any man. I and my pardners will defend this claim with our lives, and I say to the fust man that strikes a pick into these diggins that he had better fust make his peace with God, for sure as my name is Abraham Slocum I'll send his soul to meet his Jesus."

5

There was a pause for a moment. The determination of our leader was impressive. He sat himself down upon the rock, and with a quick, nervous movement, slung his weapon to the full cock.

I cannot describe the surprised look that ran over the faces of our brigand jumpers. I saw the fading out of the bravo into pale-faced cowardice, and after some bantering words our prospectors pushed on. We were never disturbed afterward, and I have never questioned the fact that a man who prays might also fight.

Abraham Slocum is now enjoying, upon a small New England farm, the competency acquired by his bravery and his toil in the gulch of Weaver Creek in the county of El Dorado.

## Camp Equity

During the later part of 1850 the Klamath River in northern California was prospected by a party of miners, and a mining boom of short duration took place. In one of the river camps, two mining partners, unable to cease their mutual recriminations, were brought by friends before the local Justice of the Peace, but the judging of the dispute proved to be too difficult for him and the assembled miners undertook to probe for the truth in their own spontaneous manner. ("Two Miners on the Klamath," San Francisco *Argonaut*, October 25, 1879.)

In the early days of California two old and experienced gold diggers, named Jake and Jim, had been patiently working to "make their pile" in the Klamath diggings. They were called simply Jake and Jim because few of the California miners were commonly known by their proper names; generally some fanciful sobriquet was the only title by which they were known among their fellows, and thousands of graves may be seen in the Sierra Nevada and Rocky Mountain mining regions of those whose fate will ever remain unknown to their distant relatives or friends. You see by the wayside a little mound that marks a grave, and if, as rarely happens, an old settler is asked who lies there, he

6

answers: "Don't know. A party came along one day, miners, and a man called Jake took sick and died, and they buried him there." And that is all is known of a lost pioneer.

Jake and Jim had a good claim that paid, and had built a comfortable log cabin, and even had a small enclosure where they cultivated a few vegetables; for, being no longer young, having families in the East, and also having found this spot that paid fair wages, they wisely agreed to stick to it until each had got a certain amount of gold dust, which amount they had decided would be enough to return with to the old homes in the East. Every Saturday night for over a year, after their evening meal was over and the pipes were lighted, their day's work in gold dust was carefully weighed and divided, after enough had been deducted to pay their expenses. Then each one put his gold away in some place known only to himself for safe keeping.

On a Saturday afternoon in the latter part of June Jake and Jim cleaned up and washed the last spoonful of pay dirt scraped from the bed-rock of their claim. It had been a paying claim well worked out; and, as they took their tools and bag of dust to their cabin for the last time, with the pleasant verdure and flowers of summer that were around them in the grand mountain scenery of California, they felt themselves among the lucky ones that had been successful and "made their pile." Their evening meal was eaten in a jolly mood; and then their last day's work in gold was to be divided, their hidden deposits of dust to be dug up, and the next morning they would be ready for a start on the long journey to their Eastern homes.

"Well, Jim," said Jake, "as we never happened to know where each other put his dust, I reckon I'll go to my bank and remove the deposits."

So, taking up his shovel, he went to the door step, which was a large flat stone, and carefully moved it aside, and commenced digging down into the somewhat light earth. While all this was being done by Jake, Jim sat with an amazed expression watching him, but said not a word. Jake dug down three feet, and, stooping

7

in the hole, removed some earth and took out a tin can, which was heavy, and placed it on a log. Jim now found his tongue, and spoke:

"Well, Jake, if that ere ain't the dog-rotted, coolest thing I ever seen a human critter do, you can shoot me. Do yer mean ter say that tin can is yourn, and that yer put it under that ere stun?"

"Of course I do, Jim; and why shouldn't I hev done it?"

"Because, old pard, that can, I will take my Bible oath, I put, with my dust in it, buried in that hole jest three feet, by a foot rule. It was that identical tin mustard can."

"After all these years together, Jim, do yer mean ter call me a liar; and, worse, a thief?"

Both now became heated, and their passions aroused. Each word led to a worse one, and in five minutes they drew their bowie knives, and clinched in a deadly struggle. Luckily the noise brought in some miners from their camp near by, and, after a fierce resistance, they were separated, and taken before the justice at their own request. As this was not a case for Judge Lynch to decide, it was brought before a Justice of the Peace in the camp, called by the miners "Old Blowsy." The miners crowded into the Judge's cabin, and old Blowsy put on his judicial dignity, with an old, rusty black coat he always wore on such occasions, lit his pipe, filled a tumbler with whisky, and was ready to decide the case.

Jake, on his oath, first swore he put the tin can of gold dust exactly where he had taken it from. It was the identical can—a mustard can—and he would stake his life upon its being the same.

Jim swore to do exactly the same thing as regards himself.

Both the men were steady, honest miners, of unquestionable character, veracity, and well known to all.

The Judge and all present were confounded at the positive, sworn evidence of the two men, and all kinds of opinions were advanced noisily, amid confusion, tobacco smoke, and the fumes of whisky.

Sitting on a barrel in the corner, listening, but saying not a

8

word, was a well known character in the camp, known as "Whisky Bob." Bob had been a sailor, miner, packer—in fact a little of everything. But one thing he always was—lucky in mining; and whenever he chose to work, would take his rocker and tools, and disappearing for a time, return with a full bag of dust. Then Whisky Bob would go on a long spree through the mining camps, until his gold was spent, and, dead-broke, he was ready to loaf, drink, but not work unless forced to do so. It was a proverbial saying in the mines: "A sailor or a nigger for luck," for they generally were lucky in finding the gold, and the former ever ready to spend it for whisky.

Judge Blowsy was not equal to the emergency of deciding the case, and the opinions advanced to explain it were wonderful to hear. One miner said he thought the coyotes had dug up the dust, as they had been known to do it when it was buried in greasy bags. In the midst of this confusion Whisky Bob entered the room, pushing all aside, went to the Judge, and putting a package folded in an old newspaper upon the table said:

"Look a here, Jedge and feller citizens, I kin settle this ere case, I kin; if I don't, ye can bust my top lights. What's my fee for acting as jedge."

"You do that ere thing," answered Jake, "and I and my pard will give yer two ounces each."

"Yes," said Judge Blowsy, "and all the rest of us will put in four bits a piece."

"Well, then feller citizens," said Bob, "ye see, I hearn all your jabber about this ere case, and holds a court of my inward senses to justify the matter. When men gets mad and hasty like they forgets reason, 'cordingly I went to that ere hole where Jake and Jim hid their dust to prospect it judgematically. I gets down the hole, takes my knife, and there, three inches under the dirt, I finds this ere tin mustard-can of dust—just 'dentical with that ere one on the table."

And sure enough, there were two tin cans exactly alike, holding some forty pounds of gold.

"Well, that beats my time," said the Judge. "Two men take two cans, exactly the same, and hide 'em in the same hole without knowing it within three inches of each other! It's what the books call a coincidence, sure. And now, Whisky Bob, I say, jest ye take the five ounces ye've earned as jedge and make a fresh start, leaving whisky behind, and save yer money. Ye've got inward sense enough to make yer pile without whisky."

"That's so, Jedge," said Bob; "an' if I don't do it, bust my top lights."

### A COURT OF APPEAL

Jackson Creek Camp, a settlement in the Rogue River Valley of Oregon, was the scene in the autumn of 1852 of a popular call for a Court of Appeal. The creation of a new court on the authority of a mining assembly to re-examine a dispute between Sims and his partner Sprenger overrode legal and constitutional formalities. Though the case had been tried by the local alcalde, there was a strong suspicion in the camp that the alcalde had conspired with Sims to wrong Sprenger, and the miners acted vigorously to right matters. Charles Shinn used this incident in *Mining Camps* to demonstrate the power residing at the popular level in these communities. The source for his evidence is given in its entirety in this text. (William M. Turner, "Pioneer Justice in Oregon," *Overland Monthly*, First Ser., Vol. XII [March, 1874].)

Prior to January, 1852, there were no county organizations south of the Calapooia Mountains, a range stretching from the Cascades to the Pacific, and dividing western Oregon nearly midway between the Columbia and the California boundary; and for nearly a year later no courts were held in that region, other than those of the local *alcaldes*. In the summer of 1852, a rich and expensive discovery of gold on Jackson Creek, within half a mile of the present site of Jacksonville, had brought a large number of miners to that locality, both from other portions of the territory and from California. At this time, justice was dispensed within the new district by an individual named Rogers, who had been elected prior to the gold discovery. Rogers was known as a man of stubborn, willful nature, and not credited either with discernment or honesty; but, hitherto, his decisions, involving no considerable amounts of property and not outrageously unjust, had passed unquestioned by the people. When, in the fall of 1852, the mining camp was at the full tide of prosperity, a complication arose between two mining partners, involving the right to a mining claim and the settlement of a partnership, the adjudication of which was finally taken in hand by the people, and resulted in stripping a dishonest judge of his undeserved honors.

Two miners, named respectively Sprenger and Sims, owned and worked in partnership a valuable mining claim on Jackson Creek, and, late in the fall, Sims, taking the partnership funds, started for Portland to purchase a supply of provisions, leaving Sprenger at work in the claim. During his partner's absence, Sprenger met with a serious accident, which confined him to his cabin, crippled and helpless. There was a "lack of woman's nursing" in the wild mining regions, but there was no lack of kindly, generous sympathy for the unfortunate among the rough miners, and Sprenger was nursed and cared for with all the proverbial humanity of this class of people. When Sims returned, finding his partner likely to be a burden on him for the coming winter, he at once ejected him from the cabin, and took possession of the claim. Sprenger appealed to Alcalde Rogers for restitution, but appealed in vain. His suit was conducted with considerable skill by a fellow miner named Kinney. Every point of law, both territorial and local, were on his side; every principle of equity in his favor; but the pleadings of his advocate fell on the ears of a corrupt and unfeeling judge, whose decree stripped him of every dollar of his worldly possessions. His counsel, suspecting the credibility of some of Sims' witnesses, and satisfied that the trial was as unfair as the decision was unjust, demanded a new one, which was refused by the *alcalde*.

11

Poor Sprenger was almost in despair. He was a cripple, dependent on public charity, his means entirely exhausted—cheated and robbed by the man who should have stood by him in his misfortunes. In his distress, he sought the services of a neighboring miner named Prim, who, report said, was a lawyer, but who, for the sake of avoiding annoyance in petty trials where the fees were not commensurate with the lawyer's services, had kept his true calling a secret. Sprenger found the disciple of Blackstone in a tunnel, vigorously swinging his pick among the muddy and dripping boulders, looking more like a Cornish miner than an expounder of legal perplexities. Prim was disposed to disavow any knowledge of law for the sake of saving himself the trouble of a case, where, under the circumstances, defeat was certain; but his humanity overcame his selfishness, and, moved by the recital of Sprenger's grievances, he threw down his pick and espoused the injured man's cause as zealously as if expecting a generous fee. Kinney, the former counsel of Sprenger, was sought, and a consultation entered upon. Every known point of the law bearing upon the case was discussed. Every familiar maneuver or pretext, likely to assist in obtaining a new trial, was proposed, and the advocates waxed more earnest upon each examination of the subject. All, however, to no purpose. The known obduracy of the *alcalde* and his suspected collusion with Sims rose everlastingly before them, presenting an impassable barrier between them and justice. A protracted and exhaustive view of the case only left the attorneys less hopeful than ever—when Prim, in a half-soliloquy, remarked: "If we only had a Court of Appeal."

"Great God, sir!" exclaimed Kinney, springing to his feet in a state of intense excitement. "Why did we not think of that before? We will have a Court of Appeal, sir!"

Prim did not understand him, thinking he referred to a probable election and the organization of the regular judiciary, and suggested, gravely, that their client would probably starve, and reach the Court of Death, before they would get it before any earthly tribunal.

"No, sir!" continued Kinney, with increasing warmth; "I say we will have a Court of Appeal within twenty-four hours. Who made the d——d scoundrel *alcalde*? We, the people, sir! and if we have the power to create one court, we can make another high enough to try and hang the one below it, if necessary."

A new light dawned upon Prim. Kinney was right. His strong good sense, by going back to first principles and invoking the power of the people to correct an abuse which was the result of their own short-sightedness, had solved a problem that to the lawyer was full of stubborn impossibilities. A Court of Appeal was resolved on. Sprenger was immediately dispatched to summon the "boys" to a miners' meeting. He was not armed with any wordy legal process, with its angular and imperious verbiage, but with a writ that found a soft spot in every rough breast among the mining population; a writ that the miners never resisted—an appeal to their sympathy and sense of justice. Never was imperial ukase more potent. Never did the fiery cross on highland height rouse the clans more effectually than this simple appeal did the mining population in the early days; and the crippled envoy was as successful as his advocates could wish. The "boys" threw down their tools, and, deserting their claims, flocked to the town nearly a thousand strong, and in a perfect ferment of indignation. A committee waited on the *alcalde* to demand a rehearing for Sprenger; but he declined to open his court for the purpose of reversing his own judgment. Kinney at once sprung upon a stump, called the meeting to order, and suggested the organization of a Court of Appeal, and its investment with full power to review the proceedings of the court below. The proposition struck the popular chord, and the affirmative response that swelled up from the crowd, which was now in ill mood for trifling, almost drowned the speaker's voice. A gentleman named Hayden, a native of Connecticut, known for his uprightness and probity, was unanimously pointed to for the position of Chief Justice. In vain did Mr. Hayden protest and decline the proffered honor; in vain did he modestly insist that he was ignorant of law and unwilling to bear so grave a responsibility. The popular current was too strong; a wild yell of acclamation proclaimed him Judge of Appeal, investing him, in a limited sphere, with a power as supreme as ever clothed czar or sultan. The new justice did not wait for a formal certificate of election, but proceeded with the organization of his court in a manner that showed him to be a man of no ordinary business capacity. A clerk and sheriff were at once appointed, a record opened on which was spread the extraordinary proceedings of the hour, and when the court was in working order, a *mandamus* issued commanding Alcalde Rogers to appear with the records of his court. The writ was disobeyed, the *alcalde* refusing to recognize the appellate powers of the new court. An unexpected complication having thus arisen, the process was about to be enforced by the excited people, when Justice Hayden, maintaining the dignity of his court amid the greatest uproar, solved the difficulty by ordering the parties in equity to appear before him for a new trial. Sims dared not disobey, seeing that the dissolution of the high court would be the signal for popular violence, and securing the services of Orange Jacobs, a young attorney from Michigan, promptly responded, and the trial at once went on. A venire was issued for a jury— twelve good and lawful men—subpoenas issued for witnesses, and the case formally opened. Jacobs, of whom little was known except that he was recognized as a quiet, unassuming miner, appeared with an able and apparently exhaustive argument, protesting against and denying the extraordinary jurisdiction assumed by the court as contrary to the organic law of the territory, and therefore against public policy and revolutionary; and moved that the case be dismissed for want of jurisdiction. He pleaded as one wedded to his profession as an abstract science, jealous of the law's infringement for its own sake; but he appealed to a judge who sat for the dispensation of justice more than for the vindication of law, and, as might have been expected, his motion was overruled. Prim and Kinney managed the case with the skill of veteran attorneys, and in knowledge of the peculiar circumstances surrounding it overmatched their opponent, who deftly and courageously met every argument and sifted every witness with all the adroitness of a thorough legal expert. During a stubborn argument on a law point presented by Jacobs, he became so earnest as to venture to bet a small sum that it was good law and supported by ample authority. Kinney sprung to his feet triumphantly; he knew the point was law, but he knew his man, and understood the composition of the jury. Drawing his buckskin with an air of the most supreme confidence, he flung three of the old-fashioned fifty-dollar slugs upon the table, and demanded the amount of his opponent's bet. It was bluff against knowledge, and bluff won. Jacobs was a recent immigrant, without "color" in his wallet, and responded not; there was an audible smile on the faces of the jury, and the court, with becoming gravity, pronounced the point "not well taken." Jacobs fought over every inch of ground and opposed every effort of Sprenger's joint counsel with a moral heroism, that, in the face of an angry and excited crowd of spectators, was almost sublime; but he was at a sad disadvantage, and talking to a court and jury who did not care a fig for law when conflicting with their ideas of right and wrong.

The witnesses examined and the issue made, Kinney presented the case to the jury. He dwelt on the right of every citizen to the peaceful possession of his property, and on the duty every man owed to society in the protection of his neighbors' rights; but it was when he referred to the relations existing between the two men that crude human nature triumphed over legal science and skill. Drawing a distinction between partnerships in civilized communities and those in the wild mining region, where the social amenities of life were uncommon, he showed the former to be mere commercial and financial connections among men, while the latter were ties of brotherhood, sanctioned and pre-

15

scribed by custom, and imposing obligations than which there were none stronger. He told the jury that a man's partner was required to be his friend, to sustain him in evil and in good repute, to share with him in health, to nurse him in sickness, to divide his last ounce of dust with him, and to stand by him when all others had deserted him. He summed up the evidence clearly and forcibly, showing the jury, who were becoming each moment more impatient to render their verdict, that Sims had disregarded his neighbor's rights, violated the common law of the region, and robbed and abandoned—not Sprenger—but Sims' partner. It was then that decorum ceased, and the honest manhood of the rough crowd found vent in applauding cheers. The jury rose and swung their hats, forgetting the dignity of their position, while Justice Hayden with difficulty restored order, and informed them that the case was only half tried. It was now Jacobs' turn. He rose, quiet and self-possessed, conscious of a strong prejudice against himself and client, and presented an array of legal objections that under other circumstances or before another tribunal would have been most formidable; but he forgot that he was talking law to a court sitting only for the purpose of doing equity, and he talked to listless ears. The court charged the jury—an unnecessary proceeding, perhaps, so far as their understanding of the case was concerned, but necessary to sustain the proper dignity of the court, which would have been infringed had this important formula been dispensed with. The charge was one that might be a model for higher courts. His Honor instructed the jury that they must strip the case of all the legal mystifications with which Sims' counsel had surrounded it, regarding no law but that of right and wrong, and decide upon their belief of an existing state of facts established by the testimony, and in such a manner that justice would be done, though all the law in Christendom fell to the ground. And they did so decide it. At first, they experienced great difficulty in their finding. Some of them were in favor of recommending the hanging of Sims; others stoutly demanded the punishment of Rogers as *particeps criminis*. One or two suggested the mercy of the court; but the difficulty was solved by the permission of special instructions. Jacobs again objected, but he looked askance at Kinney's plethoric buckskin, and his now feeble protest was again overruled. Of course, the verdict was for the complainant, and the court at once ordered his reinstatement in possession of his claim, his share of all partnership property, and an allowance of all charges during his sickness. The decision was received with a deafening yell of applause, amid which the court adjourned. It was then that the half-smothered feeling of indignation against Rogers found vent. The evidence had disclosed unmistakable rascality and malfeasance on the part of that official, and his contemptuous noncompliance with the order of the superior court could not be passed in silence. A low sullen murmur, like the sweep of an approaching storm over a treeless prairie, was heard. Knots of angry men gathered together; louder and louder grew the tumult, till a fierce, determined voice rang out, "Hang him!" and five hundred voices hoarse with rage echoed the dreadful words that nearly paralyzed the poor wretch with terror. It was a fearful moment for Alcalde Rogers. The excited throng swayed to and fro like angry human waves. The cry swelled into maddened fury, and his life was not worth a minute's purchase, when Jacobs, Hayden, Prim, and others, sprung among them, and begged them not to stain the record of a noble day's work by the commission of a terrible and unnecessary crime. Fortunately, their counsel prevailed, and after the most strenuous exertions, Rogers was allowed his life on condition of his resigning the alcaldeship, which he immediately did without a single demurrer, glad to escape so easily. The case, however, was not over. The functions and existence of the Court of Appeal had by no means ceased, and it appearing that Rogers was in possession of part of the property of which Sprenger had been robbed, he was forced to disgorge the last dollar, which was only done by means of an execution, and justice was satisfied.

The principal parties to this case have disappeared from sight, but the remembrance of it is yet fresh among the old settlers of southern Oregon, and the proceedings therein are still of record in the archives of Jackson County. Some of the actors in this little drama are still among us. Jacobs, who stood before that exasperated mob and pleaded in behalf of the sacred principles of law, now occupies the position of Chief Justice of Washington Territory. Prim has been Chief Justice of Oregon, and is now associate Justice on the Supreme Bench of that State. "Chief Justice" Hayden has held the honorable place of Recorder for the principal town of southern Oregon for nearly twenty consecutive years, having repeatedly refused higher honors; while Kinney has long since gone to plead, in obedience to a resistless mandate, before a higher tribunal than all.

The day of the Pioneer is over. The star that he followed has reached its zenith, and he can go no farther. We may now regard him as a soldier in the cause of human advancement, whose battles have been fought and won, and he may well look back in surprise at the wonderful social and material results that have followed in his wake. The shifting sands of the desert have covered up his footsteps, but the solid and substantial foundation laid by the Pioneer for the social structure of the Far West will be as lasting as it is surprising. Separated by thousands of miles of lofty mountains and barren plains from the ties and influences of civilization, these wild rough men in the early days established a code of ethics for the regulation of the social duties, that was founded on the soundest principles of morality. Without written law, they enforced justice, and decided all questions relating to individual rights with that unerring judgment which springs from a keen discrimination between right and wrong, and is worthy of the jurisprudence of the highest civilization.

A Pioneer Justice of the Peace

Sonorian camp in Tuolumne County was organized by a

small group of miners in the spring of 1849; they elected R. S. Ham their alcalde. In the autumn of the same year there were five thousand people in camp, among whom were many Mexicans and Chileans. A town government was organized with a mayor and a council, but when the legality of its existence was called into question the government was dissolved, leaving justice for a few months in the hands of Justice Barry. This Justice of the Peace, the successor of the first alcalde and later a member of the Court of Sessions meeting at Sonora, held a court that exhibited the contemporary bias against Mexicans and a desire on his part to collect the court fees at any cost. But in spite of his eccentric manner he showed great firmness in his office and at least in this characteristic he was typical of a great number of the frontier justices of the peace. ("Pioneer Justice," San Francisco *Argonaut*, December 15, 1877.)

Judge Barry was a Justice of the Peace in Sonora, in the country of Tuolumne, in the years from 1850 to 1853. Not one of your narrow-minded, technical judges whose genius was circumscribed by the formula of precedents, or who permitted the great stream of justice to be d——d by the narrow interpolation of merely judicial minds. He was the Haroun al Raschid of the Bagdad of the southern mines. Like Ned McGowan, his jurisdiction was co-extensive with the boundaries of the State. His was not the even-handed blind justice that is idealized by a good looking female with a bandage over her eyes and a pair of evenly balanced scales. His idea of administering the law was of the aggressive character, and had he been called upon to devise an ideal representative of the law, he would have made of him a broad-shouldered, keen-eyed, double-breasted, strong-fisted, well-muscled, stalwart figure, well mounted to hunt down fugitives, with a lariat to catch them, or a good thick-lashed black whip for punishment. The only use he would have had for scales would be to weigh out the gold dust for costs.

Mr. Justice Barry kept a docket—not a thing of scraps, but

each case was carefully written out in a good round hand—and it was his pride to claim that he put everything down in black and white for reference.

To give an idea how justice was administered in Tuolumne in the good old days of '50, we print the following extracts from Justice Barry's docket, preserving his orthography, and assuring our readers that it is a literal transcript:

"No. 101. This is a case where one James Knowlton brings sute again Jose —— for feloniously and surreptiously taking, steeling, and robbing the said James Knowlton, late of San Francisco, one Buckskin purs or sacks of gold-dust of the value of 4,000 dollars.

"After heering the evidense projuced in the case, I demand of Jose —— whether he was going to plead guilty or not. Jose answered me thus: 'You find out.' For which insolent and abominable contempt of coort I find him 3 ounces, and adjudged him guilty. I sentenced him to restore the goold-dust to the court, and to receive, well laid on, 40 lashes on his bear back, and to pay the cost of the court.

"Cost of court, 5 ounces, which Jose not having I rooled that James Knowlton should pay. Deducted the amount and returned the balance to the owner, James Knowlton.

"July 9, 1851. Rec'd C. Barry, J.P.; U.H. Brown, constable.

"No. 516. This is a suit for mule steeling, in which Jesus Ramirez is indited for steeling one black mare mule branded O, with a 5 in it, from Sheriff Work. George swares the mule in question is his'n, and I believe so to on hearing the caze. I found Jesus Ramirez gilty of feloniously, and against the law made and provided, and the dignity of the people of Sonora, steelin the aforesaid mare mule. Sentenced him to pay the cost of court— $10—and find him $100 more as a terrour to all evil-doers. Jesus Ramirez not having any munny to pay with, I rooled that George Work should pay the cost of coort, as well as the fine, and in default of payment that the said one mare mule be sold by the constable, John Luvey, or other officer of the court, to meet the expenses of the costs of court, as also the payment of the fine aforesaid.

R.C. BARRY, J.P.

SONORA, August 21, 1851
JOHN LUVEY, Constable

"N.B.—Barber, the lawyer for George Work, insolently told me there was no law for me to rool so. I told him I didn't care a damn for his book law; that I was the law myself. He continued to jaw back. I told him to shut up, but he wouldn't. I fined him $50, and committed him to goal for 5 days for contempt of court, in bringing my roolings and dissions into disreputableness, and as a warning to unrooly persons not to controdict this court.

"No. 606. This was a suit between two gamboleers. E. Kroke, the gamboleer who sooed Sam Heed the gamboleer, to recover 3,000 dolers won at ceards. After much swarin one way and another the lawyers, H. P. Barber and Leander Quint, argooed the caze which, after a long time, they got through with. I descided that Barber was right, whereupon Quint said please, your honor, I never can get justice in your court—putting out his finger and thumb. I told him the likes of him in my country often lost their fingers tealing corn or chickens, and that if I had anything to say he never should have justice here. I ordered him to hold his tung and shet up. When he went out of court he began to grumble again. I ordered John Luvey, the constable, to arrest him and bring him into court before me—which he done— and I then fined him $25 for contempt of court.

"Cost of court, $100—which was paid."

R.C. BARRY, J.P.

SONORA, September 19, 1851.

### A MOB SCENE AT ROUGH AND READY

T. H. Hittell, in his *History of California*, related that in 1850 in Nevada County a band of cutthroats known as the "Forty

Thieves" seized an innocent man to cover up their own malodorous trail, tried and convicted him of stealing three hundred dollars, and inflicted fifty lashes upon him while the real culprit stood by. The event described by Hittell coincides with the details of a story that appeared years later in the San Francisco *Call*. The author recalled the winter of 1850 as the time, Rough and Ready in Nevada County as the scene, the "Sydney Ducks" as the mob, and an innocent man as the victim. The year 1850 in Nevada County saw lynch law becoming the strong arm of both honest men and rogues, and the story printed by the *Call* reconstructed an obscure incident, probably the one cited by Hittell, which throws light on the clandestine operations of bands of desperadoes roaming the Sierra Nevada during the early mining days. (Thomas N. Wand, "Early Days in the Mountains," San Francisco *Call*, July 21, 1889.)

One morning during the winter of 1850, "after the water came," I broke my long-handled mining shovel, and to get it mended, as well as to purchase a pair of red blankets and a paper of tacks, left my cabin and went down to Rough and Ready, Nevada County—a place that still bears the same name as it did in early days. Leaving the shovel with a blacksmith for an hour or two, I went up to Donohoe's store—Joseph A. Donohoe, now of the firm of Donohoe, Kelly & Co., bankers, in San Francisco—bought my blankets for an ounce (gold), and the tacks for a quarter-ounce. Tacks were tacks in those days, I can tell you. Having got through with my limited business I loafed 'round the little settlement, taking in such points as it afforded. It being early in the morning, there were few people astir. The old California pioneers and the natives were not early risers. Like most of the old proverbs brought from the East, the well-known one of "Early to bed and early to rise will make a man healthy and wealthy and wise" had been set aside for a new reading, which a mountain wag did in this fashion, "Early to bed and early to rise will give you a headache and a pair of sore eyes." However, the gambling-houses, saloons, and all such places were closed, but pretty soon I saw a commotion close to where I was standing, at the intersection of the Red and Blue ravines. Something was up. Having nothing else to do I followed these exceptional early risers, and soon found myself on the hill above and on the outside of a tumultuous mob of "Sydney Ducks," as a certain class of adventurous gold-seekers were called in those days. Probably there were twenty-five or thirty of these fellows. I was an un-armed boy, and alone, as I supposed, from an American point of view; consequently, I had to remain silent and witness an awful sight. A word or any sign would no doubt have given me a dose of the same medicine they served out to a hapless victim in their clutches.

What occurred, and the cause of it, I will endeavor to relate as briefly as possible. It appears that two or three of the "Sydney Ducks"—miners as they pretended to be, but, in reality, generally thieves and gamblers—had really a rich claim in the main ravine, which they occasionally worked, and on the previous afternoon had found a nugget worth two or three hundred dollars. Feeling elated by their good luck they went up to a little store on the side of the hill kept by a young Missourian named Wright—if my memory serves—and had it weighed. Having no immediate use for the gold, they left their prize with Wright, and he carelessly threw it into a drawer underneath his Chinese gold scales, and went about his business for the rest of the day, probably never thinking of it again. Such occurences were common enough in those times. About dark, the same day, ten or fifteen of the party went to Wright's store and asked him for the nugget. He opened the drawer, and, to his utter astonishment and consternation, could not find it. At once he was accused of theft, and he, of course, protested his innocence, and to prove his sincerity offered to pay more than the value of the nugget in coin. "No," was the response; "we want only the nugget we left with you—that par-ticular piece of gold, or nothing." They swore and raved. Wright was helpless. Some one—probably one of their own gang—had, without doubt, secretly abstracted the specimen while his back

23

was turned during the afternoon. With many threats, they finally left the store, giving the young proprietor till next morning to produce the nugget or else take the consequences.

As stated before, it was early in the morning—the morning the party had fixed—that I first noticed the commotion; and I soon learned that the roughs had seized, bound and were taking young Wright to the top of the hill to whip him till he gave up the sought-for-nugget. Curiosity led me to follow the crowd and witness their doings. To this day the remembrance of what I saw sickens me. The poor fellow begged and pleaded, avowing his innocence and at the same time offering them the contents of his little store and all he had in the world in satisfaction of the loss if they would only let him go; but it was useless. They were determined to whip him, and there was no power then and there that could prevent them carrying out their purpose. To say I was mad with rage, and that every drop of blood in my body boiled, but feebly expresses my feelings. But what could I do against such a blood-thirsty mob? Nothing. Interference on my part would have only brought down on my head the fate they had in store for Wright. I would have been whipped to death without benefiting the victim already in their power. So I was compelled to look on in silence.

When the mob reached an old oak on the summit of the hill they stripped Wright to the waist and tied his body to the bole of the tree, so that his white skin was fully exposed to the sweep of the lash. Once more the nugget was demanded, and again the unfortunate young Missourian told them he could not produce it if it were to save his life. In his desperation, he even importuned his brutal assailants to kill him.

"It were better for you to do so," he said, "than to torture me as you propose."

But denial of guilt and appeal for mercy were alike useless. Finally a burly looking ruffian, with a most fiendish expression of countenance, whom the gang called "Captain," took both ends of a rawhide lariat in his hand and struck the shrinking skin be-

24

fore him the first blow, leaving two great bloody wales clear across the back. Heavens! how the warm blood spurted as blow followed blow on that quivering flesh. After three or four strokes the flogging was suspended and the demand for the nugget renewed, the tortured wretch feebly shaking his head in reply, being too weak to answer in words. The flagellator paused in his infernal work; he paused some three or four times to demand the missing gold, with the same result, and was about to commence lashing a fifth time when I saw a man whom I had not noticed before break through the circle formed around the victim. He had a revolver in his hand, and in a loud and peremptory tone of voice called a halt.

"I am a doctor," he said, "and know that you are committing murder. Every time you strike this man the loop of the riata falls immediately over the liver, and if he be not already dead, another blow or two will finish him. I will kill the man who attempts to strike him again." And he brought his revolver to bear on the "Captain."

Quick as a flash I was by the doctor's side with my sheath-knife in hand, determined to die with him if he were attacked. But there was no danger. The "Sydney Ducks" had satiated their thirst for blood, or else they were scared, for they all scattered off down the hill, yelling like demons, and left the doctor and myself alone with the apparently dying man.

As soon as the murderous band were out of sight, the doctor, seeing my drawn knife, said quietly:

"Cut the cords that bind him to the oak, and bring water, strips of cotton cloth and get some brandy or whisky, or anything in the shape of spirits, as you can."

The cords were cut at once, and the poor fellow dropped forward into the doctor's arms, instead of into a pool of his own blood at the foot of the tree, as he might have done. A hatful of water was procured from a neighboring spring, and the patient laid on the fresh grass with his head on the doctor's knee, and while he bathed and cleansed his horrible lacerations I ran to a little

25

roadside inn about a quarter of a mile off and, without saying a word to the landlord—there was no time to parley—snatched a bottle of whisky from behind the counter and a cloth from one of the tables and returned as soon as possible to the scene of the tragedy. Gradually, by the aid of the water and stimulants, the scourged man partially recovered, and we dressed and took him down to his little store, which we found looted. The robbers, as well as would-be murderers, had taken everything they could lay hands on. This, coupled with the agony and the disgrace, made the situation too much for the poor fellow to bear. He determined to leave the scene of his misfortune and did so as soon as he could, saying he would send a friend from Bear River to take charge of any effects he might have left. We never saw him again. He died the same night of his departure at a place called Round Tent, some fifteen miles away from Rough and Ready, on the Sacramento road.

On Saturday, the day we heard of poor Wright's death, the doctor and myself, after consultation, concluded to call a meeting of the miners in the district for the next day (Sunday). He undertook to stir up the law-abiding (or respectable) element—there was very little law in Rough and Ready during 1850—and I to arouse the denizens of the surrounding mining camps, tasks which we performed so effectually that by noon a large concourse of determined men had assembled to avenge the outrage on Wright. Early in the morning, accompanied by two or three trusted friends, I had been searching for members of the gang of "Sydney Ducks," especially the "Captain," so that I might identify them at the proper time, but we could not find a man. They had evidently taken fright and were cached somewhere. I was particularly disappointed in not finding the "Captain," as I wanted to see him swinging from the same oak where he had tortured the young Missourian. When the meeting was organized the doctor made a speech, describing graphically the scene on the hill; and I followed in the same strain, as best I could, and we soon had our audience roused to such a pitch of righteous indignation that if any of the miscreants had been in the vicinity they would have been strung up out of hand. As it was, the best we could do was to pass a resolution banishing all who were engaged in the whipping outrage. They were given three hours to leave camp, and told not to return at the peril of being hanged at sight. There were several ownerless claims about Rough and Ready before the three hours expired, and none of the gang was seen there again.

I left the mountains soon after, and was living in Sacramento City in the fall of 1851. One afternoon the news was spread through the city that three men had been caught in the act of garroting and robbing a miner in a clump of willows back of and a short distance from the celebrated Horse Market, corner of Sixth and K streets. There was, of course, great excitement, as people were getting tired of marauders. In a short time quite a number of citizens had assembled determined to hang the robbers. Before the assemblage had time to organize, the Governor of the State, John MacDougal, and the Mayor of the city, J. R. Hardenberg, with many other prominent men, appeared, and pledged themselves that the law—death for highway robbery— would be speedily enforced after conviction. On this the crowd gradually dispersed, and the accused men were sent to jail. According to the promise given, the culprits were tried and condemned to hang within a month or so after the commission of the crime; but, for some reason, Governor MacDougal reprieved one of them, named Robinson, for thirty days.

On the day of the hanging idle curiosity led me to the jail-door when the condemned men were brought out. Before knowing it I found myself within a dense crowd, from which there was no escaping. I was forced down to M street, where the gallows was erected. When I looked up at the closing scene—Great Scott! what was my astonishment and nearly joy, to see the burly form of the "Captain"—the same ruffian who had whipped Wright to death nearly a year before at Rough and Ready, standing on the trap with a rope around his neck, and side by side with a fellow-ruffian. In the midst of my feeling of surprise and gratification the trap was sprung and down they went to death and eternal despair. [A description of vigilante action in Sacramento follows, but the Rough and Ready part of the story ends here.]

### BOOM AND BUST

Prentice Mulford, a prolific contributor to the California press, wrote often about the played out placer miners and camps. As a young man in 1856 he came to California from Sag Harbor, Long Island, found employment at a variety of jobs from sorting sea-bird eggs to cooking aboard a whaling ship and mining in the Mother Lode country. He arrived in the mines in 1858 and worked at placer mining for three years. The returns were small and the once booming mining towns had passed their days of glory. Mulford in his tales preserved the humdrum existence of the decaying camp. (Prentice Mulford, "Camp," *Overland Monthly*, First Ser., Vol. 6 [May, 1871].)

The "Camp" of 1850 was flush, lively, flourishing, and vigorous; buildings growing, claims yielding richly, dust at a dollar a pinch for currency, monte, faro, fandango. The "Camp" of 1870 is quiet, sleepy, shrunken, poor, "gone in," "gone up." We speak of "Camp" as it is and has been, say, since 1863.

After the first harvest of gold in California came the harvest of individuality. In "Camp," as it were in one household, met men from the North, the South, the East, the West, and from every nation in Europe. In 1857, or thereabouts, the excitement attendant on the first flush of the gold discovery had abated; many men were lying on their oars, knowing hardly what to do; their natures rebelled against further continuance of the toiling and exhausting miner's life; they demanded more employment for mind, and less for muscle. So, some took to law, some to medicine, some to theology, some to politics; and many, who had no idea for what purpose they had been fashioned, to mischief. "Camps" contained two classes of people: the outsiders and insiders.

The outsiders were hard-working miners, dwelling around within a radius of a mile or two, coming into "Camp" chiefly on Sunday, or perhaps for an hour or two in the evening, to hear the gossip and to read the papers. They constituted the financial backbone of the country. It was their dust which still refreshed the till of the trader and the saloon keeper.

The "Camp" insiders were made up of more or less doctors, lawyers, saloon-keepers, town and county officials, hotel-keepers, gamblers, one Express-agent, one stage-agent, one school-master, one postmaster, and a reserve of clever fellows, with nothing to do, not wishing for anything to do, living along from hand to mouth, they scarcely knew how. All these dwelt within a stone's-throw of the Express-office, which may be considered the proper nucleus of "Camp."

A "Camp" is disposed to combustibility; the hot summer sun, which beats down steadily for six or eight months, so drying the shingles and clapboards that a match will set them ablaze. For this reason there is a camp-watchman, who walks up and down the street the whole night, clad in a great-coat and carrying a bog cane; stopping occasionally at the "Riffle," to watch the progress of a poker-game, and with familiar audacity taking a quarter from the "pot," as it lies on the table, to treat himself at the bar. The camp-watchman has many little responsibilities. He calls up the Express-agent for the early morning stage; and as the heavy Concord coach thunders over the bridge at the farther end of "Camp," the two commence the exercises of the day with early morning bitters at the "Union"—always accessible to them, at night, by a private, back passage-way to the bar. He keeps a strict watch on all suspicious nocturnal movements. He knows and reports who goes in and out at unseemly hours. He knows when every bedroom lamp should be extinguished. He knows when such lamps ought not to be extinguished. He has many of the "Camp" secrets in his possession. He ends his duties for the night by calling up the butcher. Before the first streak of the summer morning's dawn, the early candle flares in the place of beef, pork, and mutton; the sound of saw grating through bone, of cleaver upon the meat-block, falls short and sharp upon the sleeper's ear. The camp-watchman, like a bird of night, disappears, and is seen no more until late in the afternoon. Then comes the dawn, and the front-doors of the "Magnolia" open silently, and the half-dressed, frowzy-haired, unwashed proprietor is seen behind his bar, putting down his dose of bitters, and stirring up the internal fires for another day. The camp-butcher slips across the street for his dram. The Justice of the Peace crawls out, and stands in his accustomed place before that bar— exactly where he has stood of a summer's morning at the same time for nineteen years past; and then the hot sun wearily rises above the horizon; the cool of the dawn almost instantly gives place to a glow of heat, and these town worthies say languidly to each other, "Another scorcher today." The mercury at nine o'clock stands at 90°; at eleven, 100°; at twelve, 105°; and until four or five o'clock, anywhere from that point to 115° to 120°.

By nine or ten the "Boys" commence working out. There are breakfasts cooked in tenantless stores and offices. The "Camp" has passed its maximum of greatness, and there are many empty buildings. In these the "Boys" drift as naturally as the burrowing owl finds the ground-squirrel's hole on our arid plains. Rents are very low, being little or nothing. The stove has seen better days; so has the crockery; one end of the house sometimes furnishes fuel, the other shelter. The "Boys" number from two to four in a mess; and all share in the labor of preparing breakfast. Each one has some favorite duty. Smith's knack is that of slicing tomatoes; Sutton can fry potatoes better than any man in the Southern Mines; Brown prides himself on Chile stews, learned in South America, involving a strong application of red peppers; Dan's forte is broiling steak. They are long and social meals: there is no business to hurry one off; nothing to do save wash up the dishes, light the pipes, and then sit on the street in the shade of the locust-trees, talk over last night's game, and watch dusty horsemen and jingling mule-teams plodding through "Camp."

These are a keen set of men. Involuntary their minds turn to the study of human nature. When a stranger comes in their midst, they set to work and analyze him, and sift him down, until he is thoroughly known. Has he any special weakness, it is discovered. These little, lazy "Camps" become select schools for the study of character. New material wanting, they study each other. They know, and comment upon, and relish each other's peculiarities. There is Green, a tall, gaunt man from North Carolina—a man profoundly wise in ignorance. Green cannot read. But he watches narrowly the newspaper as others read it; he notes the location of stirring paragraphs which have been read aloud; he fastens upon them with his thumb and finger, and then, awaiting his opportunity until some unemployed bystander saunters into the "Magnolia," he knowingly and triumphantly hands him the sheet and remarks, "Here, sir, read that!" Green's ruse lasts for years, and is often revived and acted over, ever retaining all of its original zest and freshness.

Idle men are more mischievous than idle boys. The inside modern California camp-life proves that. The natural inclination of its human nature seems to be that of extracting all the amusement and comfort from the surroundings. At least, we live up to that rule in "Camp." The simpleton, and the worthless loafer, wandering reckless and aimless about the country, are taken in, fed, clothed, and entertained, so long as they afford amusement. Judge T——, as he announced himself, was once found in "Camp" one evening. No one knew who he was, or where he came from. His hat was battered; his garb seedy; he wore spectacles; and he made his debut by an unsuccessful attempt to negotiate with the saloon-keeper. The boys measured this character instantly. One after another they wormed themselves into acquaintanceship; they heard his story; they became his friends; for three days Judge T—— was the lion of "Camp;" he was well entertained; introduced with distinguished consideration to all the leading men; flattered, praised; consulted as to important matters; seated by the side of the Justice of the Peace during the progress of an important mining suit; but on the fourth night the end came. Judge T——, in the center of his circle of new and admiring friends, was giving a lengthly opinion with regard to the political outlook, when the heavy boots of his particular friend, the ex-sheriff, were laid across his lap, as if it were a common social habit of the country, and another pair of boots settled on his right shoulder, and another on his left; and in five seconds he found himself covered with boots. He arose, shook off the load, gave one reproachful look, darted from the saloon, and was never afterward seen in that "Camp."

There are men in "Camp," also, not gregarious, living by themselves in solitary cabins. These have been lone housekeepers for years, with fair prospects for remaining so. Middle age, hard labor, and hardship are stamped in the lines on their faces and the silver tinge in their beards. The young man of twenty-five came to "Camp" in 1850. In 1870, he finds himself, at forty-five, the owner of a rough cabin, a stove, a bed, two chairs, crockery, one six-shooter, a month's provisions, an indifferent wardrobe, perhaps a two-dollars-per-day claim; this is all he has to show for twenty years of life in California. He cannot get out of "Camp." The invisible, but strong thread of habit and old association keep him there. He has mined a little, maybe held office, speculated, kept a saloon, been a rough carpenter, worked in quartz mill; hied off to more or less new diggings—to Fraser River, Arizona, Cariboo, Washoe; but finally drifts back to the old "Camp," where he pulled up the virgin gold in the grass roots in 1849.

Sometimes he becomes the last man in "Camp." Men, life, buildings—all, save his old log-hut, his dwelling, have disappeared. All about are the pits digged in former days, but they are smoothed by the hand of time, and overgrown with the thickly springing vegetation. There are great piles of boulders, heaped up years ago; but even in their interstices the weeds are springing. In the gulches, the rivulet trickles faintly in summer, or rushes and roars, muddy and turbid, in winter. The rugged

32

mountains look down with the same stern composure as they did upon the excited crowd who dug, and drank, and fought in this ravine twenty-odd years ago. The "Last Man" rocks his cradle in the silent gulch alone. He finds the remnant of a pay-streak here, a half-worked crevice there, not worth attention in more prosperous times. He runs through sluice or rocker two or three hundred buckets of dirt per day, gathers therefrom perhaps a dollar in fine dust, tramps wearily back to his lone cabin, cooks his solitary supper, sits in his doorway, smokes his pipe, thinks of home, digs a little in his garden, feeds his chickens, and goes early to bed. This, from day to day, from year to year, varied only by an occasional visit to the nearest neighbor, some other "Last Man," a mile or two away, or a trip to "Camp" to purchase provisions, is the life of "The Last Man in the Dead Camp."

He ceased years ago to write home; Eastern friends and relatives have lost all trace of him. The "Last Man" came here to make a fortune. He meant never to return home without one. He has endured privation, hardship, loneliness; he has worked, planned, fretted—and failed. He will not go home poor, and wealth retires farther in the distance. Yet he clings to the deserted bar: there he is at least his own master, so long as the oft-turned, oft-dug-over dirt will yield a dollar or two per day. Sometimes, he is not seen for days; the house is barred and silent; they commence asking, "What's become of ——?"

They break open the cabin: the "Last Man in the Dead Camp" lies there: he has taken his departure: the few remaining relics of 1849 bury him in the little grave-yard on the red hill-side. Its fence is tumbling down; the wooden head-boards lie prone to the earth, split, and the inscriptions erased by time, the sun, the rain. One old, familiar sound is heard: the roar of the river below over the riffle—roaring as it roared in the ears of the "Last Man," when in 1850, from the brow of yonder hill he first caught sight of its glittering line, and the grating of pebbles from a thousand rockers sounded like the din of a cotton-factory—roaring as it fell upon his dulled and dying ear, the last sound of earth—roaring an eternal requiem in the long years to come, while in a far-away Eastern home mother, wife, daughter, sister, still long, and wait, and weep, vainly hoping for the return of the "Last Man of the Dead Camp."

# Placer Miners

## DIGGING SONGS

J. M. Hutchings, an Englishman who made and lost money in California, devoted *Hutchings's Illustrated California Magazine* to the natural beauty and grandeur of his adopted state. He did a great deal to advertise the wonders of California and to popularize the workaday activities of the miners. The digging songs published by him preserved the rhythms of the mountain trail and the miners at work.

### I

("The Miner's Song, Words by J. Swett and Music by Jas. C. Kemp, *Hutchings's California Magazine*, May, 1859.)

The eastern sky is blushing red,
    The distant hill-top glowing,
The river o'er its rocky bed
    In idle frolics flowing;
'Tis time the pickaxe and the spade
    Against the rocks were ringing,
And with ourselves the golden stream
    A song of labor singing.

The mountain air is fresh and cold,
    Unclouded skies bend o'er us;
Broad placers, rich in hidden gold,
    Lie temptingly before us.

We need no Midas' magic wand,
    Nor wizard rod divining;
The pickaxe, spade and brawny hand
    Are sorcerers in mining.

When labor closes with the day,
    To simple fare returning,
We gather in a merry group
    Around the camp-fires burning,
The mountain sod our couch at night,
    The stars keep watch above us,
We think of home and fall asleep
    To dream of those who love us.

## II

("Miners' Song on Frazer River," *Hutchings's California Magazine*, September, 1859.)

Where mighty waters foam and boil,
    And rushing torrents roar,
In Frazer River's northern soil,
    Lies hid the golden ore.

    Chorus
Far from home, far from home,
    On Frazer River's shore,
We labor hard, so does our bard,
    To dig the golden ore.

Far, far from home we miners roam,
    We feel its joy no more;
These we have sold for shining gold
    On Frazer River's shore.

Each mountain height is shrouded white
    From the Snow-King's icy store;
At them we gaze, thru' storms and haze,
    And wish the winter o'er.

*Placer Miners*

At times we hear, with startled ear,
    The avalanche's roar
As thundering down from the mountain's crown,
    Its crashing billows pour.

In cabins rude, our daily food
    Is quickly counted o'er;
Beans, bread, salt meat, is all we eat—
    And the cold earth is our floor.

Lonely our lives—no mothers', wives',
    Or sisters' love runs o'er,
When home we come at set of sun,
    To greet us at the door.

No woman's smiles our hearts beguile,
    No books, with wisdom's lore;
Silent we sit, while visions flit
    Of loved ones seen no more.

At night we smoke, then crack the joke,
    Try cards till found a bore;
Our good-night said, we go to bed,
    To dream of home once more.

Home's dearest joys Time soon destroys,
    Their loss we all deplore;
While they may last, we labor fast
    To dig the golden ore.

Early and late it is our fate
    To toil for Fortune's store;
We find it hard, so does our bard,
    To get the shining ore.

With luck at last, our hardships past,
    We'll start for home once more,
And greet the sight, wild with delight,
    Of California's shore.

And when on shore, we never more
Will roam through all our lives;
A home we'll find, just to our mind,
And wake our sweethearts—wives.

Last Chorus
Then home again, home again,
From a foreign shore,
We'll sing how sweet our heart's delight,
With our dear friends once more.

EMORY'S BAR, FRAZER RIVER, July, 1859.
(I have not drawn on my imagination for this song; it is truthful. Every feeling, incident or scene has come within my observation or experience, except what relates to the future, and that I trust will.)

## THE MINERS' COMMANDMENTS

The "Miners' Ten Commandments" was written by J. M. Hutchings, the founder in 1856 of *Hutchings's Illustrated California Magazine*. Hutchings worked in the mines and while there he hit on the idea of a Ten Commandments that would meet the moral needs of the miners. His decalogue was printed on letter writing paper and sold almost a hundred thousand copies in a single year. ("The Miners' Ten Commandments," *The Golden Era Pictorial*, January, 1854.)

A man spake these words and said: I am a miner, who wandered "from away down east," and came to sojurn in a strange land and "see the elephant." And behold I saw him and bear witness that from the key of his trunk to the end of his tail, his whole body has passed before me; and I followed him till his huge foot stood still before a rusty clapboard shanty; then, with his trunk extended, he pointed to a candle-card tacked upon a shingle, as though he would say read, and I read:

38

## The Miners' Ten Commandments

I. Thou shalt have no other claim than one.

II. Thou shalt not make unto thyself any false claim, nor any likeness to a mean man, by jumping one; whatever thou findeth on the top above, or on the rock beneath; or in a crevice underneath the rock—for I am a jealous dog, and will visit the miners round with my presence, to invite them on my side; and when they decide against thee, thou shalt have to take thy pick, and thy pan, thy shovel and thy blankets, with all thou hast, and go "prospecting," both north and south, to seek good diggins; and thou shalt find none. Then when thou hast returned, in sorrow thou shalt find that thine old claim is worked out, and no pile is made thee, to hide it in the ground, or in an old boot beneath thy bunk, or in the buckskin or bottle underneath the cabin; but hast paid all that was in thy purse away, worn out thy boots and thy garments so that there is nothing good about them but the pockets, and thy patience be liked unto thy garments; and at last thou shalt hire thy body out to make thy board and save thy bacon.

III. Thou shalt not go prospecting before thy claim gives out. Thou shalt not take thy money, nor thy gold dust, nor thy good name, to the gambling table in vain; for monte, twenty-one, roulette, faro, lansquenet and poker, will prove to thee that the more thou puttest down, the less thou shalt take up; and when thou thinkest of thy wife and children, thou shalt not hold thyself guiltless, but insane.

IV. Thou shall not remember what thy friends do at home on the Sabbath day, lest the remembrance may not compare favorably with what thou doest. Six days thou mayest dig or pick all that thy body can stand under, but the other day is Sunday, when thou shalt wash all thy dirty shirts, darn all thy stockings, tap all thy boots, mend all thy clothing, chop all thy whole week's firewood, make up and bake thy bread and boil thy pork and beans, that thou wait not when thou returnest from thy long tour, weary. For in six days' labor only thou canst not work enough to wear out thy body in two years; but if thou workest hard on Sunday also, thou canst do it in six months, and thou, and thy son, and thy daughter, thy male friend, and thy female friend, thy morals and thy conscience be none the better for it; but reproach thee, shouldst thou ever return with thy worn-out body to thy mother's fireside, and thou strive to justify thyself, because the trader and the blacksmith, the carpenter and the merchant, the tailors, Jews, and buccaneers defy God and civilization by keeping not the Sabbath day, and wish not for a day of rest, such as memory, youth, and home made hallowed.

V. Think more of all thy gold and how thou canst make it fastest, than how thou wilt enjoy it, after thou hath ridden rough-shod over thy good old parents' precepts and examples, that thou mayest hath something to reproach and sting thee, when thou art left alone in the land where thy father's blessing and thy mother's love hath sent thee.

VI. Thou shalt not kill thy own body by working in the rain, even though thou shall make enough to buy physic and attend-ance with—neither shall thou kill thy neighbor's body by shooting him, except he give thee offense—then upon the principle of honor; without principle thou mayest, even though, by "keeping cool," thou hadst saved his life and thy conscience.

VII. Thou shall not grow discouraged, and think of going home before thou hast made thy "pile," because thou hast not "struck a lead," nor found "a rich crevice," nor sunk a hole upon a "pocket"; lest, in going home, thou shalt leave four dollars per day, and go to work, ashamed, at fifty cents, and serve thee right; for here, by staying, thou mightest strike a lead and fifty dollars a day, and thy manly self-respect, and then go home with enough to make thyself and others happy.

VIII. Thou shalt not pick out specimens from the company pan and put them in thy mouth or in thy purse. Neither shalt thou take from thy cabin-mate his gold-dust to add to thine, lest he find thee out, and straightway call his fellow miners together, and they hang thee, or give thee fifty lashes and two hours to leave the country, or brand thee like a horse-thief, with R upon thy cheek, to be "known and read of all"—Californians in particular. And if thou steal a shovel or a pick or a pan from thy toiling fellow-miner, hanging will be too good for thee, and thou asked to be kicked and cowhided for thy pains, and forever hang down thy head.

IX. Thou shalt not tell any false tales about "good diggings in the mountains" to thy neighbor, that thou mayest benefit thy friend who hath mules and provisions and tools and blankets he cannot sell; lest, in deceiving thy neighbor, when he returneth through the snow, with aught save his rifle, he presenteth thee with the contents thereof, and like a dog thou shalt fall down and die.

X. Thou shalt not covet thy neighbor's gold nor his claim, nor undermine his bank in following a lead, nor move his stake, nor wash the tailings from his sluice's mouth, nor throw up dirt upon his bank. And if thy neighbor hath his family here, and thou love and covet his daughter's hand in marriage, thou shalt lose no time in seeking her affection; and when thou hast obtained it thou shalt "pop the question" like a man, lest another more manly than thou art, should step in before thee, and thou covet her in vain; and in the anguish of disappointment, thou shalt quote the language of the great, and say, "Let her rip!" and thy future life be that of a poor, lonely, despised and comfortless bachelor. The end.

The popularity of the original "Miners' Ten Commandments" inspired an elaborated "verse-ion" for the columns of the *Golden Era*. The new version, lengthier but more jocular than the original, included a preamble, by-laws, and decree written by Cadiz-Orion, a pseudonymous writer for the *Era*. ("The Miners' Ten Commandments; a New Version," *The Golden Era Pictorial*, January, 1854.)

> Away "deown east" there dwelt a man,
>   E'en over in the State of Maine,

Who had enough of tall pine trees
    Himself and wife to well maintain.

But years rolled by and children came
    Around the little fire-side,
And claimed a right to eat and drink,
    Nor could such wants be well denied.

The pine trees grew and children too—
    Though in their manner far apart:
The trees grew thin, the children thick,
    And thus from Maine were doomed to part.

"Old Zenas" to his wife did say—
    "I'll move you all to Michigan,
And California I will seek,
    And dig until a richer man."

Across the Plains he bent his steps,
    And passed large droves of buffalo,
Wild horses, turkeys, very fine,
    And tigers, jackalls, Indians, too.

At times he hadn't nary piece
    Of meat whereby to feed upon,
Nor any water for his thirst—
    And thus he saw the old lion.

At last his clothes in tatters hung
    About his sore and weary form—
His "harp of hopes" was soon unstrung,
    And fancied nigh the gathering storm.

He mourned his lot and often wept
    To think he ever took the jaunt—
And then he'd rave, and swear he b'leaved
    He's soon to see the Elephant!

And thus "Uncle Zenas" soliloquized:—"I onc't lived in peace and prosperity away deown in the State of Maine, and owned

tew ceows, ten oxen and three shoats—besides dear Polly, and
Ike and Jake and Tabitha and Sarah Ann and Eliza Jane, together
with the darling babe that was named Rachel, because she lifted
up her voice and wept when I kissed her and departed for Californy! Y-a-s, 'tis even I, 'Old Zenas,' that is neow in Californy and
hain't struck a single pocket nor crevice yet, and I've traveled
e'en a'most as fur as 'tis tew hum. And here the road forks!—
Wonder which of these onlikely roads nears off to Hangtown?
Hellow! I'm blazed ef here ain't jest the sarkumstance I'm looking for, by golly! A guide-board, sartin as preachin!—No 'taint,
nither—coz the fingers are pintin up, and it reads—

'Behold a new verse-ion of the Miners' Ten Commandments,
By-Laws and Decree! Which reads as follows:

## By-Laws

One claim thou mays't own, and there drive your stakey
And coyote and crevice till you make or you break;
Always find the bed-rock, keep at work and pump out—
Do anything rather than be running about.

If the gold isn't there, keep cool and don't swear;
Nor either get tight and say you don't care,
Nor practice the art of 'salting' your claim—
For by such practice you'll get a hard name.

Climb out very cool, with pick, pan and shovel,
And don't seek the cabin and pore over a novel—
But mark a new claim and pitch in again,
And never have doubts of striking a vein.

Should you strike a rich pocket, a crevice or lead,
Don't drink quite a barrel on the fortunate deed—
But pocket your dust and go whistling away,
Content to enjoy it at some future day.

Should you venture your luck in damming the rivers,
And work in the water, getting colds, coughs and shivers,

43

Let 'old rye' alone with wisdom of thought,
Sell out if you can, and bless him who bought.

Wend your way to dry-diggings, purchase sluice-box or 'tom,'
And a claim too, if rich—judge of those you buy from—
Hire eight or ten 'Coolies'—come the cooly at once,
Thus showing the people you are not quite a dunce.

By 'Johnny Celestial' make two dollars per day,
On the labor of each, you see that will pay;
Whereas, if you hire Uncle Sam's sturdy son—
You would pay more for labor, and hardly make one.

And lastly, thus reads the Decree:—

*Firstly*—It is decreed unto all the people of California, that ye
do observe all that is herein written, that ye avoid some of the
shoals and quicksands of this life, and especially during your
sojourn in California, where a lesson of warning cannot be given
too soon. California is one vast amphitheatre—containing an
assemblage of human beings from every land and every clime.
All classes, all colors, and all conditions, are each day before
your gaze, and soon they are associated more or less with you all.
And now, my disciples, this is why I publish this Decree, and give
you this warning that ye may be prepared to meet the tempters.

*Secondly*—It is decreed, O ye Miners, that I first publish unto
you the decree; as yet are the most numerous of any of the tribes
of California; and I pray you will hearken unto me with an atten-
tive ear, that ye may be profited thereby. Ye are indeed mighty,
and the wise men and the counselors of ten, have sought thine
abode to teach ye wisdom and understanding.

*Thirdly*—And thus it is decreed that thou shalt not labor to
thine discomfiture and bodily pain. Thou shalt labor as becometh
good disciples, and shall not exceed ten hours each day. Thy
food shall consist of that which is most wholesome and nourish-
ing, and thy raiment shall be of woolen and of firm texture, and
each week thou shalt cleanse thine apparel.

44

*Fourthly*—In default of the same, thy brother miners shall take thee down, even unto Feather River, and there cleanse thee,— apparel, body and all together, until thou wilt lend thine own exertions to do it thyself.

*Fifthly*—If vermin infest thee or thy blankets, thou shalt be banished from the cabin, thee and thy raiment until thou shalt rid thyself of thine unwelcome visitors. And on the day—yea the hour—in which it shall appear that thou are ridden of all plagues, —then in solemn procession shalt thou be marched with thy brother miners even unto the cabin, and all feast sumptuously.

*Sixthly*—It is decreed that thou shalt not be made servants one to another, only as each serves the other in his turn. Neither shalt thou forsake thy brother miner while on the couch of sickness and pain, but shall carefully watch over him, and administer unto every necessary want, until he shall be able to rise again, and proclaim himself well of his malady.

*Seventhly*—It is also decreed that thou, O Miner, who hath a family in a distant country, shall, whenever in thy power, remit the avails of thy labors, to keep them in food and raiment during thy sojourn here. Thou shalt not neglect thy wife and children, and go after strange women, who, with a Syren's tongue and winning smiles, would lure thee to her snares of shame and degradation, and rob thee of thine honor, thy virtue and thy gold; and at last would despise and curse thee, and turn thee away empty handed. Beware lest thou are overtaken in thy secret wanderings, and lose thy life and thy friends mourn thy untimely end.

*Eighthly*—And it is also decreed that thou, O young man, who hast left thy father's house, to sojourn in the land of California,— even in the mines thereof—thou, too, I pray take heed. Remember the counsel of thy mother and sisters, and forget not thy solemn promises and pledges of affection. Nor shalt thou forget to pen an epistle each mail to thy kindred, that they may know how fares the wanderer and when he is to return. Neither shalt thou forget that young and comely maiden who gave to you her warm and trusting affections, while you vowed to remain true and never forget that starry night just on the eve of thy departure. Remember all these promises, that in thy after life thou mayst be blessed with future generations likened unto thee.

*Ninthly*—It is decreed that thou, O Bachelors, shalt be banished for a season, working out thy salvation here in the mountains, even among the eternal snows of the Sierra Nevada, and here remain for a while until you come to the sage conclusion that there is a more congenial atmosphere by the side of the gentler sex. If such is the result of thy experience, thou mayst take up thy bed and walk, leaving thy tools for others of thy kind. Ever after thy works shall be judged, and when a certain period of time shall expire, and thou hast not employed the time profitably, and obeyed the Scriptures wherein it reads "multiply and replenish the earth," if you have failed in this thou shalt again and forever serve among the snows of the Sierras. Therefore, ye bachelor miners, take warning.

*Tenth* and last Decree—for the people—It is now lastly decreed, that thou, Californians all, male and female, who comest hither to better thy fortunes—thou art commanded to pay especial attention to this Decree. Thou—a certain class—journeyed hither to repair thy ruined circumstances, to pay off old debts which have hung like a heavy weight over the horizon of thy future happiness. Thou hast come hither, willing to brave the storms and tempests, both of nature's warring elements, and also the "party feuds" and "political gusts" that so often lend violent commotion to this golden land. Thou, O Politician, who, in thy Atlantic home, didst crave office, and thy ambitious desires were not gratified—thou who labored so energetically for the *good* of the people (and thyself, too)—thou, who wert beaten by thy political opponent, thou comest hither to retrieve thy fortunes, to build up thy high minded hopes, to court Dame Fortune's smiles once more, and to raise up unto thyself a great name. But beware, thou lofty aspirant of fame; there are those here who art long before thee, who have their wires laid, and now have wealth on their side. Take heed; be wise; do thou go to one

Bryant, and there select a pick, pan and shovel, and sojourn a while in the mountains, for there thou wilt have an equal chance among thy fellow laborers. And thou, O Speculator from Gotham, thinkest thou in California, even in San Francisco, thou canst succeed, and have built up thy broken fortunes by thy schemes and thy small capital? Thou, too beware, for in San Francisco are speculators congregated from all countries, even of the shrewdest kind, and have studied and practiced all manner of devices. Take heed, therefore, and invest thy small capital in miners' supplies, and flee to the mountains, or to some inland village and there be content with health, good cold water, and fair profits.

And thou, pilgrims to the Eureka State, tarry not at the Bay, but pierce the northern wilds and the mountain scenery; rush for pure air, health, wealth, and plenty of labor. Despair not in the hour of thy afflictions, but brave the storm manfully, and soon thou art safe. And thou fair maidens, daughters of Eve, who hast braved the hardships and dangers of a voyage to our golden shores, and thou heroines and pioneer mothers, we greet thee— thrice welcome are ye all. Thou whom in memory we cherished— thou, whom we so much wished for, who are so highly prized and cherished in every land—thou art indeed here. And thou aged, thou single maidens, thou art here, too; nor wilt not meet with so many fair competitors to bear away the prizes from you, but will soon be heard exclaiming, Eureka!

### FORTUNES OF A PILGRIM

Alonzo Delano, who wrote under the pen name of Old Block, described the ups and downs of mining life. He had crossed the plains with an ox team, suffering many hardships on the way and later in the mines. Eventually he set up in business selling squashes and cabbages on Long Wharf in San Francisco and when he found time depicted the Argonauts for the *Pacific News* and other journals. His descriptions of the California frontier types, combining skilfully humor and bathos, won widespread popular-

47

ity in California. (Old Block [Alonzo Delano], *The Miner's Progress*; or *Scenes in the Life of a California Miner* [Sacramento, Daily Union Office, 1853].)

A Pilgrim from the Eastern shore
    Stood on Nevada's strand:
A tear was in the hither eye,
    A pickaxe in his hand.
A tear was in his hither eye—
    And in his left, to match,
There would have been another tear,
    But for a healing patch.

And other patches, too, he wore,
    Which on his garments hung,
And two were on that ill-starred spot
    Where mothers smite their young.
His hat, a shining "Costar" once,
    Was broken now, and dim,
And wild his bearded features gleamed,
    Beneath the tattered rim.

The Pilgrim stood: and, looking down,
    As one who is in doubt,
He sighed to see how fast *that* pair
    Of boots was wearing out.
And while he filled an ancient pipe,
    His wretchedness to cheer,
He stopped, with hurried hand, to pick
    A flea from out his ear.

Then spake this Pilgrim from the East,
    "I am a wretched man,
For lust of gold hath lured me to
    The shovel and the pan.
I saw, in dreams, a pile of gold
    It's dazzling radiance pour;

No more my visions are of gold,
　　Alas! my hopes are ore."

"Thrice have I left this cursed spot,
　　But mine it was to learn
The fatal truth, that 'dust we are,
　　To dust we shall *return.*'
So, here condemned by Fates unkind,
　　I rock illusive sand,
And dream of wailing babes at home,
　　Unrocked, an orphan band."

The Pilgrim paused, for now he heard
　　His distant comrades' shout,
He drew a last whiff from his pipe,
　　Then knocked the ashes out.
And, stooping, as he gathered up
　　His shovel and his pan,
The breeze his latest accents bore,
　　"I am a wretched man!"

Once more returned, at close of day,
　　To a cheerless, dismal home,
He vows, if he was back in Maine,
　　He never more would roam.
Now hunger makes "his bowels yearn,"
　　For "yams" or "Irish roots,"
But these he looks in vain to find—
　　Then tries to fry his boots.

The night is passed in happy dreams.
　　Of youth and childhood's joys:
Of times when he got flogged at school
　　For pinching smaller boys.
His wife, whose smile hath cheered him oft,
　　And rendered light his care,
He sees, in far New England's clime,
　　Enjoying better fare.

49

But morn dispels these fairy scenes,
 And *want* arouses pluck;
He shoulders pick and pan once more,
 Again to try his luck.
He digs in dark, secluded depths,
 The spots where *slugs* abound,
And oh! what raptures fill his breast—
 His "pile" at last is found.

He drops his pick, his pan is left,
 He e'en neglects his pipe,
He leaves the diggings far behind,
 His purse he holds with iron grip.
Resolved to dig and toil no more,
 No more in dreams to trust,
His well filled bag upon his back,
 Of pure and shining dust.

His wardrobe changed, behold him now,
 In affluence and pride,
Surrounded by the forms he loves,
 With joy on every side!
Pressed closely to his heart he holds
 His wife and children dear,
The latter shouting madly, while
 The former drops a tear.


A LAST FAREWELL

Thoughts of home were ever present in the minds of the early Argonauts. The desire to return home was deeply etched in the thinking of the placer miners, as Joaquin Miller recalled in a moving sketch. Miller—adventurer, poet, literary celebrity, and eccentric—had his first experience with mining when he was not much older than seventeen. Toward the end of 1854 he ran away from his parents, who had only two years before come as emigrants to Oregon. His search for adventure took him to the Humbug mining fields, situated not too far from Yreka, in California's northernmost wilderness. In this wild region he eked out an existence prospecting, cooking for the miners, and doing other odd jobs. What he related about the miners has a certain authenticity, based on the passions and tribulations he had seen, and notwithstanding his notoriously loose respect for facts. Miller was a man of rugged talent, and he won popularity in British intellectual circles for the bold sweep of his manner as well as the merit of his *Pacific Poems* and the *Songs of the Sierras*. As a writer he was a creator of frontier folklore. ("They Were Going Home: The Climax of the California Miner's Dream," San Francisco *Call*, July 10, 1892.)

He is going home. Going home! That was the climax of his California dream; the end of the play—and the work; why nobody in the mines and mountains meant to stay there. Still many a good man stayed. But all along through the first fifteen or twenty years if every man who wanted to go home could have gone there would have been nothing left in the Sierras but graves, heaps of gravel, prospect-holes and battered old picks, shovels, toms, rockers, boots, broken bottles and so on. The whole land would have been left as quiet and empty up there as a dead man's hand.

But years later, when men left California, still fortune-hunting, and went to the northern mines, they somehow forgot all about the old world, and when fortune found them they came back to California to live and to die. There was nothing, however, very dramatic in this short, safe return from the northern mines in the days of stages, steamers and railroads back to the Golden Gate. Still it was an event and was enjoyed by all most heartily in each camp. And it always seemed to me that the men who took the deepest and tenderest interest in the "going home" of one of their number were the very men who were most helpless and most incapable of reaching this one desired end.

I know that when it began to be whispered about that Fred Adams of Canyon City had made his "pile" and was going home there was joy in the heart of many a gray-headed man who knew right well it would never be said of him that he had made his pile and that he was "going home." And when Fred Adams quietly slipped out of camp down to a friend's house and stayed all night and weighed his gold dust there on the butcher's scales before starting at daybreak the next morning, and when the news came back to town that the dust weighed well nigh to a hundred pounds, I tell you there were tears of delight in many an old man's eyes at thought of Fred's good fortune. We called him "Fred" Adams up there; but his name is Judge Adams by title and right; and he is now one of the rich big lawyers of San Francisco.

The first "going home" I ever saw was on Humbug Creek, Northern California, in the winter of 1854. I tell you it took men of grit to get there. The cowards had never started there and the weak died on the way, so they were a powerful and select lot of men, and it took nerve, time and dust, too, to get away from there. Think of it. Ten miles on foot over a mountain of snow to Yreka, then hundreds of miles through the savages by mule to Portland, then a sailing vessel to San Francisco, then the steamer, Panama, New Orleans, up the Mississippi, and so on.

I had been blown into this canyon at the forks of the Humbug, as a bird, by the winter storms and had to bridge over a mighty hard month or two I can tell you. I first got a place as cook for my board. But the provisions gave out pretty soon and I had to go. Then Frank Campbell, brother of the late Bartley Campbell, dramatist and member of the Idaho Legislature when last heard from, got me a place to sit up with a miner who had been hurt in a slide. I got no wages, but as I had to sit up at night and so didn't need a bed, and as the man was too badly hurt to eat the meals sent him from the hotel I did not suffer, but soon made friends with the poor man by reading to him. Lots of miners used to drop in after night and smoke and listen. The book was Harrison Ainsworth's novels and bound up together, "Dick Turpin," "Jack Shepherd," and so on. Never had man or boys such listeners. And when I, 30 years later, told dear old Ainsworth in London how he had been read and listened to in the heart of the Sierras, he nearly crushed my hand in his two hands. But this is scattering birdshot; let us get forward.

It is marvelous how ignorant those men were. They were from what was then the "border"—largely Missourians, and I doubt if one-half of them could write their names. I know right well what I say, for I wrote many letters for them. Of course there were other men there from other countries. Pat Flannigan, for instance, who kept the store. From France do you say? No, he was a white Irishman with a very black beard, and is now the rich and influential president of the Coos Bay Bank. He was very popular then, as he is still, I reckon, and seeing the dismal ignorance of the miners he and Frank Campbell set a committee to work to get up a "public library." And this is one of its methods: The secretary tacked up the following notice on the door of the saloon known as "The Howlin' Wilderness:"

"Know all men that enny book in this 'ere camp belongs to the publick library except the holy bibel and enny man found gilty of taking enny book except said bibel will be hung for horse stealing so help me god. (Sighned) The librarion of bored of directors and secretary of said library."

The result was, a preacher who went away as provisions got short left behind a copy of Josephus. This made three books in the library now, and Pat Flannigan employed me at $2.50 a day, or rather an hour, for the man could not stand more, to go up the creek and read Josephus to a sick miner there. "You see, he has got the scurvy, and rheumatism, and consumption; I'm afraid he's pretty sick," said Pat pathetically, as we approached the low little cabin under the dark fir trees on the hillside.

"Is Josephus the short for Joseph?" asked the long, slim and bony man, who lay there with his big bent and knotty feet sticking far out from under the blankets and over the pole that served for a footboard.

"Yis, yis, sorr; Josephus is the shorrut forr Joseph, Zeke, moi boy."

"Is it? Well, by gum! Say, I know all about that ere book, sort o' religious like; jist suit you, see now; and I'd like to hear it again; jist suit you, see now," and he looked long and meditatively at his queer, twisted toes, that were all trying to climb up on top of one another away down yonder beyond the narrow end of the narrow little bed of fir boughs and blankets in the dark corner of the cabin; then for the third time he said, talking in a whisper to those curious and multitudinous toes, "Jist suit you, see now."

And so I read and read from Josephus; and the next day I wrote a letter for him to his little sister at home; to Savannah Landing, Mo., and signed Ezekial Wells; for although he had two brothers with him, young brothers, who were busy "cleaning up" in the claim, and faithful, loving brothers they were, too, not one of them knew even so much of books as the alphabet.

Let it be noted as we go along that nearly all these men were sternly honest, and they all had more or less knowledge of the Bible; many of them, 50 per cent more than now, had Bible names. It is very curious, a thing worth noting, else I would not bother to set it down; but I reckon they must have brought these names and this tradition of Holy Writ all the way, through generations, from Virginia and the Carolinas.

In about a week the two younger brothers got all cleaned up in the claim down in the gorge under the cabin, and their friend Flannigan weighed and brought them back their dust, cleaned of black sand and stray bits of clinging quartz and pyrites of iron, nearly $4,000. Not much, it is true, for three men. But the long, slim creature in the corner, who by this time was pretty well doubled up, all except the persistent and ever-moving feet, stopped coughing long enough, as they set the dust in the gold pan by his bedside, to say, "Boys, divide up and go home."

And here was the example of another tradition that had come

54

down all the way, even from beyond old Virginia—the old English loyalty and obedience to the head of the family. It is to be sincerely regretted that this has so entirely perished from among us now.

The two young men held their heads silently for a second, then glancing at each other, they came forward.

"Yes, put her in three piles here on the table by the bed, an' Hez he'll turn his back an I'll touch one pile with the p'int of my jacknife that Pat give me to peel my toenails with when I get well next week, an' he'll say, 'whose?'"

The poor fellow was tied in a knot coughing for a time, and then he seemed to take up some broken thread of conversation with those remote and multitudinous blue acquaintances down yonder beyond the foot pole till the dust was divided. Then he turned his hollow eyes and looked on the glittering little heaps, and he smiled to see that nearly all the big pieces were heaped on the biggest heap. And he was glad, for that would go to little Hez, who had worked night and day all the time that he lay there in the corner talking to his toes. Sim, the other brother, was good, but he had a beard on his chin; and he had a baby at home, too; but this boy was as Benjamin.

"Turn your back, Hez; whose?"

"Brother Zeke's."

It was a minute or two before Zeke could see straight enough to touch another pile with any precision. But when it was all divided they came up smiling and propped him in bed.

"Say, Hez," he said, as he took the largest piece on his pile in his slim, blue fingers, "say, I want you to take this and buy Sis a pirote. Oh, wont she cavort to hear it screech and scream and cuss!"

He tossed the nugget into his young brother's heap, and then after tying up and untying himself he took up another piece, and tossing it into the other brother's heap, said: "Say, you get her another pirote. Boys, get her three pirotes when you get to the isthmus! One might die, and then the other one would be lonesome like. Yes, one might die. That happens sometimes."

He pushed his gold all over and away from him and then, with the big blade of the jackknife he divided it in two and made them put it into their long buckskin bags as they stood there before him.

"An' now you git; you git to-night; an' you git now. Provisions is short, an' I need em, now as I am gittin' well, Go! go, go to-night. There! Good-by."

One hand to each in a long, hard clasp; and as they hurried out—for their hearts were full and they would not weep, these men of old, in the presence of anybody—they heard a piping cheery voice calling after them, "Say, don't forget the pirotes for Sis, boys."

I tried to read some more to him right away to keep him from talking to his toes about Sis and the "pirotes," and was right in the midst of the struggle between Simon and John, where the streets of Jerusalem were running blood, when he suddenly turned his head and said slowly: "Say, how much more is they of that fightin' an' when will you come to where Josephus had that trouble with Potiphar's wife?"

I closed the book and tucked up his feet, telling him as I did so that I would have to ask the librarian about it.

"That's right; an' say, you bring Frank Campbell with you to-morrow. I feel kind o' low, now that the boys is gone, an' want to git some speerits to pull me up like. Yes; good-by!"

Frank Campbell laughed that queer, quiet laugh of his as we went in there the next afternoon. For those feet, as if they must surely be going somewhere, had pushed away out, and out, and out; and the man's face was entirely under the blankets. Campbell tiptoed up and began to tickle his foot a little as he laughed and laughed that low, quiet laugh of his, for he did not want to startle him. But suddenly he let his right hand fall, and with his left lifted his hat and let it hang low down by his side as he said softly to himself, looking at the poor tired feet, "Going home."

*Placer Miners*

## THE DOMINANT VICE

Gambling and drinking were the dominant pastimes of the
Americans in the mines and before them of the Spanish inhabitants of California. A skilled class of gamblers presided over the
games of chance that saw large sums of money changing hands in
favor of the professionals. An aura of fact and legend surrounded
the gamblers, whose reputation for notorious guile was almost
exceeded by their reputed generosity. The *Golden Era,* under the
management of Rollin M. Daggett and J. Macdonough Foard,
printed reminiscences of real life-size gamblers who preceded in
time the Hamlins and Oakhursts of Bret Harte's work. The gambler of this sketch, "Lucky Bill," was the legendary William B.
Thorington, whose fabulous career began in the Mother Lode. In
1853 he went to the Carson Valley in Nevada, engaged in a number of businesses, gambled with emigrants, and excited the envy
and hatred of his neighbors. A victim of vigilante action, he was
found guilty of giving aid and comfort to a murderer and was
hanged June 17, 1858. He appears here under trying, though hap-
pier, circumstances than those that led to his end. ("'Lucky Bill,'
The Thimble Rigger: A Sketch of 1850 and '51," *The Golden Era,*
July 1, 1855.)

Of all the individuals who figured in California in early
times as desperate and successful gamblers, or rather as "thimble-
riggers" and French monte dealers, none are better known than
the subject of this sketch, Lucky Bill. Many who were in the State
as early as '50 or '51 will doubtless remember him. During the
greater portion of these two years he was a resident of Sacramento City, and almost any day might have been seen squatted
in front of some of the gambling houses, or near a street corner,
with a pile of doubloons beside him, offering to bet "two, four or
six ounces" that no one could find the "little joker" which he was
artistically moving about under the three "cups" placed in a row
upon his knee, or which was ingeniously hidden under his thumb-
nail. In the spring of '51, when "thimble-rigging" and French
monte were carried on to their greatest extent, and with such

57

success, too, that the fraternity practicing them were enabled to rent the largest gambling house in Sacramento (Lee's Exchange) for no other purpose than that of securing to themselves the right of exhibiting their games in front of it. Lucky Bill occupied a stool at the extreme west end of the porch of the building, and in two months time made $24,000. This sum seems immense for a gambler to make in the short space of sixty days, yet it is hardly a tithe of the amount to which Lucky Bill victimized the unwary during the three years preceding the passage of a law by our Legislature in 1852, prohibiting "French monte," "thimble game," "pick-i'-the-loop," and similar thieving games then practiced to an alarming extent throughout almost every portion of the State. Bill understood his business as well as anyone that ever undertook to mislead the eye of the verdant miner; and although his great success may doubtless be attributed to the dexterous and well-organized gang of hired "cappers," who, disguised as miners, laborers, traders, etc., etc., went from table to table and from game to game, making sham bets (which they generally won) and inviting the looker-on to "invest," yet not a small share of it was owing to his own shrewd management. Sometimes he would assume such an air of verdancy, and handle his "cups" so clumsily, that persons well acquainted with the nature of the game (better, I need not say, than with the man dealing it) imagining that they had found some one ignorant of his business, were induced to lay down a few ounces, religiously believing that an opportunity had at last presented itself for them to get even with previous losses; and others were ensnared and relieved of many an ounce by his counterfeiting intoxication, and recklessly tossing his money around, and exhibiting "deadwoods" (certainties of winning) to their temptation. One bet generally operated as an eye-opener, however, and relieved the loser of any erroneous idea that appearances may have warranted him in entertaining respecting Bill's verdancy or intoxication, for the bet always lost. Bill's usual method of attracting custom was the cry of—"Here, gentlemen, is a nice, quiet little game conducted on the square, and especially recommended by the clergy for its honesty and wholesome moral tendencies. I win only from blind men; all that have two good eyes can win a fortune. You see, gentlemen, here are three little wooden cups, and here is a little ball, which, for the sake of starting the game, I shall place under this one, as you can plainly see; and now I shall place it under this one, as you can plainly see, and now I shall place it under this, the middle one, merely to show how much quicker the hand is than the eye, and removing it from the middle, quietly cover it with the other, thus—and thus—and thus; and now I will bet two, four, or six ounces that no gentleman can the first time trying, raise the cup that the ball is under; if he can, he can win all the money that Bill, by patient toil and industry, has scraped together."

What Lucky Bill's real name is, or where he is from, I do not know, for as I scarcely expected to become his biographer, I never took the trouble to ascertain either. The first time I ever saw him was in the spring of 1851, although I had often heard of him before that time. I had been mining some three or four miles north of Placerville, and taking a notion into my head to visit Sacramento, had arrived in town just in time for the stage. We had travelled probably six miles, when a couple of men presented themselves by the side of the road and asked a passage into the city. As there was but one vacant seat, the driver told them that he could not accommodate both of them unless the passengers were willing, which was found not to be the case. Noticing that the travellers looked wearied, and recognizing one of them, although he did not remember me, I protested against the decision of the passengers so strongly, and appealed to their humanity so earnestly, that I at length secured them seats, although I could plainly see at the expense of the ill-will of the remainder of the passengers. However, I cared but little about that, as the journey would last but a few hours. The newcomers took their seats beside me, when, after making myself known to one of them— "Sidney Charley," a French monte dealer, who more than a year

59

previous had earned my gratitude, notwithstanding his profession, by paying my stage (or rather wagon) fare into the mountains—I inquired who his companion was, and what brought them to the road-side so early in the morning. He informed me in a low whisper that the person with him was "Lucky Bill," and that they had been taking a tramp of a few weeks through the mines; that two days before, had commenced operations in Placerville, and continued there with great success until the evening of the day following, when, in consequence of relieving a prominent citizen of $2000, the popular voice was raised against them, and they were compelled to *vamose* instanter, to keep from being swung up; that they had slept in the open air that night, not daring to apply to any house for lodging, and had commenced the journey to Sacramento on foot, when they were overtaken by the stage.

While he was informing me of this, I noticed that we began to attract considerable attention, and occasion some whispering among the passengers, which Lucky Bill noticed with a deal of uneasiness. This continued for some time, until I began to suspect the reason of it, and thought of making myself less familiar with Charley and his thimble-rigging companion, when a little, wiry-looking, middle-aged man, who had been intently eyeing Bill for sometime, rose partly up and asked him if he did not go by the name of Lucky Bill.

Bill looked at the stranger a moment, and then in a civil tone, asked why he inquired.

"For nothing in particular," replied the stranger, taking his seat; "if you are not him, I beg your pardon—if you are, why—"

"Why what?" interrupted Bill.

"Why, I might have something more to say to you," continued the stranger.

"Well, suppose I was to say that I am Lucky Bill—what then?"

"Then I would tell you," exclaimed the stranger, looking savage, that you are a d——d thief; that you as good as stole fifteen hundred dollars from a brother of mine two days ago, and that if you didn't refund every dollar of it to me, I'll cut your rascally heart out of you right in this stage," and with these words he drew a long butcher-knife from his belt, and leaned over a seat towards Bill for an answer.

"Then my reply would be, that two can cut out hearts at the same time," and as quick as thought Bill had drawn a large navy pistol, which he was just in the act of cocking as I caught his arm.

The passengers then interfered, but the stranger was not to be pacified, and continued to swing his knife around, to the danger of everyone near him, and to make every attempt to get within reach of Bill, who still held the pistol, uncocked, in his hand. Finding it would be impossible to keep them apart, it was proposed by some of the passengers that they should get out of the stage and fight it out. The stage was accordingly stopped, and all the passengers alighted, which was no sooner done, than the stranger made a dash at Bill without further ceremony. Some one stepped in front of him before he got within reach of his victim, but could not prevent him from throwing the knife, and with such precision, that the point of it passed along Bill's right side, inflicting a severe wound. Bill then cocked his pistol and fired, just as the other had drawn a revolver from his belt. The stranger fell, with a ball in his right shoulder. He was taken into the stage, followed by Bill, who was not injured so much as to prevent him from walking, and after a careful drive of three miles, both the wounded men and Charley were left at a hotel some fifteen or twenty miles below Placerville.

In three weeks after, I saw Bill "rope in" a teamster for two yoke of cattle, on the corner of J and Fourth streets, Sacramento City, and then sell the loser one yoke of them for sixty dollars, which was all the money he had, and loan him the other pair to get his wagon into the mountains.

Bill had a heart, and a kind one, too, if it was touched in the right place; and it was no uncommon occurrence for him to contribute fifty or a hundred dollars towards raising a fund for the relief of a destitute family, or to enable some unfortunate individual to return to the Atlantic States; and scarcely a day passed that he did not refund to someone money which he had won from him, upon ascertaining that it left the loser destitute. In one instance, I know of his winning three hundred dollars from an old man, on his way home. After he had lost it, he turned away with such a look of misery, that Bill called him back and asked him which way he was travelling, and if he was out of funds. The old man thought he was being ridiculed, but answered that he had no money left; that he had been six months in laying up the three hundred dollars which he had just foolishly lost, and with which he expected to have paid his passage home, but that he supposed nothing was left him now but to return to the mines. Bill inquired why he was so anxious to return to his family, and with scarcely money enough to pay his passage. The other answered that a short time before, he had learned that his wife was dead, and that three of his children were without a home. Bill did not ask another question, but handed the three hundred dollars back to the old man, which he had won from him, and two hundred dollars besides, saying as he did so—"Here, old man take back your money, and here is a trifle besides, which might be handy when you get home; I don't play to win money from such as you. Take it, and never again bet at any game, however strong the impulse may be; for the game that I play is about as honest as any other, and the devil couldn't win at it if he wasn't a 'capper.' " The old man took the money, and went away a wiser if not a better man.

In the fall of 1852 Bill returned to the Atlantic States, taking with him an immense sum of money, although it is said he lost $20,000 at "faro" before leaving the State. The next we hear of him is at St. Joseph, Mo., in the spring of 1853. He had run through all he possessed, and was again hiding the "little joker," and winning scores of cattle from the migrants. He crossed the Plains that season and settled in Carson Valley, where he is at present residing. He is again wealthy, owning a saw-mill and several thousand head of cattle and horses. It is said he contemplates joining the Mormons, and taking to his heart twenty or thirty wives which he will have an opportunity of doing, now that the Mormons are settling in Carson Valley. He seldom plays, except for amusement or when in want of a few yoke of cattle or a horse or two, and these he can win without difficulty from the emigrants. Of the immigration across the Plains in 1854, quite a number entered Placerville on foot, leaving cattle, horses, wagons and all in the hands of Lucky Bill, the "thimble-rigger." The next we shall hear of him will probably be as a Mormon prophet, with fifty wives and concubines.

# Laughter of the Argonauts

PISTOLS FOR TWO

The *Empire County Argus* of Coloma, which began publication in November, 1853, presented a bizarre account of a duel between Black Bill and Carolina Bob. Dueling was in vogue during the 1850's though the first constitution of California prohibited the practice. The humorous parody published in the *Argus* ridiculed the code in a year when two frontier editors had lost their lives on the field of honor. (*Empire County Argus*, December 9, 1854.)

A duel was fought day before yesterday in Greenhorn Valley—cause of difficulty, a dark skinned beauty loved by both gentlemen—Carolina Bob and Black Bill. Weapons Allens revolvers—distance ten paces—Bob won the choice of position and the word. At first fire Black Bill hit Carolina Bob where the Irishmen hit the deer. The second fire Bill hit Bob in the same place. Great efforts were now made to reconcile the parties, but without avail, as pistols were again provided, the combatants resumed their places looking the impersonation of courage and defiance. At the word two, both fired, Black Bill hitting Bob within one inch of where he had hit him twice before, the ball lodging in an oak tree twenty paces to the right of Bill, making a severe wound in the bark. Bob's ball accidentally hit a dog square in the ear killing him on the spot. Another effort was now made at reconciliation, a rub of seven-up was played by the

64

seconds, Bob's second won the game. The surgeons thereupon produced a jack knife and cut two holes through Black Bill's coat, and besmeared his shirt with the blood of the dog. Bob having agreed to stand the liquor for six. Thus ended this fatal duel, a dog having been killed. Awful things these wicked duels.

### A GENIAL PRANKSTER

Placerville, known as the old Dry Diggin's and then as Hangtown between 1848 and 1854, was the most prosperous and populous mining town in El Dorado County. The Methodists had established a religious organization there in April, 1850, and Catholic worship began about the same time, but the religious element was not able to keep the mining population from carousing and gaming, and only a frontiersman of the stature of Black Sand Jack, the genial prankster of this story, had the hardihood to meddle with the gamblers and their patrons on home territory. ("Black Sand Jack," San Francisco *Argonaut*, December 21, 1878.)

In the booming days of Placerville—then more commonly known as "Hangtown"—during the years '50 and '51 there was an immense canvas building, devoted to all the wickedness and cussedness that could be originated or imported from any land. Twenty or thirty gambling tables were kept constantly running—music, rum, and the necessary glitter.

Near the centre of the large room was a long sheet-iron box stove—for in those early days there was no cast-iron about—around which were common benches for the habitues to sit on, and warm themselves during the damp and cold winter evenings.

One dark and rainy night, when the room was packed full a man dressed entirely in buckskin came in; he was well known—known too, as a brave, fearless backwoodsman; he always carried his rifle and powder horn, and moved and looked like a revolving arsenal. But this evening, an unusual thing for him, he appeared to be drunk; his clear, strong voice would occasionally rise above

65

the murmured din and clink of coin, so that even the sitters around the stove seemed inclined to give him all the room he wanted.

At length, in a loud voice, he called for a drink, which was given him; and then he as loudly said:

"Boys, I have lived long enough."

From his powder horn he poured a lot of powder into his hand saying, "that is all right," and touched it off—the dull puff and whirl of smoke filled the air, and it seemed as if every eye was turned toward him. Then, apparently becoming furious over some imagined trouble, he tore the large powder horn from his side, advanced to the box stove, filled with blazing wood, and threw it in, crying in a loud and stentorian voice:

*"Now, let every man wait!"*

But there was no waiting—through the windows, out of the doors, even through the side of the house, over the tables, players, gamblers, lookers-on, all stampeded! There was never such a hurried wreck of a house before!

But as no explosion took place, those who had left large sums of money gradually crept back; for everywhere gold was scattered, and, of course, much was found that never went on the tables again.

The backwoodsman meantime had quietly stepped out the back-way, mounted his horse, and rode away in the gloom. And it was well he did so, for the gamblers hunted him for a week afterward. But eventually everybody laughed at the joke, and he became known as "Black Sand Jack," for of course his powder horn was filled with sand, except the little he turned into his own hand as an experiment—but that little experiment bewildered the boys.

A PIONEER OF '49

Colusa City of Colusa County is located fifty-three miles northwest of Sacramento on the Sacramento River, and in adjoin-

66

ing Sutter and Yuba counties to the west are Marysville and Yuba City. In this general locale, Colusa Nick, the ribald comedian of this story, was famous for his jokes and pranks. (Frank W. Gross, "Colusa Nick," San Francisco *Argonaut*, November 23, 1878.)

My hero is not a myth. He is neither a "Starbottle" nor a "Hawkhurst," nor a "fighting Tarantula from Tuolumne."

On the contrary he is a veritable personage living today in the town of Colusa, in this State, and is known to nearly every man, woman, and child in Yuba, Sutter, and Colusa counties. All through that section of country his drolleries, funny sayings, and witticisms are as familiar as household words, and it is an even chance that any man selected at random from among a crowd of the older residents would regale you with one of Nick's jokes in the course of a half hour's conversation, or employ it to point the moral of an argument. Nick is *sui generis*.

In my California experience, which has brought me in contact with as many original and humorous characters as it is the average lot of ordinary mortals to meet, I have never seen his like. His humor, though sometimes coarse, is bright and crisp, and always flows without seeming effort, popping and sparkling with the effervescence of champagne when occasion prompts the discharge of the metaphorical cork.

His jokes and witty sayings are not laboriously cudgeled from an unwilling brain in the quiet of a sanctum, written, rewritten, and studiously embellished, but they burst spontaneously, and ofttimes when least expected, from the confines of an inexhaustible fund of humor, and upon the slightest provocation.

And his fun bears no sting of malice. Hit where it may, the victim never thinks of taking offense. To "get mad" over one of Nick's shafts of wit would be the height of folly, for the exhibition of the wound inflicted would provoke an avalanche of ridicule from a non-sympathizing community that would completely overwhelm the complaining party and speedily convince him that it were better to have suffered the pain in silence than

67

have sought such relief. And Nick is thoroughly impartial in the distribution of his favors, but sends his pointed arrows wherever the humor suggests, regardless of politics, creed, nationality, color, or "previous condition of servitude."

Nick is a Pioneer—an Argonaut of '49. Arriving in Marysville in the early dawn of her prosperity, his open-hearted and open-handed ways, his proclivity for fun, and his quaint and original sayings soon made him exceedingly popular. No convivial party was complete without him. Those who missed the cracking of one of his jokes listened eagerly to its repetition by others, and if the after relation was imperfect it was only necessary to disclose the name of the author to secure its acceptance and hearty approval.

One of his first practical jokes is well, and by some sadly, remembered to this day. A citizen, whom we will call Brother Randolph, fancied that a neighbor was appropriating his chickens, and confidentially communicated his suspicions to Nick.

"I'll tell you what to do," said Nick, taking him cautiously aside; "you go home and gather in your chickens, and then tie a piece of red yarn on the left wing of every one of them. Tie it under the feathers where it won't be seen, and then when you see a chicken which you think is yours, you can easily prove property if it has your mark on it!"

The idea struck Brother R. as a capital one, and he acted promptly upon it. But in the meantime Nick had not been idle. Procuring a wholesale supply of red yarn, he spent that night among the Marysville hen-roosts, and few chickens there were in town next day that did not bear Brother R's private mark.

The joke soon bore fruit. Brother R. not only claimed his own, but his neighbors, and, in fact, everybody's chickens. The best citizens of Marysville were accused of stealing his fowl. Chicken coops were invaded with search-warrants, criminal prosecutions were instituted, actions were commenced in Justice's courts for the recovery of the feathered property, suits for slander were threatened, the lawyers reaped a rich harvest of small fees, and the town was kept in a hubbub until the chicken complication was finally settled. And when it leaked out that the whole thing was "one of Nick's jokes," those who had been the maddest were perforce compelled to laugh loudest and treat oftenest to turn the tide of ridicule that threatened to overwhelm them.

Nick was never addicted to partisan politics. Being a Virginian his natural leanings are toward the Democracy; but it has always been his pleasure and his boast that he "don't care for party, but works for his friends." In 1852 he was porter and salesman with the house of John C. Fall & Co.—then doing the largest business of any concern in Northern California. Mr. Fall became a candidate for the State Senate, and Nick was of course active in his behalf. On the morning of the election Mr. Fall handed him the key to his safe and said:

"Nick, I am very anxious to win this fight. You will find about $800 in the safe. Take it and spend it among the boys where you think it will do the most good."

Nick was very active that day. Wine flowed like water, "the boys" were flush and happy, and the noisy indications were all favorable to the election of Mr. Fall. Late in the afternoon, and just before the closing of the polls, the latter stepped into the Magnolia Saloon, and there was Nick holding forth to a crowd, flourishing aloft in his right hand a bundle of ballots, and, in tones inspired by a free indulgence in wine, offering to bet on Fall's election.

"Do you think I've won, Nick?" asked Mr. Fall.

"Won? Why, of course you've won! No doubt of it. Dead sure as four aces," responded Nick.

"What makes you think so?" asked Mr. Fall.

"Why, I've plumped a hundred and twenty-four of them fellers into the ballot box this afternoon," said Nick, triumphantly shaking his tickets.

"Let me see them," said Mr. Fall.

Nick handed him a ballot; he gave it a single glance, and his countenance fell.

"My God, Nick, you've beaten me!" he exclaimed, and it was

true. Some cunning fellow of the opposition had taken advantage of Nick's hilarity and substituted for the genuine ballots bearing Mr. Fall's name bogus ones, on which the name of James E. Stebbins, his opponent, had been substituted, and John C. Fall missed being a California Senator by five votes.

There is but one well authenticated instance of Nick having ever again taken a part in a political contest, and that was on an occasion, some years since, when W. T. Ellis, a present prominent merchant of Marysville, was a candidate for the office of City Treasurer. On election day, so the story goes, he quietly slipped a twenty-dollar piece into Nick's hand and informed him that he would be glad of his assistance, which was promptly tendered. During the day the candidate visited the polling places, but saw nothing of Nick, and finally went to Nick's house, where he found him lying on the lounge, smoking and reading the paper, utterly unmindful of the political contests waging without.

"Why," said Mr. E., in surprise, "I thought you were going to work for me!"

"I have," cooly responded Nick.

"But I gave you twenty dollars to spend for me," said Mr. E.

"That's so," replied Nick. "I spent a dollar of it among the boys, and it took the other nineteen to convince me."

It might be inferred from this anecdote that Nick's political conscience was somewhat elastic, but it is probable that he preferred exposing his character to that suspicion rather than lose so good an opportunity for perpetrating a joke.

Another illustration in point: When Hon. James A. Johnson, our present Lieutenant-Governor, returned home after his second term in Congress, he desired to take the stage from Colusa to Marysville, but there was a slight obstacle in the way. Governor, then Congressman, Johnson had always been too honest a man to profit pecuniarily from his official positions, and on this occasion lacked sufficient money with which to purchase a ticket by the stage and was compelled to borrow it. Nick heard of the matter, and when next he met Johnson said to him, with great seriousness:

"Doc."—the Governor is popularly known as Doc. Johnson in the Third Congressional District.—"Doc., I've always been your friend; I worked for you both times when you was elected to Congress, but this lets me out. I'm ashamed of you, Doc., I'm ashamed of you."

"What's the matter, Nick?" asked Johnson.

"Doc., I thought you was a statesman. I thought you had a little sense; but I've come to the conclusion that you're a d——d fool!"

"Why, Nick, that's pretty hard talk. What in the world do you mean?" asked Johnson.

"Well," said Nick, "here you've been two terms in Congress, and have to borrow a little ticky two dollars and a half to buy a stage ticket. Now, I ain't no statesman, but you just bet your life if I'd been four years in Congress I'd have owned a quarter section of the Northern Pacific Railroad."

Some years since Nick left Marysville, and took up his abode in Colusa, where he opened a saloon which he now keeps, and his relation of his early experience in his new home was exceedingly interesting and amusing. I will endeavor to tell his story as nearly as possible in his own style:

"When I went to Colusa," said Nick, " I wanted to get the trade of them lop-eared Missourians, so I went down to the bay, and I laid in a stock of the best whisky that had ever been seen in that town. But, don't you know, them six-toed Missourians would come in and take a horn of that whisky, and turn up their noses, and they wouldn't come back again. I tried to find out the reason, and one day one of 'em told me. 'Why,' said he, 'it's too powerful weak!' Then I sent down and got a lot of Barbary Coast tanglefoot. That suited 'em better, but they said it didn't take a good hold. Then I mixed up some benzine and sulphuric acid, and they said it was pretty good, but it wouldn't stay by a feller.

So at last I went to work and made up a decoction of poison oak and buckeye, and called it the 'Sheep-Herders' Delight.' You oughter seen them huskies go for it. One drink of it would set a feller to turnin' flip flaps. A peddler come into the place one day and took two drinks of it, and managed to get away. About two hours afterwards he came back and said he'd been robbed of his pack. I knew the effects of the 'Sheep-Herders' Delight.' So I went out and hunted around, and found his pack where he had hid it in the bushes and forgot all about it. I tell *you* it's a mighty popular drink over there."

During the War of the Rebellion Colusa was a very hotbed of treason, its inhabitants being mostly from Arkansas, Missouri, and the Southwestern States. Shortly after the commencement of hostilities, Nick, who was an unswerving and earnest Union man, determined to celebrate the Fourth of July.

"There was one American in the town besides me," said Nick. "Well, we went and got an old anvil, and we took her down on the bank of the Sacramento River and loaded her up, and about daylight we commenced banging away. We'd fired about a dozen salutes, and jest as day was breaking we saw half a dozen things in the river that looked like ducks coming towards us. In a little while they reached the bank where we were, and we saw that they were a lot of Missourians, with their clothes tied to their heads and rifles in their hands swimming the river. When they reached the shore the head man, a big husky more than six feet high, climbed up the bank, and planking the butt of his rifle on the levee, sung out:

"I say, stranger, *whar's the war?*"

But this happened, if it happened at all, in the comparatively early days of Colusa, which has since become more cosmopolitan in her population and now boasts of all the concomitants of civilization and refinement. She has good public schools and churches and an excellent town and county government. Most of the Southwestern people are Campbellites, and they have erected a neat little church in the town for their peculiar worship.

72

Nick, for some reason, became a great admirer of "Brother Porter," the pastor, and lost no opportunity in sounding his praises. One Sunday he took a friend to his favorite church, and, after the services were over and they were walking quietly home, his friend broke the silence by remarking:

"Nick, that's a nice little church and a good preacher, but it's a new thing to me to see a congregation stand up when the minister prays. They always kneel in my church."

"Why," exclaimed Nick, "you don't s'pose Brother Porter would let them huskies kneel in that new church, do you?"

"And why not?" asked his friend.

"Because if he did," responded Nick, "John Boggs, Frank Goad, Bill Harrington, Doc. Glenn, and all of them moneylenders would snake out their pencils in prayer time *and figure up their interest money on the backs of them new pews.*"

Coming down on the Sacramento boat soon after, I was heartily glad to meet Nick as a fellow-passenger. His droll sayings and funny stories soon transformed a tedious journey to a pleasure-trip.

"And how is Brother Porter's church getting on?" I asked.

"It's all right *now,*" said he; "but it had a mighty close call a while ago, and-you-hear-me!"

"How so?" I inquired.

"Well," said Nick, "you see ther was one o'them cussed Missourians come to town with a jackass, and bought a lot right alongside the church, and every time that jackass would squeal the whole congregation would run out doors. For a little while 'twas a question whether the church or the jackass would have to move, but Brother Porter he jes threw hisself and rassled with the Lord and *you bet that jackass had to go.*"

Up to a very recent date most of the light freight destined for Colusa was taken there on the tops of the stage from Marysville. On one occasion a Colusa undertaker was the consignee of several burial caskets, which loaded on the top of the stage gave it a decidedly funereal appearance and attracted the attention of an old lady passenger on the back seat. Nick was her *vis-a-vis*, and her extreme nervousness soon excited his interest and curiosity.

The old lady finally spoke to Nick in a tremulous tone. "Are those—those—*corpses*, on the top of the stage?"

"Oh, no, marm," replied he. "They're only empty coffins."

Both relapsed into silence for a few minutes, when the old lady asked: "Why do they carry them on the passenger coach?"

At this moment the spirit of mischief took possession of Nick. His eyes twinkled, and his sympathies for the elderly female's nervous sensibilities vanished in the provocativeness of a practical joke.

"You've never been to Colusa, have you, madam?" he asked, confidingly and mysteriously.

"N–n–no, sir!" she stammered.

"Well, yer see, it's very dangerous going up and down, and around these mountain curves, and so they take them coffins along for the passengers in case of accident," said he softly.

"To–to–to send the bodies to Colusa?" she inquired.

"Oh, no!" said Nick. "They bury 'em right alongside the road. 'Twouldn't be any use to take 'em to Colusa when they was dead, you know. *They wouldn't enjoy their visit.*"

The old lady buried her face in her handkerchief and when, with a sigh of relief, she alighted from the stage at the end of her journey, she was utterly ignorant of the fact that the entire distance traveled had been across a plain.

One more of Nick's jokes, which will be best appreciated in San Francisco, and I will close. Your readers doubtless will remember the Pioneer celebration of 1875, the twenty-fifth anniversary of the admission of California into the Union the '49 ers congregated here from all parts of the State and were *not* received by their metropolitan brethren; but they couldn't get any lunch at Woodward's Garden; how mad they got thereat; how the balloon collapsed, and Tommy Newcomb got his arm broken; and how the failure of the celebration was made entirely disastrous through the mismanagement of the excursion around

74

the harbor on the steamship *Great Republic*. Nick was one of the pilgrims and came as a member, or guest, of the Society of Pioneers of Colusa.

The morning after the trip around the Bay I met Nick on Montgomery Street, and as the affair was the greatest object of adverse criticism I was curious to see what he would say about it.

"Well, Nick," I said, "I suppose you went on the excursion. How did you enjoy it?"

"Yes," replied he, "I went, and had a bully time. I just rung in with the Cap'n, and had all the boned turkey and champagne I wanted." And after a pause he added: "But a lot of our party from Colusa made a mistake and didn't go."

"What mistake did they make?" I asked.

"Well, you see," said Nick, "a lot o'them six-toed, lopeared Missourians had come across the plains in bull teams and never seen a steamship, and they mistook the Lost Bridge for the *Great Republic*, and thought that a pile-drive was the smoke-stack, *and I'm d——d if them huskies didn't stand on that bridge all day long waitin' for 'em to to cast off the lines.*"

I have presented these few jokes as samples called from a seemingly inexhaustible stock that increases as the days go by, for Nick, although fairly advanced in years, has lost none of that keen sense of humor and love of fun that have made his name famous where he has lived. Kind-hearted, open-handed, chivalrous, and brave, he is a fair specimen of a large class of Pioneer Californians who are rapidly yielding to the inexorable march of old Father Time, and who are erroneously supposed to have lived only in the creations of romantic brains.

FORTY-NINER'S LAMENT

A newspaper in eastern Nevada, two decades after the forty-niners had tramped the Sierras, printed a lament intended to mark the passing of the old breed. To many of the early California miners, hustling about in the mining camps of Nevada in the

75

prime of their manhood, the verses might have reminded them of the gray hair on their own heads and the irreversible passing of their youth. The verses have been attributed to the minstrel singer, Charles Bensell, known to stage audiences as Charley Rhoades. This version antedates, with some minor stylistic differences, the song printed in the *Great Emerson Popular Songster*, issued by the San Francisco publisher S. C. Blake in 1872. The song has undergone textual changes in various reprintings and has had in truncated form a curious half-life of its own. (Elko *Independent*, September 16, 1871.)

> Oh, here you see old Tom Moore,
>    A relic of former days.
> And a bummer, too, they call me now!
>    But what care I for praise?
> For my heart is filled with the days of yore,
>    And oft do I repine
> For the days of old, the days of gold,
>    And the days of Forty-nine.
>
> I'd comrades then who loved me well—
>    A jovial, saucy crew;
> There were some hard cases, I must confess,
>    But still they were brave and true,
> Who'd never flinch, whate'er the pinch—
>    Would never fret nor whine,
> But like good old bricks, they stood the kicks
>    In the days of Forty-nine.
>
> There was Kentuck Bill, I knew him well—
>    A fellow so full of tricks;
> At a poker game he was always thar,
>    And as heavy, too, as bricks;
> He'd play you draw, he'd into a slug,
>    And go a hatful blind;
> But in a game with Death, Bill lost his breath,
>    In the days of Forty-nine.

There was Monte Pete, I'll ne'er forget,
    For the luck that he always had;
He'd deal for you both night and day,
    Or as long as you had a scad.
One night a pistol laid him out,
    'Twas his last lay-out in fine;
It caught Pete sure, right in the door,
    In the days of Forty-nine.

There was New York Jake, a butcher boy,
    So fond of getting tight;
And whenever Jake got on a spree
    He was spoiling for a fight.
One day he run agin a knife
    In the hands of old Bob Cline,
So over Jake we had a wake
    In the days of Forty-nine.

There was Rackensack Jim, who could outroar
    A buffalo bull—you bet;
He roared all day, he roared all night,
    And I believe he's roaring yet.
One night he fell in a prospect hole—
    'Twas a roaring bad design—
For in that hole Jim roared out his soul
    In the days of Forty-nine.

There was poor old Jess, a hard old case
    Who never would repent;
Jess never missed a single meal
    Nor never paid a cent.
But poor old Jess, like all the rest,
    Did to Death at last resign,
For in his bloom he went up the flume
    In the days of Forty-nine.

Of all the comrades I had then
    Not one remains to toast;

77

They have left me here in my misery,
　　Like some poor wandering ghost;
And as I go from place to place
　　Folks call me a traveling sign,
Saying, "Here's Tom Moore, a bummer, sure,
　　Of the days of Forty-nine.

# PART TWO

# Hard Rock Mining

# Hard Rock Enterprisers

MINING PROVERBS

These proverbs appeared in newspapers published in Lake and Red Mountain cities, located in Colorado's rugged San Juan mountain country. The earliest of the two camps to come into existence was Lake City in 1874. The mineral wealth of the district was sufficient to support two newspapers and four churches by the early 1880's. The continuous search for the precious metals led to the opening of the Red Mountain district during the winter of 1883, when prospectors staked claims in ten feet of snow and two newspapers started publication in the midst of feverish activity. The nuggets of advice printed in the columns of the *Mining Register* and the *Pilot* spoke the language of the industrious hard-rock mining community. ("Mining Proverbs," Red Mountain City *Pilot*, June 2, 30, 1883. Reprinted from the Lake City *Mining Register*.)

You can't knock a ten-foot hole into a lode and then sit on the dump and talk about your "mine" without becoming a subject of ridicule.

You can't sell a confectionery on a stick-of-mint-candy sample; neither can you sell three hundred by one thousand five hundred feet of a mining claim on a vest-pocket specimen.

An assay certificate for 1,000 ounces silver to a ton of 2,000 pounds is about as valuable in the mining market as a ten thousand dollar Confederate bond on Wall street.

When you tell a purchaser how your property can be developed by a two hundred foot cross-cut tunnel that will intersect the vein a thousand feet deep, you cross-cut the trade and had better cut your throat. That class of idiots died last year.

Sharp drills and a hammer are like unto the business end of a wasp: they create a sensation when they commence moving.

A fool and his hard-earned assessment money are soon parted. Stud-horse poker hasn't temper enough to develop a bonanza.

When you send a two thousand dollar superintendent from a grocery store in the East to work your property in the mountains, you have put the fire-end of the cigar in your mouth and you won't be a year discovering that fact.

A good trail to your prospect is a good thing if there is a good prospect at the upper end of it. Business people don't climb trails for scenery.

The drill has the only eye that can fathom the wealth of a prospect.

The ore purchaser's certificate of a five-ton mill-run and his check for the ducats will recommend your property where an expert's gush fails.

When you leave the prospect you have clung to five years to seek a fortune in a new excitement, you follow the example of the greedy dog with his breakfast in his mouth who saw his shadow in the water.

The prospector, like the cavalryman in the army, leads the advance and covers the rear. It is the settler and the tin-horn "capitalist" who carry off the spoils.

A location certificate and a location stake are of equal value: but a good pay-streak outstrips them in a sale.

Whenever you see a man tearing around with a pound specimen in his hand, claiming he "struck it rich," you may set it down in your book that he has just passed out of barren quartz.

When a prospector tells you with a tired sort of satisfaction that he has just completed his annual assessment, you can bet your bottom dollar he will never "get there."

Success in the mountains is only secured by untiring preservence, steel, grit, hope, faith and eternal vigilance.

The boys who worked their claims last winter on grub stakes laid up riches for the future.

One foot of giant powder is worth more than ten thousand yards of gush. Drill and blast is the music that charms.

Blessed is he who mindeth his own business and back'cappeth not his neighbor.

Flood and tornado are less to be feared in the mountains than fraud and idleness.


MINER'S CREED

The groans, gripes, and disappointments of the Pikes Peak miners who rushed to Colorado were many. The majority of the men in the mines were young and strong, but they found good paying claims in the mountains hard to come by. Rather than give up and turn back many went to work for the more fortunate, laboring ten hours a day at the rate of four to six dollars per week and subsisting upon bread, beans, bacon, and black coffee. Even with the bad luck and attendant hardships the search for new mining fields was pursued avidly by those who had failed to make a stake in the first strikes. ("Articles in a Miner's Creed," *Rocky Mountain News*, June 8, 1861.)

He believes in fifty cents to the pan and the bed rock "pitching."

He believes that feathers in straw pillows should not be over six inches long and an inch square.

He believes in the top dirt paying wages, and the water money; and the bottom dirt—a fortune.

He believes that sheets in hotels should not be considered clean after five weeks use without washing.

He believes that Gold is found in Quartz, but he would be satisfied to find it in pints—or, even half-pints.

He believes in going to bed to sleep, and not to chase fleas—even in dreams—moreover.

He believes that all over a quarter of an inch should be caught by the—landlady.

He believes there is plenty of gold here, but precious little falls to his share—somehow; yet.

He believes that it don't pay to sell out everything to come to Pike's Peak, and then go home without the "ore."

He believes that butter sent to the mines should not be used as a motive power—although strong enough for anything.

He believes that labor is not the only capital now required for a good claim.

He believes in "the good time coming"—but thinks it must have started for the San Juan on a prospecting trip, and got lost in a snow storm.

He believes that if old Father Time had any regard for our prosperity, he would take the juvenile by the ear and thus admonish him,—"My son, if you're coming, why don't you come along?"

He believes that hard work, hard prospects, hard beds and hard living will harden him into premature old age. Still . . .

He believes after all that three or four dollars a day is better than six bits.

He believes that hash set upon the table twice a day for two weeks, after that, should be considered pickles.

He believes that "prospecting" may have paid others, but it never did him.

He believes that a good Sunday dinner is not hard to take after a week's work and fasting on slap-jacks and molasses.

He believes in Hope, but thinks he has lived on that long enough, and would now like something a little more substantial.

He believes it uncomfortable to feed flat-backed live stock in beds, after being charged for his lodgings.

He believes that every man separated so long from his family or friends, and the comforts and pleasures of a good home, deserves to be well paid, after striving hard for it, if he isn't.

He believes—or rather thinks—that those who labor the hardest are not always the best paid—at least that's his experience.

He believes in big vegetables, because he sees them; but wonders if there is any other kind of fruit than dried apples, dried apples scalded, and dried apples with the strings in.

He believes that every man who plays at cards, when he should be at work, would look rather foolish and ashamed if his friends could just drop in and see him.

He believes that nine persons sleeping in one room, only twelve by ten, should not allow the landlord to double the number—at the same charge.

He believes that hill diggings will last for ages, and quartz diggings forever; and that all the waters of every mountain stream will yet be required for mining purposes.

He believes that blankets used over three years, without washing or airing, are entitled to "walk off" on their own account "for parts unknown;" and that no sadle horse or lasso should be kept in readiness for their re-capture.

He believes that his cabin looks rather lonely at night; and further, that it would not, if someone that he knows lived within it.

He believes that man to be a knave who foolishly squanders his hard earnings here, and allows his wife and children to be starving at home.

He believes that the cooks in hotels should not always be known by the different colored hairs in his pudding.

He believes that no able-bodied man need want in Pike's Peak—if he is willing to work. Moreover,

He believes that it is better not to wait for "something to turn up," but in going to work at once and turning something up.

He believes that where he is, there his family should be—and that one home for one family has less expense and immeasurably more comfort than two can have.

He believes, too, that with gentle hands to aid him, gentle

words to cheer him, and gentle smiles to welcome him, he could enjoy life as it passes, and work hard and willingly until fortune should crown his labors with success—for

He believes that Pikes Peak, with all its social drawbacks, is not only a "great country," but that it is in every sense the best in the world for a working man, and only awaits the coming of a good, sensible, intelligent, and contented class of noble-minded women to make "the desert to blossom as the rose," and man to become rich, contented and happy.

So mote it be.

### Enterprise and Enterprisers

The assessment system of raising money for opening a mine was used extensively in the era of hard-rock mining. The officers of a company would levy a sum on the stock held by the shareholders. This system of amassing capital was the subject of satire in a story printed in the Salt Lake *Tribune*. At the time of writing in 1881 the center of mining activity in Utah was Silver Reef, located in the vicinity of present day Zion National Park. Though mining districts were organized near Salt Lake City in 1864 and 1865, the development of silver mining in southwestern Utah did not occur until the late 1870's. ("Two Kinds of Mining," Lake City *Mining Register*, December 20, 1881. Reprinted from the Salt Lake City *Tribune*.)

A few evenings since a couple of mining men, both strangers to each other, met in the reading room of the Walker House. The conversation turned to the mineral development of the west, and presently one of the men remarked, "If you want to see mining on a big scale, just go to southern Utah.

"How big?" said the other quietly.

"Why, the Big Hole mine that I am connected with, has the deepest shaft and biggest workings in the world."

"How deep?" said the little man.

"You can't measure it, because if we stopped work long enough to see how deep the shaft was, it would materially interfere with the bullion product. We dropped a line down once and reeled it out until it broke with its own weight. When a boy falls down that shaft he strikes the bottom as a grandfather."

"Must have a big pay roll?"

"We used to send the money down to the hands in cages until the workings got so deep that we didn't get the winter account settled until way long in the spring. So we started a bank and telegraphed the money orders. That system saved us an awful wear and tear on the cages. The miners live down there and rear their families. They've got an underground city bigger'n Salt Lake, with a regular charter, and hold municipal elections twice a year. They publish two daily papers down there and a literary magazine."

"I never heard of the magazine," said the stranger.

"Of course not; it would be a year old when it got to you. Besides, they hold a fair there every year and horse-racing every Saturday. Finest four-mile track in the world, lit up with electric lights. No mud, no dust, always in the same condition. Perfect paradise for sports. What do you think of that for a mine?"

Here the stranger, who was a Californian, threw his leg carelessly over the arm of his chair and, lighting a fresh cigar, replied in a deep, earnest tone:

"I don't think much of your mine. You work too much for small results. When your mine plays out you have a lot of old machinery on your hands, and where are you? You mine after primitive methods, like all new countries. It takes experience and headwork to tackle the industry in proper shape. With your mine you must be on the ground in person, and have any amount of men to look after this department or that. Now I have a bigger mine than yours. It is located in Storey county, somewhere in the northern part, I believe, and I run it quite up to the handle with one or two assistants."

"How deep might the shaft be?" asked the other.

"It might be pretty deep if I allowed the men to rush forward and overdo the thing, but at present there is no shaft."

"Hoisting works up?"

"No, no hoisting works—not if I know it. You can fool away a great deal of hard coin on hoisting works."

"How in thunder do you work your mine?"

"On the assessment plan, sir. That's the latest and most approved method. We have a big map of the mine hung up in the company's office, made by one of the most competent artists on the coast. Now when we have a good map of the lower workings we don't need any workings to speak of. We photograph the Savage hoisting works from the top of Hale and Norcross trestle work—an entirely new view—and call it by our own name, the Bullion Brick. I keep a man in Virginia at $60 a month to superintend the location and write weekly letters, and I stay in San Francisco in my office on Pine street, and levy the assessments every sixty days, that's as often as the law allows. I'm the president, board of trustees, secretary, treasurer and everything. Of course, I draw a salary for all the offices, and when I get through drawing salaries, I turn the rest over to the agent in Virginia to pay off the hands. By not employing any hands he saves enough to pay himself. My regular income from that mine is $200,000 a year and never a pick stuck in the ground. This is what I consider scientific mining, sir. You get the silver out of the pockets of the stockholders and leave the vast argentiferous and auriferous deposits in your claim for your children, who can go right ahead and develop the mine just as soon as the public quit putting up. As soon as a man drops on the game he dies, and the newcomers all have to learn for themselves."

"But," said the Utah man, "my style of mining keeps a lot of men at work."

"So does mine," quoth the Golden Gate chap. "Thousands of men are working night and day to pay assessments. It keeps the country as busy as a bee hive," and the speaker sauntered to the telegraph office to order assessment number 36.

## A Mining War

A mining war, which occurred in 1868 in the comparatively quiet town of Austin, Nevada, was fought underground with spectacular pyrotechnics. The battle between the men of the Buel North Star and the Plymouth mining companies led to the death of George Cook, foreman of the Buel North Star Company. The death of Cook took place under the following circumstances. The Buel North Star miners drifted into the works of the Plymouth Company. Hostilities were engaged in by the men in the employ of both companies, prompting the building of a fire at the mouth of the shaft by the Plymouth men. Cook, who had unadvisedly entered the mine, was overcome by noxious gases. A coroner's inquest probed the causes of death and the report was published in an Austin newspaper. (*Reese River Reveille*, July 20, 1868.)

Inquest held by Justice W. K. Logan, Acting Coroner, on Saturday, July 18, 1868, over the body of George Cook, who was found dead in the Buel North Star mine, on Friday, the 17th of July.

*Verdict of the Jurors*: In the matter of the inquisition upon the body of George Cook deceased, we the undersigned, the jurors . . . having been duly sworn according to law, and having made such inquisition after inspecting the body and hearing the testimony adduced, upon our oaths each and all do say that we find that the deceased was named George Cook, was a native of Scotland, aged about 27 years; that he came to his death on the 17th day of July A.D. 1868 in this country, by suffocation, having been found lying in the Buel North Star mine, about eighty feet above the sump of the main incline, suffocated by inhalation of deadly gases generated by the burning of charcoal by the Buel North Star Company and burning wood by the Plymouth in their respective works; and that this disastrous event was caused by a persistent and reckless attempt of the superintendents of said companies to smoke each other out.

*Testimony Leading to the Foregoing Verdict*: Hugh McLane, being sworn, deposed substantially as follows: I was working for the Buel North Star Company of which George Cook was foreman; I think it was at 9 o'clock yesterday morning that George Cook went down the incline of the mine; he was down about 15 or 20 minutes before I went down; could not see the wire shake or hear the ringing of the bell; asked the carman to hoist the car; he did so, but Cook was not upon it; I was then sent down, and I took two lighted candles with me, but they went out; I was lowered slowly to the sumphole; I halloed "George" three times as loud as I could, but there was a big gale of smoke which stifled me; I pulled the wire three times but the car did not start, and I then wrapped the wire around my wrist and pulled it with all my force, but the car did not start; I thought then it was time for me to make tracks; I had my senses pretty well then, and I started up the incline following along the air box and keeping a look out for Cook; I was getting weak in the legs and I had to sit down; after resting I traveled up again; my legs got very feeble and I fell down and I had hard work to get up; I heard a voice hilloa, which I answered, and climbed towards the man while he came towards me; I caught hold of his waistband and he pulled me up, but I fell and lost my senses, and I don't know how I got out of the incline. Cook went down to see if he could stand the air; it was very good when he went down and also when I went down; it was not clear of smoke or vapor, but was the same as the day before; Cook did not come up because he pulled the wire and it did not act; the smoke killed George Cook; it came from the Plymouth mine; the kind of smoke yesterday, as far as I could judge, was created by different sorts of acids; it was not the same as the day before; I had gone down about 250 or 300 feet when the candles went out; the incline is 500 feet deep; I believe the volume of smoke which stifled me was driven from the Plymouth shaft; every few minutes a heavy gale of wind would come from the Plymouth works, with smoke and vapor; a current of air constantly passes from the Plymouth works up the incline of the Buel North Star; we could not work in the smoke until yesterday except to draw water; a candle would burn.

T. F. Fuller sworn and deposed substantially as follows: I have not been in the employ of the Buel North Star since June last; was at the mine yesterday but did not see any fire at the mouth of the incline; I saw Cook when he was brought out of the mine; I think his death was caused by suffocation; the smoke was not sufficient to cause death when he went down the mine but it was afterwards; a current of air passes constantly from the Plymouth works into the Buel North Star, caused by pouring water down their shaft; I was in the Plymouth company's works last Tuesday; I went in first and Mr. Lane and Mr. Cook came in afterwards; the Buel North Star people worked into the Plymouth works; I stayed there about an hour, called the men to stop the drift, and then built a barricade to prevent ingress from the Plymouth works; our object was to keep possession of the property and prevent them taking out the quartz; don't know how long it was after we broke through that they built the fire; I believe their fire was built to prevent our men going in there as they might take out the quartz; the men who went into the Plymouth ground were not armed; I believe weapons were found in the drift; I asked Mr. Scrimgeour for them; I furnished the weapons to two of the men to hold possession of the drift, and to prevent the Plymouth men from getting in while we were absent at court; I went there to hold the ledge, and did not suppose there would be any trouble. . . .

Marcus Lane sworn and examined, deposed as follows: Am Acting Superintendent of the Buel North Star Company; I had given orders that nothing should be done to disturb the Plymouth Company in their possession; night before last Cook stated that he wanted to put a fan in for the object of driving back their smoke on the Plymouth Company so that they could not build any more fire; he stated that during the day and evening two men had been brought up insensible, and he could not keep the water out of the mine unless this smoke was driven back, and he intended to build a small fire at the mouth of our incline to make certain that they could not start more upon us; I gave my consent provided that no attempt should be made to take possession of the smoking part of either mine; when the fan was started Cook built a small fire; I saw the materials of which it was composed, but did not see him put them on; he had about a hat full of shavings and two shovels full of fine coal in a box; saw the box after he had built the fire, and should judge about half of it was left; stayed there about three-quarters of an hour and only saw him replenish the fire once; it was done from the box without refilling; I then went home; next morning was informed that the fan broke down a short time after I left; the fire was placed within 15 feet of the mouth of the incline; this was the fire I talked about with Dr. Wixom; think it was not replenished after the fan stopped; left there about 2 A.M.; if the fire had been replenished after then it would only have blown out into the building, for the current was changed. . . .

Francis Barkle sworn: I have been in the employ of the Plymouth Company some time; had orders on Tuesday afternoon to take a number of men and see what could be done with the barricade; I thought the best way would be to put powder under it and blow it down; about 30 pounds of powder were sent down for that purpose; the men of the Buel North Star were told of our intention, and they were allowed plenty of time to get out of the mine; we set fire to the fuse and went to the surface until the explosion took place; after it occurred we went down again, and there was no one in the drift, but our men picked up two loaded revolvers; the men kindled a fire in the drift; a small fire was kept burning just close to the hole made by the Buel North Star men. . . . the object in making a fire was to keep out the Buel North Star people after they had taken forcible possession; the fire was made of pine and cedar wood; nothing was used by our men except common timber; yesterday morning the smoke came back almost suffocating; I received no orders from Mr. Scrimgeour in regard to arms, but he told me to get possession in the best way we could; I don't know who suggested the building of the fires; a small fire was kept up from Wednesday until Friday, on which day another fire was built by our men. . . .

R. J. Moody, sworn and examined, testified substantially as follows: Had conversation with Lane yesterday about fires; he was denouncing the Plymouth Company for burning tar and brimstone in their mine; I suggested it was in his mine that was done; he denied it; asked him what he was burning, he said he was burning coal. . . .

(John H. Boalt testified that charcoal produces carbonic acid and carbonic oxyd. Both gases are fatal to human life when present in any considerable amount.)

# Prospectors and Miners

## AN ARIZONA PROSPECTOR

The mind and manner of a desert prospector are portrayed by James W. Gally, a Nevada pioneer of the 1860's. Gally lived with his wife and two children at Hot Creek in southeastern Nevada, where he was for a few years Justice of the Peace, and at various times part owner of a mine, a rancher, a teamster, and a correspondent for the *Territorial Enterprise*. After ten years in Nevada he bought a fruit ranch in the beautiful Pajaro Valley, near Watsonville in California, and it was there that he raised his two children after the death of his wife. Always a man of many intellectual interests, he made a joint project of running the ranch and writing about politics, horticulture, his own rambling travels, and now and then the mining life of prospectors and miners. (James W. Gally, "A Listening Loafer," San Francisco *Argonaut*, October 2, 1880.)

I t's all well enough to talk about living on nothing for forty days and nights, but you don't get none o' that soup into me," said Colddecker, as he and "Big Bill" sat with their booted legs across opposite corners of the same table in Squeakem's bar-room.

"O' course not—not into you," said Bill. "You're mor'n twict as smart as most other people. I've knowed you a long time. Nobody can't fool you. You never invested your money in 'white heat'—a

94

patent fire what was to burn water and wind (mostly wind), and smelt ore for less'n nothin' a ton. Oh, no! can't nothin' fool you. Your other name is Solomon."

"Well, now, look here, haven't I got a stummick?"

"I shouldn't say 'at you hed—ef you leave it to me. Talk about havin' a craw, er a bellony, an' ye kin summon me on behalf of the defense. An' ef ye hed a stummick, it wouldn't be ol' Tanner's stummick—an' ye haint got his sand ner his imagination."

"What good'd his 'magination do him? A feller can't live on that."

"He can't?"

"No, he can't."

"Well, a dern sight of people comes mighty nigh Livin' on it now, ef ye're liss'nen' to me."

Perceiving the possibility that this nervy style of dialogue would drift into something better than average ennui, I took a seat at the same table and threw my booted legs across one of its unoccupied corners. Outside, in the streets of the California village the threshing machines were yawning for repairs, the mechanics were busy, the laborers were lounging, while all abroad was the yellow promise of a good year's yield.

The ruralist was rejoicing, the merchant was merry, and, take it all together, it wasn't a bad day for a listening loafer.

Therefore I loosened out under the soothings of a shortening cigar, and let myself listen.

"I've knowed men not quite as smart as you are, 'at has married on imagination," said Bill.

"Don't doubt that," said Colddecker. "No, I wouldn't doubt that. That's what 'magination is for. Love and religion is imagination. But grub is a solemn fact—particulary solemn when you can't reach it. Was you ever without grub?"

"Often when I've had it within," said Bill, gently caressing the region of his diaphragm.

"Pshaw! No more fooling. Come down to cases. Was you ever plumb empty? That's what I ask you."

"Better ask me somethin' hard! I've been wher' I hain't e't nothin' but a pair of rawhide Ingin moccasins for four days. How's that for a fancy menoo?"

"Good strong diet, moccasins is. How'd ye have them—boiled or broiled?"

"Bilt or briled?" exclaimed Bill, derisively. "You're a bigger fool 'an the feller 'at baked the dry 'bayons' afore he bilt 'em. The way to cook moccasins is to break 'em fresh and scramble 'em. But we didn't cook these yere'ns I'm talkin' about. We soaked 'em over night, an' e't 'em raw as we was trampin' all day diggin' out o' Arizona deserts—er ruther, I should say, we soaked 'em over day an' e't 'em trampin' at night; for the country was too hot in day time. An' you talk about imaginin'! A hungry man can imagine a dinner fit for a million-dollar weddin'. Why, when I was fattenin' on them moccasins—they wasn't no new moccasins from Niaggery Falls, nuther—I laid down one day on my stummick, or ruther on the awful holler place wher' my stummick hed moved away from, 'an I hed a dream. I s'pose dreams goes fer imagination, don't they?"

"Yes."

"Well, ef I hed that dream painted out, in full, on a big piece o' dry goods, I could git a million—er million an' a half—fer it. Ther' was everything on the biggest table you ever saw—everything. I don't except nothin'. Ther' ain't nothin' 'at a white man ever liked to eat that wasn't on that table—nothin'—nary damned thing. And—cooked? Dished up? Why, you couldn't think of anything half equal to the cookin'. All the air in the world was jist a welpin' an' rainin' down with the smells o' good cookin'. And the waiters was jist a gittin' up an' dustin', a-bringin' in more an' more. An' them waiter-girls! Talk about yer sweet sixteens, yer lovely twenties, yer alabaster shoulders, yer dimples, yer peachblooms, yer orange-blossoms, yer heavy-hooded eyes 'at broods on passion-flowers, yer grace of motion, an' yer faultless forms—why they was all ther—every one of 'em—comin' an' goin', and flingin' kisses to me from luscious lips with lily white hands.

96

Why, you never see such hands an' necks as them waiter-girls hed—white an' soft, an' round an' warm, an' taperin'. An' they was all a-waitin' on me—gittin' my dinner ready; and none of 'em was jellus of one another. They hedn't no need to be jellus, fer I had appetite enough fer all that dinner in my stummick, and love enough fer all them girls in my—"

"In your what?" suddenly exclaimed Colddecker.

"In my dream."

"Oh!"

"Why, wher'd ye s'pose I had it?"

"I didn't know but you was going to play a heart on me."

"No, sir. Hearts has nothin' to do with love or appetite. It's stummick. Hearts doesn't do nothin', only pump. But stummicks is boss. A empty stummick in a cast-away boat at sea will eat a Christian feller-Christian, an' the heart can't do nothin' to stop it; but a full stummick loves all good things, an' the heart only keeps on a-pumpin'."

"Well, never mind about hearts. What did you do about that dinner the pretty girls were setting out for you?"

"What 'id I do? Why I jist laid ther' under that old palm-cactus an' watched 'em. One of the girls—a regular Menken—come in with her bare arms over her head, and' her breast standin' out under her white satin dress shinin' like twin buttes of pearl statuwerry, an' she had a done-brown roast turkey on a chiny dish trimmed with sparegrass an' sallery, an' I couldn't wait to be called to dinner, so I jumped up a hollerin', 'Hold on my darling—don't go to no more trouble on my account;' then I rubbed my eyes an' looked at the damn cactuses standin' 'round over the desert, smacked my dry lips together till the dust flew out between 'em, an' cussed the country."

"Did that imaginary dinner do you any good?"

"Yes; done me just as much good as it does you to lay abed an' imagine what a purty girl you could marry ef ye hed a chanct. An' ye don't deny takin' comfort out o' that sort o' thing, do you? An' it made me ambitious to hang on an' hold out fer better days,

97

like a warm Christian bound fer hallelujah. What's heaven but a dream of glory? I wouldn't take a thousan' dollars fer that dream, an' ef I could tell it to you just's I dremp it ye could make big money lecturin' on it."

"And you were lying on your stummick?"

"Yes, I was."

"Well, how is it now?"

"Oh, youbedam!"

"Where did you get something to eat when you did get it?"

"Didn't get nothin' to eat, only moccasin, till we came to Gorgonio Pass. Know wher' that is?"

"No, I don't."

"Guess you're like a heap more Amerrikan citizens, of the smart kind—don't know much about Amerriky. You'd better 'prentice yourself to a statesman, an' learn how to whip ten Amerrikan States with seventy-five thousand men in sixty days. Amerriky's a hell-snortin' big piece of land you might remember, ef you knowed anything about it."

"Well, show your learning. There's no strings on you. I'm sittin' here list'ning, a'n't I? Where is Gorgonio Pass?"

"It's between the Chabazon and the waters of the Santy Ana. Now d'ye know?"

"No; I don't know any more than I did before."

"I s'pose not. That shows 'at a feller can't even lis'en with sense, ef he don't know nothin'. I reckon now you know wher' Judear is, an' Mount Sineei is, and Nazareth, an' Jerusalem, an all them places; but ye don't know nothin' about the Chabazon, ner Gorgonio, do ye?"

"Can't say that I know much about any place you've spoken of."

"Great thunderation! Wher' was you raised—in Amerriky?"

"Yes."

"How long 'a' you been in Californy?"

"Fifteen or sixteen years."

"Well, I'll swear! You don't know as much as 'll do fer this world er the nex'. Them first places I was speakin' of is on the straight road to heaven—them's Bible towns; but Gorgonio an' the Chabazon is on the rough road from Southern Californy to the last place this side o' hell's delights."

"How many people are there in Chabazon? Is it a place of any importance?"

"Place! People! It's a desert. It's a big piece of Californy. It's drier an' hotter'n a bake oven. It's the bottom of a dead lake, wher' the smiggymagurian an' the mastomathirryum used to wobble in the mud among the geolergy bugs, forty thousan' years afore Moses's great-gran'-daddy lost his tail."

"Oh, is that the place where they found the ancient ship keeled over in the dry desert?"

"Wher' who foun' it?"

"I don't know who. I read about it."

"Well, I'm dern glad they foun' it. I helped to put it ther'," said Bill in his iciest manner.

"You did?"

"That's what I aim to say."

"Why, the ship I read of was a big vessel—supposed to be ancient Phoenicia."

"All correct," said Bill, nodding his head; "that's the one 'at Tim Dix an' me put ther'."

"It is?"

"Yes, sir, it is—the identical same. You needn't stare at me. I know what I'm talkin' about. An' ef you knowed the histerry of your country, you'd remember that John P. Jones an Ike James was a-goin' to flood that country onct with the Gulf o' Californy. That's the time we put the ship ther'—so's to get the bulge on the inland navigation. I've heerd since that a feller named Miller writ a pome on it."

"You said," Bill added, after taking a new chew of the popular weed—"you said ol' Tanner couldn't live on imagination. Now, what's that feller Miller livin' on?"

99

"Him? Oh, he lives on his earnings and his bummings, I s'pose, like the other Bohemians."

"Well, I don't know nothin' about Boheemyans; but I do know 'at these writin' roosters lives mos'ly off ther' imaginations. That's one o' the pints I'm makin'. I'm not talkin for nothin'."

"Well, all right! Let it go at that. Don't let us wander off the subject."

"It's your fault. I'd 'a' gone on an' told a straight story of you'd 'a' let me alone. But you don't understand conversation."

"Very good; I'm not saying I do. Let us go back to Gorgonio Pass. That's where you left yourself, isn't it?"

"No, it isn't. I never leave myself anywher'. That's wher' I left you."

"Yes; that's where you left me. All right—go on."

"Well, Tom Dix an' me come acrost the Chabazon, shufflin' for God's country, an' we struck a big spring in the Chabazon. We hed an ol' mule, an' we lost him ther'—busted hisself drinkin' water an' eaten' grass on an empty stummick, 'cause he had no watermillon to start in on. Wher' that mule died we must 'a' been, in the way 'at we wandered about from water to water, nigh on a hundred miles from Gorgonio. We knowed when we left the sick mule that we didn't have no grub left, but we wasn't hungry enough yit to think of eatin' sick mule—thought of it afterward, though, many a time you bet you—and we struck out across the infernal dry country, a s'posin, er, ruther, imaginin', we could make some kind' o' camp in twenty-four hours. Well, we tramped and tramped; we tramped for four solid days and nights—that is we tramped all we was able to in such a country. Tim Dix told me of'en, afore that, 'at a man could live a week on water, an' average twenty miles walkin' in each twenty-four hours, right along, ef he'd divide his time right and not fret. Frettin' is what kills people. Talk about walkin' on water. It's no trick at all. The way you do is this way: You know you must hev a belt—a leather belt with a buckle to it—around you to hang your knife an' pistol on. Well, then, say you come to a spring; you walk right down to the water an' take a moderate drink, an' let your belt out one hole. Then you go an' set down an' think about somethin'—mostly about somethin' to eat—for nigh about a'hour. Then you git up, go the spring ag'in, an' drink enough to let your belt out two holes more—and so on till you git full enough to stop the hunger gnawin'. Then you go to sleep a while, till that water 'vaporates, when you go it all over again an' sleep some more. When you git rested, and begin to feel yourself gittin' too fleshy, you rise up, like your Mr. Riley, go the spring, fill your stummick and your canteen—I didn' mention a canteen before in this conversation—did I?"

"No, not that I heard."

"Well, a feller has to be mighty keerful talkin' to smart people. A canteen—well, you know what a canteen is, do you?"

"I have an idea what it is; but what do you say it is?"

"Well, it's a warlike weapon. More battles has been won an' lost by canteens than was ever won by bay'nets. It was canteens 'at saved the Union. I don't care who loads the guns of a people ef you lemme fill ther' canteens. A canteen is a tin thing, holler on the inside, shape of a watch, with a cork in a hole wher' the watch-chain oughter hitch, with a strap around the edge to hold up the thing an' go over your head like a watch-guard. It'll hold from a quart to a gallon of any kind of fluid—but it'll hold a leetle more whisky than it will anything else, peticulerly in time o'battle. Vict'ry in war, er in religion, depends mos'ly on sperrets. Civil'zation goes with the stronges' fluids. Now you take Scotland—that's wher' my forefathers come from—that's the mos' pious, mos' warlike, mos' religiousest, morrel country ther' is anywher'. What's the cause? It's whisky. Nex' comes Amerriky—what does she take in hern? Whisky. You can't hev' a high state of religious morality on weak drinks. Ef ther' wasn't no saloons, nor no distilleries, ther' wouldn't be no churches. Ther' wasn't none in Chiny so long as the Chinymen on'y drank tea and smoked opium, but jes's soon as these Chinymen what's yer in Californy learns to drink whisky, an' sich like high-proof leckers, an' goes back home wher' they come from, the gospel will begin to flourish in Chiny like it does in Scotland."

"Do you advocate whisky?"

"No; I don't. Ner I don't advocate war, ner religion. It takes very little whisky, er war, er religion to do me; but that don't alter the case, ner it don't prevent them three things from bein' trumps in the same hand. Now you look," added Bill, waving his hand abroad, "you look all over the world an' show me any religious nation 'at isn't jist hell on the fight—they all foller the Prince o' Peace with muskets on their shoulders an' carry their Bibles in catteridge-boxes, an' ef you put the cork of their canteens to your nose you'll smell—whisky. It ain't no use fer to try to hide it, for it's so. Religion may be good, but honesty is better. Let us have truth."

"How, often?"

"Well, onct in a while. The man 'at pretends he can hit the truth every time, he's a dern fool—er thinks I'm one. The man 'at says he never tol' a lie is the champion liar of the universe, an' the truth isn't in him. He might as well say he had walked thirty or forty years an' never stumbled, er took a false step. Ther' ain't no animal, tame er wild—no bird, no bug, no insec', no fish—but what'll lie an' make false moves to deceive the innemy an' protect its own. These yer truthful fellers is the kind 'at says they have lived ten married years with a live woman an' never had a cross word with her." Here Bill laughed loud and long, not so much at what he had said as at what he had suggested, and finally wiped his brimming eyes with a spotted, red bandana handkerchief, exclaiming, as he did so, "The damn lying fools!"

"Well, let us get back to the text."

"The tex'! What is the tex'?"

"The text of this talk—'Starvation.' "

"No—there you go wrong agin. The tex' o' this conversation is 'Imagination'."

"Founded on fact?"

"O' course. A lookin'-glass can't make no reflections with

102

nothin' to reflec'; nuther kin a man. No new thing can't be got up by no man without puttin' ol' things together. Everything that is, is—an' always was. No man kin imagin' mor'n what is, or hes been here an' ther' in pieces. He kin discover things, but no man can't make nothin'. Ef a man tries to 'magine anything, an' writes it down to his great-gran'-children, ef ther's anything in it, his posterity finds out that the ol' man's ideas wasn't mor'n half equal to the real thing. What's ol' Ben Franklin's kite and door-key to these yer tellyphones an' 'lectrick lights. 'Spose a man says he 'magines that we will yit go thro' the air direct from Frisco to New York? That ain't no 'magination o' his. That's the song o' the wild-goose. An' the goose has been a-honkin' away at that for thousan's an' thousan's of years. The guano quarries is ol'er than any dead man. Wher's the goose 'at writ the fust letter in the fust vollum of the Book of Guano?"

"Give it up."

"I reckon he was the peteryodactyle of the geolergy bugs, er some o' them long-toed roosters what the book-sharps talk about up in the quartz mines. Anyway, no man can't make no new thing in his imagination, er out of it. This yer's a fact 'at covers everything. But I jist think, an' I kin prove it, that ef he overloads his stummick, or starves hisself—either one or the other, I don't kur which—he can see some mighty fine picters, that never was painted on sea nor land. An' that's why I say 'at stummick is boss."

"The Germans have found that out some years ago."

"All right; and bully fer the Germans. Now ef everybody would quit talkin' 'soul,' which is a doubtful possession an' mostly a mighty thin property, and go to preachin' 'stummick,' they would come a dern sight nearer campin' on the real foundation of civilization."

"Now about this Gorgonio and Chabazon country."

"Well, you leave the Colorado River to go west by no'th an' you go through a lot o' hills—stone hills, sand hills, mud hills, an' all sorts o' hills, 'cept green hills; an' after you come out o' them hot hills an' barren canons, which are of all colors, 'cept any decent live color, you come down into a flat—a big dish—as white as white ashes, an' in places white as snow. This yer dish goes on no'th o' wher' we struck it, fer I sh'd say over a hund'd miles; an' it goes south fer more miles an' it goes no'th. It is the bottom of a big ol' sea. The hills put out into it—dry head-lands in a dried-up sea. An' the dry bays an' harbors put in among the dry hills, just as if the Bay o' Frisco was to dry up and leave a white bottom— on'y an awful sight bigger. It's the desolatest, the dryest, the hottest, an' the hellhantedest place that a man ever throwed his eye over. You go into the middle of it an' git ther' at noon in summer-time, the sun plumps down on your head. You look away no'th— nothin'. You look away south—nothin'. You look east—hills, all dead. You look west—hills, darker an' deader. No clouds, no shade, no shadders—just nothin' but the heat a-shimmerin' and a-shudderin'. Your eyes smartin', your lips peelin' with alkali, an' your stummick a cryin' 'water!' That's a place right yer in Amerriky, wher' if a man hain't got no imagination he's got nothin'—not even hope. At last when you get across the damn thing, you come up into Gorgonio Pass, an' ther' you begin to git the first smell o' moisture—and it is mighty faint I tell you. Ther's wher' I got something to eat after livin' four days on water and imagination, spiced with raw moccasin. Now, if ol' Doc Tanner 'd hed to paddle along over the Chabazon at twenty to twenty-five mile a day, he'd 'a' pegged in less'n forty days, you bet."

"Did you get watermelon at Gorgonio?"

"No, sir. Mutton, an' beans, 'an bread, an' *chili colorado* stew."

"What good did all that starving racket do you?"

"What good? In the first place, it give me an idea of my own country. Then it showed me 'at this is an ol', ol' world—no book ner nobody knows how ol'. Then, ag'in, it learnt me that stummick is boss. An', last of all, it learnt me what Doc Tanner has learnt you—ef ye kin take in the idea—an' that is, not to worry er git skeered when yer grub peters out. An', ef ye hear me, that's a mighty val'able lesson. A man kin do more than he thinks fer, ef he'll keep cool an' try. I tell ye, imagination 'll keep a man alive a

104

long time; an' it'll kill a man, too, ef it gits away with him. I kin tell ye a yarn about 'magination killin' me onct—er mighty nigh a doin' it—but I haint got time to tell that now. I mus' go an' water my horses;" and taking his booted feet down from the corner of the table, he started off, saying: "So long! I'll see ye again."

"Well, but—hold on here. How did you sleep under cactus trees on a naked white plain?"

"Didn't I tell ye there was headlands put out into it?"

"Yes, b'lieve you did."

"Well, what more d'yer want?"

"Ah!"

Bill went away. So did I. On reflection, I am not able to say if he is the average Far-West American, of the Jonathan stripe, or not. If he is, his information, scattering as it may be, exceeds his culture. What he knows seems more than how he tells it. If his leisurely manner and odd drawling emphasis could be conveyed in print, it would be the best part of this sketch.

### UNDERGROUND MINERS

The most dreaded occurrence in hard-rock mining was a cave-in. These were frequently the result of faulty mine management, but invariably the courage and loyalty of the miners were immediately evident in these mishaps. A cave-in which occurred in the Idaho mine of Grass Valley, California, was described graphically by a local newspaper. The mine, located in 1863, had been in operation nineteen years at the time of this particular accident and was one of the many quartz mines in a district that pioneered in hard rock mining. ("Brave Miners," Lake City *Mining Register*, October 6, 1882. Reprinted from the Grass Valley *Tidings*.)

The terrible break-down in the incline of the Idaho mine, that caused the death of Thomas Williams and the serious injury of Richard Carter, Frank Johns, and Richard Johns, called forth acts of courage, daring and heroism on the part of their fellow workmen that have rarely been equalled, even by men who have risked their lives for glory and renown. These were simply deeds of self-sacrificing devotion, without a thought of the praise that men would have for them; they thought only of their friends being in danger.

The cave occurred about 640 feet from the bottom of the incline shaft. Fortunately, there were no men in that incline at the time. If the cave had occurred an hour earlier, when the men were going to work, there might have been a dozen killed, for as the mass went down it increased in volume and velocity, carrying everything before it. Men who were at the stations of the levels as the mass went by say that it left a blaze of fire, caused by the friction of the rocks, and was terrible to see, when they knew it was rushing down on four helpless men.

William Magor deserves particular mention. He was in the 1,300 level and was informed that the mass had come down upon the shaftmen. He hurried out to the 1,000 station, and, without stopping to consider the very great danger he was in, made his way down the shaft, although the rocks and dirt had not stopped falling. When he got near enough to the men below, Frank Johns, who was severely wounded and fastened down in the debris, answered Magor and told him that he (Magor) had better get out and save himself, as by standing there he would surely be killed. To this Magor replied: "Never mind me; we will have you all out or we will all die together." Soon Magor was joined by Richard Eva and Jerry Angove, and soon all the miners came to save their comrades.

Then came the long and apparently insurmountable task of getting the dead and wounded out of that awfully dangerous place. These injured men had to be pulled out and carried up to the 1,300 level and no one knew at what moment another cave would come and sweep them all to the bottom. After they were brought up to the 1,300 level they had to be carried up to the 1,200 level, and then up the backs to the 1,100 level and through

106

the backs again to the 1,000 level and to the cage shaft. It hardly looks possible that men so badly hurt as these could be got through such places as they were.

### CORNISH MINERS

The Cornish miners brought their mining lore and customs from their homeland. They worked in every hard-rock mining area, where their skill with pick and gad, learned in the tin mines of Cornwall, was in great demand. They showed great loyalty to one another in life and no less in the solemnity with which they buried their dead. ("Beautiful Burial Ceremony," Elko *Independent*, October 6, 1869. Reprinted from the Treasure City [Nevada] *White Pine News*.)

About half-past three o'clock, Sunday afternoon everybody along Main Street paused where he stood, fastened as by a spell—reverently as the Mohammedan when the sacred call strikes the ear—all on the instinct of our common humanity. The occasion was, the soft cadence of sacred music, harmoniously rendered by manly voices, gave notice that the Cornish Miners were in a funeral march. One day last spring we witnessed this ceremony, and all who had once uncovered their heads to such a pageant remembered it. The pallbearers trode slowly with the remains of the deceased brother, and the choristers chanted a beautiful hymn as they followed on foot. Everybody stood reverently watching as the long line of stout men filed by, and all listened to catch the last swell of the sacred anthem. We are reminded by these praiseworthy observations that men need not brutalize themselves to be fit to brave the dangers of mixed society, the rigors of a severe climate, and the hardships of pioneer life; but that rather, as Bayard Taylor beautifully said it:

> *The bravest are the tenderest,*
> *The loving are the daring.*

107

## A Pocket Miner

E. H. Clough depicted in "Our Jim" the character and philosophy of Jim Gillis, a pocket miner of Tuolumne County. He and his brother William resided in the neighborhood of Jackass Hill, which was celebrated for the number of its quartz pockets and the richness of their yields. The two men counted among their friends Bret Harte and Samuel Clemens. Jim was known as "The Sage of Jackass Hill" for reasons that become entirely clear in Clough's description of him. The writer of this sketch was associated with the Oakland *Times* for a number of years. (E. H. Clough, "Our Jim," San Francisco, *Argonaut*, April 13, 1878.)

It was a magnificent afternoon in autumn—one of those sweet, calm days that Californians love to speak of when praising "the finest climate in the world."

"Hullo, stranger."

I glanced around, startled and nervous, for the voice of a human being was the last sound I should have expected to hear in this primitive solitude.

"Up here."

The voice was on my left, and turning in that direction, I saw a man stretched beneath a tall, heavily tasseled pine.

"Do you drink?"

The man held up a large flask, shaking it, and causing the contents to dash invitingly against the brown glass.

"You might as well," he continued, "though it ain't the best in the market; 'way above proof, I reckon; but you're thirsty, and it's free. Tie your animal up to that tree yonder, and take a seat. It's more sociable."

I could not resist the generous hospitality of the invitation, for its tone was even heartier than the words; besides, I was thirsty. Upon closer inspection I found that my friend—for I instinctively felt that he was a friend—was a man about forty years of age, slenderly built, but displaying a frame well knit and apparently inured by hardship. His expressive face bore that deep mahogany tint produced by constant exposure to all weathers, and his hands were calloused by hard labor. He was leaning upon his elbow, which was supported by a roll of blankets. A pick and shovel, lying near a pan for washing gold dust, revealed the probability that he was a prospector. Upon interrogation he acknowledged the correctness of my surmise, and then, with a merry twinkle in his bright, honest, hazel eyes, he added: "But the prospect isn't as bright as it might be, stranger; I haven't struck any bonanzas to speak of."

"Are you searching for quartz?" I asked.

"Yes—with gold in it," he replied, smiling at his own addition to my inquiry. "I'm a pocket hunter."

"A pocket hunter?"

"You lay in a stock of grub. You shoulder your pick, pan, shovel, and blankets, and start out on a long tramp. You wash a pan full of dirt here and a pan full there. Maybe you strike the color and maybe you don't, but if you do you look at it and think. You ask yourself, 'Where did it come from?' It is free gold. It was once in the rock. Where's the rock? You look around and find that the country slopes down to where you found the little speck. You go a little higher up and wash another pan full. You keep on washing and going higher up till the prospect is good enough to justify running a cut into the hillside. If you've gauged your prospects right you'll find a little streak of quartz—'a thread,' we call them. You follow your thread and find other threads. You follow them all. By and by these threads—prospecting first-rate all along—come together. A 'crossing' comes in. What's a 'crossing?' Why, it's some other substance cutting the vein at a right or acute angle—dyke, or sand, or granite, or maybe quartz. If those threads and that crossing come together at the same point, you'll strike it sure. Ten, twenty, or a hundred dollars to the pan. The gold has settled into a pocket, and you've got enough to pay your grub bill anyhow; but sometimes you're struck by lightning and she pans out thousands. As a general thing, though, it's only hundreds. I knew a man once down on Christy's Bar who took out ten thousand dollars in three pans of dirt. He'd worked nine years on the same lead, and owed every provision dealer from Reynolds' Ferry to Columbia hundreds of dollars each. They wouldn't trust him any more, and he killed rabbits when he was hungry, or did odd jobs around Tuttletown for his grub. He paid his bills and started for a *pasear* in Egypt, I believe—he was stuck after pyramids and crocodiles from the first time he struck the Bar. He'll spend his pile and pawn his jewelry to some descendant of the Pharoahs to get money enough to come back again. He'll come back flat broke, but I'd like to borrow his credit in this section for a year or two—it's good, you bet. What did you say? No, we don't always strike it rich twice on the same lead. That fellow I was telling you about worked his for a year after and didn't get a color, so he quit for a while and went to Egypt before he eat and drank up the pocket he'd found."

I had been so interested in the remarks of the miner that I had not noticed how low the sun had fallen. He called my attention to the fact that night was approaching, and proposed that we move. I acceded, and my companion rose, hitched up his mud-stained red "ducks," placed his wide-brimmed slouch hat upon his head, loosened a large navy revolver which he carried in his belt, gathered up his accoutrements, which he slung easily upon his shoulders, took a shot-gun from behind a tree, and strode out upon the trail, with a long, swinging, Indian stride. I untied my horse and mounted. The miner turned and inquired:

"Where are you bound?"

"To Sonora."

"Where from?"

"Cave City."

"You'll strike the stage road at Tuttletown about half-past six. It's a good seven mile to Sonora from there, and your horse is tired. Stay with me to-night."

"Where do you live?"

"At Jackass."

"Where?"

"Jackass Hill—on the Stanislaus, 'bout a mile from Tuttletown."

At this moment some quail rose from a neighboring thicket, and two reports from the pocket-hunter's shot-gun answered instantly. Three birds fell.

"You'd better come, stranger," he continued, as he held his gun in rest and drew the exploded caps from the nipples. "There's part of your supper—quail on toast—plenty of dry bread for toast at the house."

I did not resist, and we traversed the picturesque trail in the dying sunlight together. He walked ahead, and the occasional shots from his gun always brought down the swiftly moving game. He had soon piled two cotton-tail rabbits, a dozen quail, and half a dozen doves upon the pommel of my saddle. As he walked, he conversed in a free, breezy manner upon a variety of subjects. I found him well informed in regard to standard English literature; he often quoted very *a propos* from Shakspeare, for whom he had the most devoted appreciation. He criticised Byron, and accused Scott of plagiarism. He gave me quaint descriptions of the habits of the birds and animals native to the section, oftentimes talking in an affectionate tone to the various animals that crossed his path, and never taking his gun from his shoulder after we had jointly agreed that there was more than enough for supper and breakfast on my saddle.

"I love these little birds," he said, "and I wouldn't harm one of them for the world, if I didn't intend to eat them afterwards."

He discoursed about the country around us, and displayed a complete knowledge of its geological characteristics. He gave me an epitome of the local history of the section, interspersed with pleasing anecdotes and tragic incidents; and through it all I perceived the true stamina of the man's character—a deep and abiding love for his fellow man in every condition and under every circumstance. But what interested me most of all were his epigrammatic character sketches. He seemed to consider every man and woman in the neighborhood a character—except himself. "There's old Pat—Dave Patterson—one of the best old men in the world; but he *will* travel round on hot summer days rigged out in two heavy gray flannel shirts, and an overcoat slung over his arm. Why does he do it? Derned if I know. Nobody knows—he don't know himself. It's his way, I reckon. And there's Tom Leach. Keeps a saloon down at the camp—down at Tuttletown. He's got a heart that's worth its weight in gold. Runs the Democratic party in this precinct, pulls the wires, and sets up the liquor for the boys when times are hard, and makes the candidates set 'em up in election times. He's the little joker in politics hereabouts. Patterson's his right—no he ain't, either—Gale's his right bower, Patterson's his left. Gale's another. Owns a ditch, and supplies 'goat ranch' to the people of this section. 'Goat ranch' is a kind of wine he makes. It must be tolerably good—he drinks it himself. There's my hotel."

He pointed to a large, white-washed building on an eminence a short distance ahead. The stars were shining through the cool atmosphere of the river canon, and the crickets were chirping their evening hymn as we stood before the wide-open doors.

"Come in, stranger, everything here is yours while you stay. I'll put your horse up."

"Have you a partner?" I asked.

"No. Why?"

"How long have you been out prospecting?"

"Three weeks. Why?"

"Your doors are all open."

"What of it? I don't keep a bank. Besides this ain't the place where thieves abound. I never shut my doors, and any man is welcome to all the comfort he can find here whether I'm around or not. Come in."

He threw his pack in a corner of the kitchen and laid our game on a table. A fire was soon lighted, and a candle jammed into a spice bottle being brought forth revealed the rude but substantial comfort of the pocket-hunter's residence. A stove standing on three pieces of basaltic rock, a table probably a half century old, a cupboard in one corner, before which hung two gaudy calico

112

curtains, on the shelves of which was arranged various pieces of chinaware in every stage of incompleteness; behind the stove hung frying pans, griddles, pots, pans, broiling-irons and kettles; the house had once been lined with white-washed cloth, but it had almost disappeared, leaving the roof and rafters black and bare. The two rooms adjoining were apparently sleeping apartments, for each of them contained three bunks plentifully supplied with variously colored blankets. I ascertained next day that the walls of these rooms were covered with wood-cuts from the periodical pictorials, these artistic adornments being interspersed with charcoal caricatures of local import by free-hand designers "unknown to fame."

My host made me seat myself in an old arm chair, upholstered with goat skin, while he plucked and prepared the birds he had shot. We had not spoken for several moments, and I was reaching for a copy of Mark Twain's "Roughing It" lying on the table, when—

"Oh, Jim!"

The voice sounded shrill and querulous from the next room.

"Yes, Dick."

The pocket-miner answered unconcernedly, and placed the cover on the steaming pan of quails.

"Oh, Jim!"

"What is it Dick?"

"Is that you, Jim?

"Yes, Dick." Then apologetically, "It's Dick Baker, home again. He's been on a spree, and he's come to me to sober him up. He always does. He's another character. You'll find him mentioned in that book—Tom Quartz, Dick Baker, and—me." . . .

The next morning I parted with my kind and hospitable host. Since then I have become better acquainted with him, and find that he is fully entitled to the affectionate regard which all who know him bestow upon him. They call him "Our Jim," and love to dwell upon "his way"—his Bohemian characteristics, his philanthropy, and his genial, quaint, whole-souled qualities.

## A Fallen Comrade

Among the hard rock miners emotions were often expressed in the language of manly humor. Mark Twain had skilfully rendered in "Buck Fanshaw's Funeral" the place humor occupied as a vent for feelings among the miners. A story imitating Mark Twain's manner in juxtaposing humor and emotion appeared in a Colorado newspaper. In all probability the story was reprinted from an unidentified source. ("He Wanted a Grand Funeral," Fairplay *Flume*, December 29, 1881.)

The sun was sinking behind the snowy peaks of the Rockies, gilding their glittering tops with rosy light, as poor Dave York was borne by the boys to his cabin. He had been terribly hurt by a blast in the mine. They carried him into the rude hut and laid him on a pile of soft bearskins before the fire. He was suffering intensely, but he bore it like a hero. There they left him with his partner, Dan Hamlin. Dan sat beside the injured man and held his hand, while the tears rolled silently down his sunburned cheek. The sun went down. The room grew dark and the dancing flames in the fireplace made the shadows leap up and down on the wall. For a long time the two partners were silent. At last the injured man spoke:

"Dan, I'm going over the range," said he.

"No, no, old pard, don't say that; you will scoop the pile yet."

"No, Dan, no. Old death holds four aces to my two pairs. I must pass in my checks. Old pard, we've worked together, gambled together, got drunk together an' fought together for four years. It's hard to part."

"You bet it is, pardner."

"But, it's got to come, old man. Dan, you've stood by me always. We've accumulated quite a little pile. There's no one on earth has so good a right to my share as you. It's yours, Dan, when I'm gone. But, Dan, promise me one thing."

"Anything, old pardner."

"Gimme a bang up funeral."

114

"I will, old pard."

"See that there's a good pair o'flyers on the hearse. Of course you'll race going to the cemetery. I never war beat in a race while livin'; don't let 'em get ahead o' me at my funeral."

"They shan't Dave."

"An', Dan, see that there's plenty o' liquor on hand at the grave."

"I'll have a barrel, Dave."

"An' in the fight at the cemetery see that there's at least three men killed. I don't want any half-way funeral."

"I'll kill that many myself."

"And, Dan, don't you think it might give tone to the thing to lynch the undertaker?"

"It might."

"And you'll do it?"

"We will, pardner. You shall have the best funeral ever seen in these parts."

"Dan, you're a true friend. Good-by, old pard, I'm goin'! Good-by' good—"

Dave York had gone over the range.


A MINER'S GRIEF

James W. Gally was living with his family at Hot Creek in southeastern Nevada when he attempted in a poem to disclose the loneliness in the heart of a miner whose last ties with home have been severed forever.

Hot Creek and Tybo were adjoining camps, looking out from mountain canyons over the expanse of interior valley to the east. The miners had built their small cabins along the sides of the canyon and in one of them in all liklihood the miner-man of the poem pursued his lonely thoughts. (James W. Gally, "A Lonesome, Homeless, Miner-Man," Sacramento *Weekly Union*, September 14, 1872. Reprinted from the Virginia City *Territorial Enterprise*.)

He was a lonely miner-man,
 Who in his cabin dwelt,
Or trod the narrow trail that ran
 Along the mineral belt;
And night and morn, with dinner pail,
 He back and forward strode,
Nor at the hour was known to fail
 To take the rocky road.

A steady-going miner-man,
 He sat at night and thought,
And many a curious miner's plan
 In fancy there he wrought;
And in his cabin, all alone,
 Before the dancing fire,
Full many a picture came and shone
 Of what he might desire.

A lonesome, homeless miner-man,
 Who cooked, and washed, and worked
Perhaps his name was John or Dan,
 No odds—he never shirked;
And why care what his name might be
 Who delved with pick and drill?
The time-book of the company
 Had put him up as "Bill."

Some said he was a heartless man,
 Who didn't care at all
How matters ended or began
 Outside his cabin wall.
But once I watched him at the store
 (Postoffice it was, too);
The keeper, as he passed the door,
 Said: "Letter here for you."

He took the letter as he went,
 Walking away alone,

And soon I saw him most intent
　　Sit reading on a stone;
And as he read, the rolling tears
　　Came coursing down his face—
His heart had traveled back for years,
　　To childhood's tender place.

Now, when that miner raised his latch,
　　What sorrow entered there,
To bow his head beneath the thatch,
　　Re-reading it with care?
How weary sat he by the fire,
　　Too sad and faint to cook
His lonely meal, and then retire
　　Without a voice or book.

Ah! miner, you and I, and all,
　　Can never, if we would,
Shut up the heart, whate'er befall,
　　Against the true and good;
And when the world looks worse and worse,
　　The farther off we roam,
We still have something that we nurse—
　　The love at "mother's home."

# Mining Population

## MINING EXPERTS

Mining "experts" were hired freely by the litigants in a lawsuit arising over a rich mass of ore located in White Pine County, Nevada. The litigation between the Eberhardt and Richmond companies in an Austin, Nevada, court was engendered by a geologically determined set of circumstances. Several claims known as the Eberhardt group of mines were made on croppings that covered a single horizontal deposit rather than separate definable ledges. The discovery of ore in a "blanket deposit" was a real problem to miners who were accustomed to thinking in terms of locating title by feet along a defined ledge, and in the ensuing struggle for the control of property the mining "expert" hired out to anyone who had need of his services. ("Lo! A Daniel," *Reese River Reveille*, January 15, 1869.)

On Wednesday a prodigy of science appeared before the District Court, to testify in the case between the Eberhardt and Richmond. His name—is it not written in the chronicles of the Court? The man of science, pregnant with simple laws and recondite studies, was a trump card; but he was "played out" before the "trick" was taken home. The cross-examination of this "expert" was so infinitely amusing, so overflowing with the creamiest of fun, that we shall never cease to regret that we were not present. We are able, however, to present a few of its salient points for the especial benefit of "scientific cusses" everywhere. The "Encyclopedia" testified substantially as follows:

Q. Are you a graduate of an academy or school of mines?

A. Yes; of the Collegio de Mineria of Mexico.

Q. What was your course of studies?

A. Oh, everything pertaining to mining and the working of ores.

Q. What were your standard works? Mention some of the books.

A. Books—(with a puzzled air)—ah—yes; let me see. Well, there was Lyell's Mineralogy, and—the works of—Castillo, and—many others.

Q. You say you studied mineralogy; what is quartz?

A. Quartz is—quartz.

Q. What is its chemical composition?

A. I—don't—know.

Q. What is the composition of cale spar?

A. Cale spar is lime and mica.

Q. You don't know anything about mineralogy, do you?

A. No, not much; indeed, the course at the Collegio de Mineria was wholly practical.

Q. Well, you learned something: perhaps you are a mining engineer?

A. Yes; I studied mathematics and am a mining engineer.

Q. A mathematician, are you! Can you square the circle?

A. Oh yes, if I had my instruments—(with exquisite naivete).

Q. Will you sit at this table and square the circle if I procure a set of instruments?

A. Certainly I will.

Lawyer. That will do, sir.

During the cross-examination the inmates of the court-room were convulsed with laughter; and it is doubtful if any parallel scene ever happened before in any court in Christendom.

SANCHO PANZA OF RUBY CITY

The representatives of various national groups imparted color in the mining scene. Henry Bloom, the very confused German witness for the prosecution in a murder trial, was a resident of Ruby City, Owyhee County, Idaho Territory. For a little less than two years Ruby City was a county seat until it lost its pre-eminence, population, and county government to neighboring Silver City. ("Henry Bloom in Court," Ruby City *Owyhee Avalanche*, February 3, 1866.)

During the examination of John W. Pratt last week in Ruby, for the murder of Anderson, Henry Bloom, *a very German* individual, was called as a witness for the prosecution. Bloom was not exactly tight according to the Silver City standard—where one is supposed to be sober as long as he can make a noise—but he had evidently taken several drams that morning, sufficient to make him talkative. On the direct examination, he testified that he had seen and closely examined the body of the deceased a few hours after the killing; that there was a bruise on the face, and a knife wound on the left breast which had went *through the heart* and had *cut off the leaders of the heart*—pointing to the front base of his neck to illustrate his idea! The Prosecuting Attorney having drawn out all the evidence he desired, turned the witness over to Judge Miller, who appeared for the defence when the following dialogue took place:

Question—Mr. Bloom, are you a surgeon?
Answer—Yesh, sir; I beech a surcheon.
Q—Where did you study your profession?
A—I stud sh in ter old guntrish, and some in dish guntrish.
Q—At what school in the "old guntrish" did you study your profession?
A—Oh! vel I studish pout two years py Hampurgh and sixsh months py Preemen.
Q—At what particular schools did you study?
A—Vel, I didn't sthudy moosh at no very barticular school;

120

I vorked pout du yearsh py Hampurgh and sixsh monts py Preemen.

Q—Are you a regular graduate, Mr. Bloom?

A—Vel, I tinks I am shust so goot a pootcher ash vas round tere.

Q—State whether you probed the wound on Anderson's body?

A—Brope him; no, I tidn't brope him.

Q—Did you hold a *post mortem* examination—did you cut the body open to ascertain the depth and extent of the wound?

A—Gut oben ter pody; No,—*I didn't gut oben ter pody.*

Q—How, then, do you know that the knife *went right through his heart?*

A—Vel, der man vas den tead; I could see der plood coming out of de hole—de plood vas all over de man. I could see he vas tead ash could pe—ov gourse he must pe stuck in de heart.

Q—Can you, as a surgeon, from the surface appearance and the amount of blood drawn, tell the depth and extent of a wound on the body or chest?

A—Ov gourse, ush so vel as any oder man. I kill more ash du tousand ox shen; I always sticks dem in de heart and dey pleeds like der tyfel—stick dem in der shzoulder and dey pleeds not moosch.

Q—You seem to be more of a butcher than surgeon, Mr. Bloom?

A—I pe shust so goot a pootcher ash any oder man. Vat you call a surgeon, eh?

The Court here interposed and explained to the witness that the counsel *meant Doctor* when he *said Surgeon.*

A new light seemed to break in on the intellectual vision of the demoralized Bloom, and he "put in" with much emphasis:

"Ah, ha! you call doctor, surgeon, what you call pootcher in English, eh? You mean toctor all de dime; vat vor you no say tocdor. I pe shush so goot a pootcher ash any oder man on dish creek. I peesh no toctor. I knowsh de man vas tead—he mush pe sthuck in de heart; vot shood kill him, eh? I tid see der plood."

The witness was proceeding at a rapid rate to explain his

theory, much to the delight of the counsel and audience, when he was rather abruptly told by the Judge to take his seat.

### ANTICS OF A "CHIEF"

The "chiefs" of the hard rock mining camps were picturesque outlaws as Bret Harte, Mark Twain, and E. H. Clough have shown admirably. Frontiersmen hoped to see them paid back in their own coin and E. H. Clough in this story expresses the desire and the fulfillment. There is more fact than fiction in locating the action of the story in Bodie, a town in Mono County, California, which was known for its bad men and prosperous mines during the 1860's. Clough contributed numerous stories of mining life to the San Francisco *Argonaut*, and he inherited with James W. Gally the local mantle of mining camp bard after Bret Harte departed California for foreign shores. (E. H. Clough, "The Bad Man of Bodie," San Francisco *Argonaut*, June 1, 1878.)

Washoe Pete was generally considered a "bluffer" by the critics of Bodie, and his wild exaggerations were the subject of merriment only in that "high old town." He was allowed to swagger and boast to his heart's content; and even when he drew his "nobby whistler" and shot the lights out of all the lamps in Ryan's saloon, the action only evoked a grin and the doubtful compliment that it was "purty fair shootin, an nigh as stiddy narve as Irish Tom showed when he popped away at that 'bad man' from Deadwood."

One day last summer Pete walked into Strobridge's saloon with the remark that he had "heerd the Last Chance was goin to be sold, and they've sent up an expert to look into it."

The expert, a pale, small man, dressed in dusty gray, was standing at the bar and looked around as the tall, would-be ruffian uttered these words.

"Thet's so, Pete," said one of the men present, "an' thet's the expert," pointing to the small man.

"You're an expert, eh?" shouted Pete eyeing the man menacingly; "you're one o' them fellers as allows he knows payin' mines, are ye?" Then, after a pause, during which he surveyed the stranger from head to foot, "Well, ye're the wust I ever saw. Experts is bad enough, but you're the slinkiest, meanest, wust coot to set yerself up to report on a mine I ever laid eyes on."

"I don't want to quarrel with you, sir," answered the expert.

"Ye'd better not, young feller, ye'd better not. I'm a whirlwind of the desert in a fight, and don't ye forget it."

"I'm a man of peace; I carry no weapons, and of course I could not hope to stand before even a zephyr of the desert—let alone a wild, untamed whirlwind."

These deprecatory words only incensed the "bad man" still more, and feeling that he had a "soft thing," proposed in his own mind to "play it for all it was worth," and gain a "record" by "whipping his man."

"Look a hyar, stranger, I don't want no insinuations. Do I look like a zephyr? Say!" Here Washoe Pete shook his fist in the expert's face. "What d'ye mean by talkin' about zephyrs? I'm a tornado. I *tear* when I turn loose. Zephyr—(sneering). Why, I've a good mind to—"

"Please, mighty whirlwind, resistless tornado, don't hit me. You wouldn't strike a consumptive man, would you?"

"Wouldn't I!" yelled the "fighter," in a terrible voice, "wouldn't I! I'd strike the side of a mountain!"

"But a sick man!" pleaded the expert, "a man dying of consumption, an orphan, a stranger, and a man of peace!"

"What're ye giving me? Do you know who I am?" fiercely demanded the whirlwind.

"You're a gentleman known in Bodie as Mr. Washoe Peter—at least, I've heard you designated by that familiar appellation during my sojurn here," answered the expert, moving off.

"What else am I?" shrieked the rough, striding toward the cowering expert.

"A gentleman, I suppose. Honestly, I don't know your other name."

123

"Well, I'll tell you who I am"; and the tall man stood over the shrinking stranger, as if about to topple upon him and annihilate him. "I'm 'bad'; I'm chief in this yer camp, an' I ken lick the man 's says I ain't. I'm a ragin' lion o' the plains, an' every time I hit I kill. I've got an arm like a quartz stamp, an' I crush when I reach fur a man. I weigh a ton, an' earthquakes ain't nowhar when I drop."

"But I've only just been discharged from a hospital," replied the expert.

"I'll send ye back again!" and the stalwart "bluffer" caught the little man by the collar and hurled him upon the floor.

"It's unkind to use a poor, weak suffering invalid that way," expostulated the expert, as he slowly arose from the floor. "Please don't joke so roughly. Let's take a drink and call it square. I am very sorry that I have offended you."

"Ye think I'm jokin', do ye—ye take me fur a josh, eh? I'll show ye what I am afore I git through with ye. Ye don't play me fur no tender-foot. I'm a native, I am, an' I've stood this yer foolin' long enough." Saying which, he dashed the stranger against a table and drew a long knife.

As soon as the expert saw this he screwed his face into the most piteous shape, and throwing his hands up, cried: "I'm unarmed; I haven't got so much as a pen-knife on me. Please don't carve me; kick me to death if you must have my life, but for heaven's sake don't stick that terrible thing into me."

Now, as Washoe Pete had no intentions of using the knife—and thereby risking his neck to the tender mercies of a Mono jury's verdict—he was well pleased with the opportunity thus afforded him of displaying the deadly weapon and, after asserting his bloody intention, returning it to its sheaf. He flourished the knife over the cringing expert three or four times, and then lowered it with the remark: "Why, dern yer cowardly soul, I wouldn't disgrace the weepin by shovin' it into ye. No, sir; but I'll plug ye;" and he drew a revolver.

124

"I'm unarmed, I'm unarmed—don't ye hear me?" whined the expert.

"Go an' heel yerself, then," retorted the "bad man."

"I don't want to fight."

"I'll make ye fight. I'll take ye at yer word, an' kick you to death."

"Please don't."

Washoe Pete laid his knife and pistol on the counter, and then strode rapidly to the spot where the expert was half crouching, half standing. By this time the saloon was full of men, all of them smiling at the picture before them, regarding it as the height of enjoyment—this lively encounter between the greatest braggadocio in the Sierra and a small, pale, mining expert, new to the section and a stranger to the wild ways of the border ruffian.

"This thing has gone on 'bout long 'nough," yelled the "bad man," stopping before the expert. "You've bin chinain' to me till I'm riled. Squar' yerself—I'm goin' ter kick, an' a Comstock mule ain't a patchin' as a kicker to Washoe Pete, an' you hear me."

"One instant, please, Peter (I don't know your other name); are you sure you've got no other weapons on you? They might go off accidentally, and hurt some innocent party."

"Thar's all the weepins I've got, ef the information 'll ease yer sneakin' mind, an' now I'm goin' ter begin kickin. Clear the track! The wooly hoss has broke out of the kerrel, an' there'll be a coroner's inquest in jest about seven minutes."

He raised his ponderous boot, but it did not swing.

The little man straightened up like an unbent bow, and his left hand shot direct from his shoulder like the piston of a locomotive, striking Washoe Pete between the eyes, and sending that worthy sprawling on the sawdust floor.

"I'm the cyclone of the West," he shouted, as he bounded to the prostrate form of the "wooly hoss," and raised the braggart into a sitting posture. The latter was dazed by the terrible blow he had received, and did not even throw up his guard when the

125

expert drew back to strike again. The blows fell like thunderbolts upon the head and face of the "whirlwind," inducing that individual to rise once more and attempt a defence. He made an effort to reach his weapons, but the active expert flanked him and planted two terrific blows on his ear and neck. Then the "bad man" howled.

"Let up! I was only foolin'—can't yer take a joke, dern ye?"

"Ye think I'm jokin', do ye? Ye take me fur a josh, eh? I'll show ye what I am before I get through with ye. Ye don't play me for no tender-foot. I'm a native, I am, an' I've stood this yer foolin' long enough."

This apt reproduction of the "native's" speech a few moments previous, and its almost perfect similitude as regards tone, was too much for the good natured crowd, and a roar of laughter greeted it that might have been heard beyond Bodie Bluff.

"I give in, dern ye, I give in! Can't ye take a man's word when he squeals?" shouted the "tornado," swinging his arms wildly, and staggering against the bar in his efforts to dodge the lightning strokes of the athletic expert.

"I'm a howling hurricane of wrath," shouted the expert, sending in both fists with terrific effect.

"Let up, won't you? I ain't a sand-bag."

"Not much; you are only a 'ragin' lion o' the plains.'" And a swift left-hander lit upon the bully's nose.

"I give in," hoarsely ejaculated the expert's victim.

"Come on with your quartz stamps, old 'wooly hoss.' When you hit you kill, and you weigh a ton. Fetch in a couple of your earthquakes. Why don't you chew my mane? You're 'chief,' are you? All right, chief, there's a neat one for you, and there's a couple more."

With these words the expert "countered" on the "bad man's" cheek, and then stretched him panting for breath on the floor with a "stinger," straight from the shoulder, inflicted upon the lower portion of the chest. Then the expert cooly called all hands to the bar to drink, and as the "bad man of Bodie" crawled away he was heard to mutter that he "didn't lay out to fall up against batterin'-rams, no more'n he 'lowed he was game in front of a hull gymnasium."

FREEBOOTING SERMONS

The "Poker Bill" sermons, printed by newspapers as widely separated as the *Mining Register* of Lake City, Colorado, and the *Epitaph* of Tombstone, Arizona, portrayed a gambler of Leadville, Colorado, in an unaccustomed role. The chief of the profession, a rough, untutored character, was represented finding religion and aspiring in his fashion to bring it to the rough men of Leadville. The gibe was a clever hit at Leadville's tough gambling fraternity.

I

("Faro Bill's Exhortation," Lake City *Mining Register*, July 30, 1880.)

I was standing in front of the hotel when my attention was attracted by a dilapidated, antiquated looking specimen of a saloon bummer, who was passing along the street ringing a bell. At intervals he would cease ringing and shout:

"Religious racket right away at the big tent: Roll up, tumble up, or slide up on yer years, fur we'll have a bang-up dish o' gospel talk from Faro Bill; an' d-o-o-n-t you forgit it!"

Turning to a dapper little gambler who stood near, I asked: "Who is this Faro Bill?"

"Who is he? Well now, if that ain't the boss play for high. You kin break me right here if I thought there was a bloke in the mines that didn't know Bill. He used to be one o' the boys, but got capped into a religious game by a slick tongued gospel sharp about two months ago. He's chopped on all his old rackets, an don't stand in with nothing now that don't show up a bible or a prayer book in the lay-out. Billy used to be the boss gambler of camp, and warn't afeared to sit in a game with the flyest sport that ever slung a card: but he is a clean gone on the pious by now, and seems to have lost all the good that ever was in him. The boss mouthpiece of the heavenly will has gone done to Denver, an' Bill is a goin' to stand in an' sling gospel for the boys as well as he can."

This explanation, given in the most earnest tone, started me instantly for the big tent. It was used at night for a variety theatre, where artists of a questionable character performed acts of still more questionable decency and was rented for religious services every Sunday morning. I found the tent filled to its utmost capacity. Many had, no doubt, come through curiosity to see how Bill would deport himself in this his initial sermon. Upon the stage sat a burly, red-faced man, with arms folded in a careless manner, who looked over the large audience with an air of the most decided independence. This was Faro Bill, the speaker of the occasion. When he arose, he glanced around the tent for a moment evidently collecting his thoughts, and began:

"Feller citizens, the preacher bein' absent, it falls on me to take his hand and play it for what it's worth. You all know that I'm just learnin' the game an' of course I may be expected to make wild breaks, but I don't believe there's a rooster in the camp mean enough to take advantage o' my ignorance and cold deck me right on the first deal. I'm sincere in this new departure, an' I believe I've struck a game I can play clear through without copperin' a bet, for when a man tackles such a lay-out as this he plays every card to win and if he goes through the deal as he orter do, when he lays down to die, an' the last case is ready to slide from the box, he can tell the turn every time.

"I was readin' in the Bible to-day that yarn about the Prodigal Son, an' I want to tell yer the story. The book don't give no dates, but it happened long, long ago. This Prodigal Son had an old man who put up the coin every time the kid struck him for a stake, an' never kicked at the size of the pile, either. I reckon the old man was purty well fixed, an' when he died he intended to give all his wealth to this kid an' his brother. Prod give the old

128

man a little game o' talk one day, and injuced him to whack up in advance o' the death racket. He'd no sooner got his divy in his fist than he shook the old man an' struck out to take in some of the other camps. He had a way up time for a while, an' slung his cash to the front like he owned the best payin' lead on earth; but hard luck hit him a lick at last, an' left him flat. The book don't state what he went broke on, but I reckon he got steered up agin some brace game. But anyhow, he got left without a chip, an' a granger then took him home an' set him to tendin' hogs, an' here he got so hard up an' hungry that he stood in with 'em on a husk lunch. He soon weakened on such plain provender, an' says to himself, says he: 'Even 'f the old man's hired hands are livin' on square grub, while I'm worryin' along here on corn husks straight, I'll just take a grand tumble to myself, an' chop on this racket at once. I'll skip back to the governor an' try to fix things up, an' call for a new deal' so off he started.

"The old man seed the kid a coming and what do you reckon he did? Did he pull his gun and lay for him, intending to wipe him as he got into range? Did he call the dogs to chase him off the ranch? Did he bustle around for a club and give him a stand-off at the front gate? Not to any alarming extent he didn't. No, sir. The Scripture book says he waltzed out to meet him and froze to him on the spot, and then marched him off to a clothing store and fitted him out in the noblest rig to be had for coin. Then the old gent invited all the neighbors and killed a fatted calf, and gave the biggest blowout the camp ever seed."

At the conclusion of the narrative the speaker paused, evidently framing in his mind a proper application of the story. Before he could resume a tall, blear-eyed gambler with a fierce mustache, rising, said:

" 'Tain't me as would try to break up a meeting, or do anything disreligious. No, sir; I'm not that sort of a citizen. But in all public hoodoos it is a parlimentary rule for anybody as wants to ax questions to rise up an' fire them off. I don't desire to fool away time a questioning the works of religion, oh no. As long as it is kept in proper bounds, and does not interfere with the boys in their games, I do not see as it can do harm. I just want to ax the honorable speaker if he has not given himself dead away? Does it stand to reason that a bloke would feed upon corn husks when there was hash factories in the camp? Would anybody hev refused him the price of a square meal if he had struck them for it? Would any of the dealers that beat him out of the coin see him going hungry? As I remarked before, I do not want to make any disrespectable breaks, but I must say that the speaker has been a trying ter feed us on cussed thin taffy, and no one but a silly would take it in."

Bill glared upon the speaker and fairly hissed:

"Do you make to say that I am a liar?"

"Wal, you can take it just as you choose. Some would swallow it in that shape."

Bill pulled his revolver and in an instant the bright barrels of numerous weapons flashed in the air as the friends of each party prepared for active duty. The brevet preacher was the first to fire, and the rash doubter of the spiritual truth fell dead on the ground. Shot followed shot in quick succession, and, when quiet was again restored, a score or more dead and wounded men were carried from the tent. Having secured attention, Bill said:

"Further proceedings are adjourned fer the day. You will receive the doxology."

The audience rose.

"May grace, mercy and peace be with you, now and forever, amen, and I want it distinctly understood that I am going to maintain a proper respect for the gospel if I have to croak every son-of-a-gun of a sinner in the mines. Meetin' is out."

The crowd filed from the tent as cooly as if nothing had happened, and as I gained the sidewalk I heard a man remark:

"Bill has got the sand to make a bang-up preacher, and I would not wonder if he made a big mark in the world yet."

II

("Poker Bill's Sermon," Tombstone *Epitaph*, September 24, 1880. Reprinted from an unidentified source.)

"Poker Bill," having procured bail since his last sermon, preached in Leadville the first Sunday after martial law was proclaimed. On ascending the platform he unbuckled his revolver and laid it on the table, with the remark that he "kinder thawt concealed weapons warn't the right outfit for a gospel preacher."

His text was from Matthew XX., 1 to 15. He said: "Partners, this text rites about a man that owned vineyards. As most of you are more convarsent with straight red licker and shafts, I will read 'mines and prospect notes' instead of 'vineyards.'"

"Thar was a man who, who was a householder, who went out early one morning to git men to work on his claims.

"And he seed two tenderfeet, and he struck a bargain with them to work on a prospect fur $4 a day.

"And he went out again and seed three miners standing by the Tontine saloon, and he sed: 'Ain't you afraid of martial law? Ain't you red Order No. 6? Go to the Buckeye shaft and work a week and I will giv yer what is squar.'

"And they went.

"Partners, I will jest say har that I kinder don't swallow that ar last line—but its scriptur.

"Nevertheless, and he went again at 6 o'clock and did the same.

"And he went again at 11 o'clock and he seed two miners and one tenderfoot loafing, and he sed: 'Why don't yer go to work? Sargint Grant will come along and hist yer in the calaboose.'

"And they said, 'we want to work, but are a leetle afeered of the Miners' Union.'

"And he sed, 'yer got yer guns, ain't yer? What are you afeered of? Go to the Buckeye shaft, and what is squar I will give yer,' and they went. Now, when pay-day come, things got mixed. He wanted to pay the miners in the Buckeye $2 a day, but partners, they wouldn't have it, and allowed as how one miner war worth two tenderfeet, and as he paid tenderfeet $4 a day, miners were worth $8 a day."

Here "Doc" Riley rose and said: "Bill, I left my gun at home, because I knowed how hard it was for yer to get bail last time, and I don't want ter discuss, but I want to ask a question."

"Go ahead," said Bill.

"Was that ere mine owner (continued Doc) a tenderfoot or a practical man?"

"Hy! hy! hy!" shouted a score of voices.

"Now, see hyar, pards," said the preacher, "you kinder got me. But it war my certain opinion that he war a practical miner, and had been around the camp saving, saving all he could, called mean, because he wouldn't jine the boys in 'freeze out,' working for $2.50 a day in wet shafts and drinking cheap red licker ontil he was afeered his breth would pizen the man at the windlass. I don't suppose he ever played a game of keerds, except seven-up—which puts me in mind how I got skinned at that ar game on the Arkinsaw. I hope none of this congregation—but I have got off the trail. Mister (to an Eastern man), whar war I?"

Eastern man—"You were speaking about paying the laborers of the vineyards."

"Beg yer pardin," said "Doc" Riley. "Bill war speaking about lodes; wineyards warn't in question. I asked him if that ar mine owner war a tenderfoot or a practical man. I and him don't agree. No practical miner would put a tenderfoot on a prospect. He'd be a darned fool to pay him $4 per day. That ar is played."

"See hyar, Doc," said Poker Bill, "another break like that and there will be trouble in this tabernacle. I want no discussion. You all know I had a ——— of a time raising bail, and further I want this congregation to understand I can caboose the whole durned lot under Order No. 6, and—"

Here the preacher was interrupted by the sharp crack of a revolver. Trouble followed. No words; no furniture broken; no

132

noise, except a score or two of sharp explosions. Luckily none of the wounds were mortal.

When the provost guard took charge Poker Bill (who was only slightly wounded) was notified to stop preaching while martial law prevailed.

### HARASSED CHINAMEN

The Chinese in Rico, a camp in the San Juan mountains of Colorado, were literally driven out of town in the dead of night. As the editor of the town's newspaper made abundantly clear, they were not guilty of any offense, but they did provide by their presence opportunity for the ruffian element to find an excuse to engage in deviltry. This was nothing new in the West, since the Chinese were the victims of beatings and homicides from the beginning of the gold rush days. Though the hatred of the Chinese stemmed largely from economic motives, the ill will shown to them was rooted in the complex pattern of American racial prejudice. ("Disgraceful Doings," Rico *Dolores News*, May 13, 1882.)

Last Saturday night about 12 o'clock was commenced one of the most shameful affairs that ever disgraced any so-called civilized country and would have met the hearty approval of the most barbarous savage. At about that time a mob of masked men, whose number is variously estimated at from forty to sixty, went to the Chinese laundry in the rear of Davis's old blacksmith shop, with the professed intention of running the Chinamen out of town, but it seems from their actions that plunder, robbery and the gratification of a brutal desire to abuse some poor creature when completely in their power were the real motives which actuated them. Arriving at the house, these miserable miscreants dragged the slumbering celestials from their bunks and hustled them from the house without even allowing them to put on their clothes and commenced to kick and beat them. One of them, braver than all the rest, drew his pistol and shot at one of the Chinamen, the powder burning the shirt on the man's back and

133

tearing a large hole through the garment, as well as grazing the skin on the victim's back. Leaving its intended mark, the bullet entered the body of J. F. Hume, standing on the other side of the Chinaman and inflicted a terrible wound. The two Chinamen inhabiting this house were then kicked, cuffed, dragged over the ground by the hair of their heads, clubbed with pistols and sticks and otherwise maltreated and abused by their vindictive captors. A squad was detailed to continue the punishment, while the larger portion of the gang repaired to Lee Sam's laundry on upper Glasgow Avenue. Six Chinamen resided there and were routed from their bunks in much the same manner as their brethren of the opposition house, except that no shots were fired at their place, it being nearer residences, and that the half-naked Mongolians were thrown into the icy waters of Silver Creek. Each one of the heathens was honored and waited upon by a separate escort of still more heathenish men, and the programme of kicking, cuffing, beating, etc., was carried out until the fiendish hearts of the ruffians were satisfied. Others of the gang were busily engaged in plundering the laundries and met with very fair success. From Chang Lung's place $57 was secured in two packages of $25 and $32. At Lee Sam's place $413.40 was found under one of the beds and appropriated, of course. Many bundles of clothes, washed for customers, as well as an overcoat, clothes and boots and shoes belonging to the Chinese were taken. Some of the bundles of clothes were found next morning in the stage barn of the Pioneer Co., in all probability deposited there by Sam McClemmends, since arrested for complicity in the Utah cattle stealing.

Taken all in all, it is the most disgraceful piece of business that ever occurred here, and no pains should be spared to ferret out the offenders and to see that the severest punishment known to the law be meted out to them. We always knew that there were some mean men in Rico, but did not know that they could muster such a force. If they were half as good citizens as these Chinamen have been, Rico would be a better town to live in. If they were half as industrious as the Chinamen have been, it would not be necessary to rob them. We are not advocates of Chinese cheap labor, but want to know where to go when we have a shirt or pair of socks to be washed and done up as they should be. So far as we know, the almond-eyed have not cut the prices of washing, and we need a few of these natural-born laundrymen in a country like this. Whenever it becomes necessary to clear a Western town of its Chinese there is a way to do it. Give them a reasonable time to settle up their business and leave, and they are generally gone when the time is up. But to jerk them from their beds, and drag them for miles barefooted, bare-headed and thinly clad, is not the work of human beings—it would take a brute to treat even a brute in that manner.

One of the Chinamen crawled back to town about daylight Sunday morning, more dead than alive, and the others were brought back later in the day in a wagon sent after them by the town board.

### OLD ZACK TAYLOR AND BILLIE SMITH

C. C. Goodwin, teacher, mill man, rancher, judge, and editor, thought the world knew too little about the generosities of the mining folk. Many of these people toiled in common spheres and yet they showed greatness of heart. Goodwin himself was a man of many charities, and when a freshet of water swept away his newly built quartz mill and drowned six of the men on the location, he adopted the orphaned boy of one of the victims. He was celebrated in the West for his wide-ranging sympathies and also as the editor of the *Territorial Enterprise* and the Salt Lake City *Tribune.* (C. C. Goodwin, *The Comstock Club* [Salt Lake City, 1891], 90–96.)

"Three or four years before Zack's death, a courier announced to the people of Susanville that three days before, out near Deep Hole, on the desert eighty miles east of Susanville, a man had been killed by renegade Pi Ute Indians. The announcement made only a temporary impression, for such news was often brought to Susanville in those days. In a very few years eighty Lassen county men were murdered by Indians.

"A few days after the news of this particular murder was brought in, Susanville began to be vexed by the evident presence of a mysterious thief. If a hunter brought in a brace of grouse or rabbits and left them exposed for a little while they disappeared.

"If a string of trout were caught from the river and were left anywhere for a few minutes they were lost. Gardens were robbed of fruit and vegetables; blankets, flannels and groceries disappeared from stores. The losses became unbearable. At length, everybody was aroused and on the alert, but no thief could be discovered, though the depredations still went on. This continued for days and weeks, until the people became desperate, and many a threat was made that when the thief should finally be caught, in disposing of him the grim satisfaction of the frontier should be fully enjoyed. Old Zack was especially fierce in his denunciations.

"One morning a horseman dashed into town, his mustang coming in on a dead run. Reining up in front of the main hotel, he sprang down from his horse and to the people who came running to see what was the matter, he explained that half a mile from town, around the bend of the hill, in the old deserted cabin, he had found the widow of the man killed weeks before by the Indians; had found her and a nest of babies, and none of them with sufficient food or clothing.

"When the story was finished, men and women—half the population of the village—made a rush for the cabin. It was nearly concealed from view from the road by thick bushes, but they found the woman there and four little children. The woman seemed like one half dazed by sorrow and despair, but when questioned, she replied that she had been there five weeks. 'But how have you lived?' asked half a dozen voices in concert. Then the woman explained that she and her children would have

136

starved, had it not been for a kind old gentleman who brought her everything that she required.

" 'Indeed,' she added, 'he brought me many things that I did not need, and which I felt that I ought not to accept, but he over-persuaded me, telling me that I did not know how rich he was, that his supplies were simply inexhaustible.'

"When asked to describe this man, she began to say; 'He is a heavy-set old gentleman; wears blue clothes; his hair is white as snow, but his eyes are black, and—' but she was not allowed to go any farther, for twenty voices, between weeping and laughing, cried 'Old Zack!'

"The widow and her children were taken to the village, a house with its comforts provided for them, and there was, thenceforth, no more trouble from the ubiquitous thief.

"Living on charity himself, with the wreck of a life behind him and nothing before him but the grave, which he was swiftly nearing, this greathearted, old heavenly bummer and Christian thief, had taken care of this helpless family, and had done it because despite the dry rot and the whisky which had benumbed his energies, his soul, deep down, was royal to the core.

"It is true that he had robbed the town to minister to the woman and her babies, but in the books of the angels, though it was written that he was a thief, in the same sentence it was also added, 'and God bless him,' and these words turned to gold even as they were being written.

"When Old Zack was asked why he did not make the facts about the family known, after waiting a moment he replied:

" 'You see I've been tossed about a powerful sight in my time; have drank heaps of bad whisky; have done a great many no-account things and not a great many good ones. Since I wus a boy I have never had chick or kin of my own. I met the woman and her babies up by the cabin; they wus as pitiful a sight as ever you seen; and besides, the woman wus jist about to go stark mad with grief and hunger and anxiety and weariness. I seen she must have quiet and that anxiety about her children must be soothed some way. Then I did some of the best lyin' you ever heard. I got her to eat some supper and waited until the whole outfit wus fast asleep. I watched 'em a little while and then I got curis to know what kind of a provider I would have made for a family had I started out in life different, and that wus all there wus about it.'

"Is it a wonder, then, that when the old man died his body was dressed in soft raiment, placed in a costly casket, and that, preceded by a martial band playing a requiem, all the people followed sorrowingly to the grave; and that, as they gently heaped the sods above his breast, they sent after him into the Beyond heartfelt 'all-hails and farewells'?"

"You see your man through colored spectacles, Colonel," spoke up Brewster. "From your description, I think there was more of the border deviltry in the old man than there was true royalty. Life had been a joke to him always; he played it as a joke to the village; had there been a dozen more like him they would have become intolerable nuisances."

"That," said the Colonel, "only shows how miserable are my descriptive powers. There are not a dozen other such men as old Zack Taylor was among all the fourteen hundred millions of people on this sorrowful earth."

"No," interposed Miller, "you told the story well enough, but it was only descriptive of a good-humored bummer at best—of one who was warm-hearted without a conscience, of one who was more willing to work to perpetrate a joke on others than to honorably earn the bread he ate.

"I will tell you of a royal fellow that I knew. It was Billie Smith. He lived in Eureka that first hard winter of '70–71. He was not a miner as we are, receiving four dollars per day. He and his partner, a surly old fellow, had a claim which they were developing, hoping that it would amount to something in the spring. That was before smelting had been made a success. The ores were all base and of too low a grade to ship away. These men

*"First news from Frazer! Strangest tales are told!*
*Of gold on river bars, and bars of gold!"*

This page and the two following are from "The Frazer River Ther-mometer," an illustrated poem about the woes of the mining com-munity in 1858, published by Street & Butler, San Francisco.

*"Just wait your turn we'll give you all a show!*
*See what a rush!—will everybody go?"*

*"Of accommodations here's a token—*
*Both floor and slumber here is broken!"*

*"Confound yer Steamboat! guess I'll show my pluck!*
*Come on, old woman, let us try our luck!"*

*"I ain't a goin' to wait for her, 'I swow.'*
*There's gold ahead—oughter be there now!"*

The following illustrations are from "Life Among the Miners," published by Hutchings and Rosenfield, San Francisco.

*Seen here are many changing scenes.*
*Met with in Miner's life,*
*Some of his comforts and his joys,*
*Some of his toils and strife:*
*And by the pictures they present,*
*A truthful tale is told,*
*Of joys and sorrows incident*
*Of those who dig for gold.*

*Returning from their daily toil,*
*Though tired as dogs they feel,*
*Contentedly they build a fire*
*And cook their evening meal.*

*The miner's pastime, which too oft,*
*Is spent in reckless play,*
*In which they hazard on the cards*
*The proceeds of the day.*

*Saturday night they weigh their dust—*
*All anxious faces there,*
*While waiting for the truthful scales,*
*To give to each his share.*

*His home a village rudely built upon auriferous soil,*
*His life is one of changing scenes—of hard, unceasing toil.*

*The washing dirt for gold is well,*
*When well they make it pay,*
*But few attractions unto them*
*The red shirt washing day.*

Letters from home—there's nought can give
   The miner joy like this;
Good news from loved ones far away,
   Is ecstasy and bliss.

He's made his fortune, and to seek
   His home he now intends;
See how genteelly now he meets
   With all his city friends.

*Upon a bed of sickness, now—*
*No loving friend is there;*
*How much he needs a sister's aid,—*
*A mother's anxious care.*

*Fatigued, the miner falls asleep,*
*Upon a mountain high.*
*His bed, the ground, his covering,*
*A blanket and the sky.*

The following are illustrations for J. M. Hutching's original version of "The Miners' Ten Commandments," which appears in full in the section on placer miners.

*"Thou shalt have no other claim than one."*

*"Neither shalt thou pick out specimens from the company's pan to put them in thy mouth."*

"*Thou shalt not remember what thy friends do at home on the Sabbath day, lest the remembrance may not compare favorably with what thou doest here.*"

*"Thou shalt not grow discouraged, nor think of going home before thou hast made thy 'pile.'"*

"*Thou shalt not make unto thyself false claim, nor any likeness to a mean man, by jumping one.*"

"*Neither shalt thou take thy money, nor thy gold dust, nor thy good name, to the gaming table in vain.*"

*"Thou shalt consider how faithfully and patiently she awaiteth thy return."*

"*Neither shalt thou destroy thyself by getting 'tight,' nor 'slewed,' nor 'high,' nor 'corned,' nor 'half-seas over,' nor 'three sheets in the wind.'*"

"*A man spake these words, and said: I am a miner, who wandered 'from away down east,' and came to sojourn in a strange land, and 'see the elephant.'*"

had a little supply of flour, bacon and coffee, and that was about all, and it was all they expected until spring.

"It was early in January and the weather was exceedingly cold. Their cabin was but a rude hut, open on every side to the winds. I was there and I know how things were. One day I was waiting in a tent, which by courtesy was called a store, when Billie came in. He had been there but a few minutes when his partner came in. The old man was fairly boiling with rage. So angry was he that he could hardly articulate distinctly. Finally he explained that some thief had stolen their mattress, a pair of their best blankets and a sack of flour. He wanted an officer dispatched with a search warrant. Then I overheard the following conversation between the two men:

" 'O, never mind,' said Billie; 'some poor devil needed the things or he would not have taken them.'

" 'Yes, but we need them, too; need them more than anything else,' was the response.

" 'O, we will get along; we have plenty.'

" 'Yes,' retorted the partner, 'but what are we going to do for a bed? Our hair mattress and best pair of blankets are gone, and the cabin is cold.'

" 'We can sew up some sacks into a mattress, and fill it with soft brush and leaves, and use our coats for blankets,' replied Billie. 'We'll get along all right. The truth is we have been sleeping too warm of late.'

" 'Too warm!' said the partner bitterly; 'I should think so. A pollar bear would freeze in that cabin without a bed.'

" 'Do you think so?' asked Billie, smiling. 'Well, that is the way to keep it, and so if any wild animal comes that way we can freeze him out. Brace up, partner! Why should a man make a fuss about the loss of a trifle like that?'

"Later I found out the facts. A little below Billie's cabin was another cabin, into which a family of emigrants had moved. They were dreadfully poor. Going to and returning from town Billie had noticed how things were. One night as he passed, going home in the dark, he heard a child crying in the cabin and heard it say to its mother that it was hungry and cold.

"Next morning he waited until his partner had gone away, then rolled the mattress around a sack of flour, then rolled the mattress and flour up in his best pair of blankets, swung the bundle on his shoulder, carried it down the trail to the other cabin, where, opening the door, he flung it inside; then with finger on his lip he said in a hoarse whisper to the woman: 'Don't mention it! Not a word. I stole the bundle, and if you ever speak of it you will get me sent to the prison,' and in a moment was swinging down the trail singing joyously:

> If I had but a thousand year, Robin Ruff,
> If I had but a thousand year.

"Last winter, after the fire, there was one man in this city, John W. Mackay, who gave $150,000 to the poor. It was a magnificent act, and was as grandly and gently performed as such an act could be. No one would ever have known it, had not the good priest who distributed the most of it, one day, mentioned the splendid fact. That man will receive his reward here, and hereafter, for it was a royal charity. But he has $30,000,000 to draw against, while, when Billie in the wilderness gave up his bed and his food, he not only had not a cent to draw against, but he had not a reasonably well-defined hope."

# Laughter in the Hard Rock Camps

### A Ricoite in Denver

A Denver newspaper reported innocently that a Ricoite by the name of Dunn had made an excursion into society with telling impact. He had buttonholed a listener in the lobby of the St. James Hotel in Denver and had proceeded to try to humbug him with a tall tale. The dimension of his effort prompted the victim to invite Dunn to join a struggling liars' club back East. This type of invitation indicated appreciation of a kind, and at the same time usually put the teller of tall tales on notice that his listeners were on to him and that his talents would be better appreciated among the less practiced liars of the eastern United States. ("Dunn's Dreadful Drop," Rico *Dolores News*, April 29, 1882. Reprinted from the Denver *Evening World*.)

C olonel David F. Gage, of the St. James, is responsible for the following:

Last night when the corridors of the hotel were filled with the excursionists, I noticed Mr. A. W. Dunn, of Rico, buttonholing one of the party and evidently telling him a yarn about Colorado. I made my way through the crowd, and took a stand near the two, without their knowledge, and overheard every word they said. Following is the conversation as near as I can remember it. Dunn was speaking while the stranger appeared to pay rapt attention to his words:

"It is a mistake," said Dunn, "the idea so universally believed in the East that these mountains were here when the first settlers arrived. I have myself watched the growth of some of the highest peaks from a mere mole hill to their present size. Some years ago when I was down at Rico, I and my partner built a cabin on a level piece of ground. One day in April as we were sitting in the cabin eating our midday meal of beans and fat pork we noticed something strange. A feeling of chilliness pervaded the cabin; and soon there broke upon our ears the sweetest imaginable sounds. We listened attentively, totally forgetting the beans and everything else. The cabin door was closed, but down the chimney came a concord of the most exquisite, musical chords I ever listened to. To say we were astonished, stranger, would be drawing it mild. All of a sudden, the tune ceased and we heard various sounds resembling the tuning of harps and violins. With our hair standing on end and our cheeks blanched, we rushed to the door, and it makes me shiver and choke when I think of it—the town of Rico was lying 15,000 feet below us; we could see the inhabitants walking around the streets, appearing no bigger than mice. Then a new light dawned upon us. The surface ground of our mine had taken a rise while we were eating; and in place of a level piece of ground on the banks of the Dolores River we were 15,000 feet up in the air. But the strangest thing of all is the fact that our bed of mineral which was about ten acres in extent, rose right out of the ground with the surface stakes. We afterwards sunk a shaft to a depth of 13,000 feet all in mineral, and drove tunnels from the surface to a distance of five miles and have not yet reached the end of the body of ore. The sounds that so captivated our ears we afterwards found out was the choir singing in the "New Jerusalem."

"Pity you didn't have your windows opened in that direction," said the stranger in a cool voice.

"Well, now, stranger," continued Dunn, "I am the fortunate owner of a one-half interest in that mine, which we call the Heavenly Harp, and if you or any of your friends have a million or two lying around loose I'll sell you a 1-1000th interest in it very reasonably. I want to sell because this thing of being over-burdened with wealth is too trying on my system."

After the speaker had finished, the stranger opened his eyes, gave a nervous twitch to his mouth, and drawing nearer to the other speaker, said:

"My corduroy friend, it is entirely foreign to my nature to call a man a liar; besides, I have been taught to believe that the inhabitants of Colorado object to being addressed in that way. But I beg your pardon if I encroach on good manners when I say you handle the truth with a great deal of caution—in fact you seem to be afraid of it. Now I'll do you a favor. Back in Boston we have a society of congenial spirits who meet once a month to tell lies. Some of the members have already obtained a great deal of celebrity in that line. Now if you will kindly give me your name, I'll take occasion at the first meeting after my arrival to propose you for membership, and have not the slightest doubt that after you have given a specimen of your skill, you will be chosen as Most Worthy High Prevaricator, so—"

But the corduroy Ricoite did not wait to hear the concluding sentence. He jumped away with his hat pulled down over his eyes, and the barkeeper was soon busy concocting a double strength cocktail.

Colonel Gage enjoyed the interview amazingly, and he laughed so much last night that his sides are sore today. The gentlemen connected with The *Evening World* don't know a lie when they see it. They met one in the street the other day and thought in their innocence it was a sunflower.

THE UPSHOT OF AN INSULT

Lake City, a mountain town of southwestern Colorado, had several churches and a large number of practical jokers. The town attracted lawyers and the sporting element, but for some reason doctors were not in practice there. When a long-legged, shabby

143

member of the profession turned up, he was treated to the humor of the place. The *Silver World*, which reported the joke on the medical man, had the distinction of being the first newspaper on the western slope, commencing publication in 1875 almost simultaneously with the laying out of the town. ("A Duel," Lake City *Silver World*, March 16, 1878.)

We are called upon to record another of those melancholy episodes in which the barbarous code of the duello was resorted to appease wounded honor, and in which one of the principals *fell*. "What a fall was there, my countrymen." Out of respect for the friends and relatives of both parties we refrain from mentioning their names because the affair occurred near the toll gate, outside of the municipal limits and additional privacy was thus secured. We have been unable after diligent search, to obtain any particulars from the spectators and must, therefore, rely on fugitive accounts of it; but the leading features of the tragic affair are about as follows:

Doctor K—— (we only give the initial) whose matchless skill with firearms was, no doubt, acquired by the professional use of the syringe, felt himself aggrieved by some sharp retorts made by Mr. The Tay——, (we give this much of his name only because it rhymes with K) and challenged him to mortal combat. The challenged party having, according to the code, the right to choose the weapons chose shot-guns at ten paces, and after settling all preliminaries the principals together with their seconds and surgeons repaired, Tuesday afternoon, to a secluded place near the toll gate. What a spectacle! Two men in the bloom of youth and beauty one or both in a few moments, perhaps, to bedew the beautiful snow with their life's blood, and all because of a few words spoken in debate. No remonstrances of friends, no tender recollections of relatives, no considerations of self-respect and reputation were of avail. The strenuous efforts of seconds and friends were rejected with scorn by Doctor K——, whose gigantic form crowned by that narrow brimmed hat which, with

144

his huge physical proportions, makes him so conspicuous. His lengthened shadow lay along the silvery surface of the snow, and as he stood with his hat on, sternly and defiantly awaiting the signal to fire, it looked like the picture of the frog at home on a Marburg Bro's tobacco placard. His opponent, T——, took things cooly, also, but was less demonstrative. Giving a few hasty directions to his seconds he took position in line with the medical Goliath and, without a tremor, awaited the fatal signal.

The surgeon's cases were open and the sunlight was reflected from the polished implements, before which the strongest men shrink even in looking upon—the shot guns were duly loaded and handed to the combatants. "Are you ready, gentlemen?" K—— hissed "yes" between his teeth, as his steely eye glanced along the barrel of his weapon in point blank aim at his antagonist's heart. T—— also quietly answered but with no air of bravado, as he felt that he was looking for the last time upon the fair scenes of this world and the friends around him. The supreme moment in the lives of both had come and both seemed to realize it. Before the final signal to fire was given, K—— removed his coat, placing it in a bundle near him and covered it with his hat, from which, however he forgot to remove the "brick" with which it is usually ballasted.

Again the awful question was put, "Are you ready?" Both answered, and then the deliberate count and signal, "one"— "two"—"three"—"fire" were given and the reverberations of simultaneous shots sped along the precipitous valley.

T—— magnaminously fired in the air, but as the powder cloud cleared away, it was seen by the horrified spectators that his form was prone upon the ground and writhing in the snow. As the surgeon felt his heart and exclaimed "He is killed!" K—— unfeelingly remarked, "I always knew I was a good shot," thus betraying the fact that he is not only an old hand at the business, but a hardened wretch whom it were base flattery to call a—doctor.

At this juncture the cry, "The sheriff is coming" rang out upon the startled ear of all concerned, and as the surgeon announced

145

the death of T——, the disciple of Galen and Bacchus frantically seized his hat and coat and started for some place of conceal-ment, and the last that was seen of him were his inordinately long legs projecting from the embankment of a cabin near the dance house. About four o'clock, however, he made his appear-ance and was astonished to perceive that he had been completely fooled by the practical jokers, chief of whom was the supposed victim of his remarkable courage and skill as a "shootist."

### CUSTOMS OF THE COUNTRY

In the two stories that follow the tenderfoot is exposed to the ridicule of the backwoodsman. The theme was an old one in back-woods humor, aimed at chastising an impolite outsider for his presumptuous manner. An arrogant tenderfoot could be made to repent while looking down the barrel of a pistol as in the first tale, but there was always a possibility too that he would be humbled by men who were his superior in wit, as in the second story.

I

("A Tenderfoot at Tombstone," Red Mountain City [Colorado] *Pilot*, April 28, 1883.)

A few days ago a flush young man from an Eastern college arrived at Tombstone, Arizona, and registered his name at the principal hotel. A socially inclined person in a blue shirt and a broad rimmed hat, who chanced to be in the office, good natured-ly answered every question and volunteered a vast amount of interesting information about Arizona in general and Tombstone in particular.

"Did you see them hills?" asked the Tombstoner, pointing through one of the office windows. "Well, them hills are chuck full of pay dirt."

The young man from the east looked shock.

"My dear sir," he said proudly, but kindly, "You should say 'those hills are'; not 'them hills is!' "

The Tombstoner was silent for a moment. He looked the young

146

man from the east critically over, as if estimating the size of a coffin he would wear. Then drawing out an ivory stocked seven-shooter of elaborate style and finish, he said in a soft, mild, musical tone of voice that sounded like Wildwood Brook coursing o'er its pebbled bed: "My gentle unsalted tenderfoot from the land of the rising sun, this here's a pint that you and me disagree on, and we mit as well have it settled right now. I haven't looked in a grammar lately, but I say 'them hills is' is correct, and I'm going to stand by that opinion while I've got a shot left. I'll give you just three minutes to think calmly over the subject, for you probably spoke in haste for the first time, and I'll bear your decision."

The young man from the east looked down the delicately-chased barrel of the revolver into the placid depths of the eye of the Tombstoner and began to feel that many points in grammar are uncertain and are liable to grow so. Then he thought of the coroner's inquest and of the verdict, "Came to his death by standing in front of Colorado Tom's seven-shooter," and of the long pine box going east by express with $99 charges on it, and before half the three minutes was up he was ready to acknowledge his error. Since he had thought it over calmly, he said, he believed "them hills is" right. He had spoken on the spur of the moment, he added, and begged a thousand pardons for his presumptuous efforts to substitute bad grammar for good.

The Tombstoner forgave him freely, and grasping his hand said: "I know'd you'd say you was wrong after you thought a moment. I admire a man who gives right in without arguing when he knows he's wrong. Come along and irrigate." And they irrigated.

II

("Culture on Bitter Creek," Lake City *Mining Register*, October 8, 1880.)

Perhaps every person who is somewhat advanced in life can remember some incident of his early years which he would really like to forget, something that resulted from the freshness and vast inexperience of youth. I remember one which I have spent a good deal of time trying to forget. Just before the Union Pacific railroad reached the Bitter Creek country, I made my first overland trip to the Pacific coast. I staged it from the then terminus of the Union Pacific to the Central Pacific, which was pushing east. The stage broke down on Bitter creek, and the passengers had to walk to the next station. I grew tired of walking before I reached the station, and coming late in the afternoon, to where some teamsters were camped, I concluded to stop with them for the night. On asking their permission to do so, they assented so heartily that I felt at home at once. Life in the west was something new to me. I was young and buoyant, and just out of college. I was fond of talking. I thought it would be novel and delightful to sleep out with these half-savage ox-drivers, with no shelter but the vaulted, star-gemmed heavens. There were four teamsters, and as many wagons, while thirty-two oxen grazed around in the vicinity. Of the teamsters, one was a giant in stature, and wore a bushy black beard; another was shorter, but powerfully built, and one-eyed; the third was tall, lank and hame-jawed; while the fourth was a wiry, red-headed man. In my thoughts I pitied them, on account of the hard life they led, and spoke to them in a kind tone, and endeavored to make my conversation constructive. I plucked a flower, and, pulling it to pieces mentioned the name of the parts—pistils, stamen, calyx, and so on—and remarked that it must be indigenous to the locality, and spoke of the plant being ondogenous, in contradiction exogenous, and they could see that it was not cryptogamous. In looking at some fragments of rock my thoughts wandered off into geology, and among other things I spoke of the tertiary and carboniferous periods, and of the pterodactyl, icthyosaurus and dinothorium. The teamsters looked at me, and then at each other, but made no response. We squatted down around the frying-pan to take supper, as the big fellow, with his right hand slapped or sort of larruped, a long piece of fried bacon over a piece of bread

148

in his left hand, sending a drop of hot grease into my left eye, he said to the one-eyed man:

"Bill, is my copy of Shakespere in yo' wagon? I missed it to-day."

"No. My Tennerson and volum' of the Italian poets is in thar— no Shakespere."

The lank-looking teamster, biting off a piece of bread about the size of a saucer, in a voice which came huskily through the bread:

"Jake, did yer ever read that volum' of po'ms that I writ?"

"No, but hev often hearn tell on 'em."

"Yer mean 'Musin's of an Idle Man?' " spoke up the red-headed man, addressing the poet.

"Yes."

"Hev read every line in it a dozen times," said the teamster with the red hair, and as he sopped a four-inch swath, with a piece of bread, across a frying-pan, he repeated some lines.

"Them's they," nodded the poet. "The Emp'ror of Austry writ me a letter highly complimentin' them po'ms."

"They're very tochin'," added the wiry man.

I took no part in these remarks. Somehow I did not feel like joining in.

The wiry man having somewhat satisfied himself rolled up a piece of bacon rind into a sort of single-barreled opera glass, and began to squint through it towards the southern horizon.

"What yer doin', Dave?" asked the stout man.

"Takin' observations on the North star. Want to make some astronomical calkilatons when I git later to Sackrymenter."

"Well, yer needn't ter made that tel'scope. I could er tuk yo' observations for yer, bein' as I have but one eye."

"Git that yer durned old carboniferous pterdacky," yelled the hame-jawed driver to an ox that was licking a piece of lariat.

"I give a good deal of my time to 'stronomy when I was in Yoorup," remarked the tall man.

"Over thar long?" asked one.

149

"Good while. War Minister to Roosky. Then I spent some time down ter Rome."

"Rome!" exclaimed the tall individual. "Was born thr. My father was a sculptor."

"Good sculptor?"

"Yes."

"Well, one wouldn't er thought it, ter look at yer."

"I never was in Yoorup," remarked the one-eyed man. "When I ocypied the cheer of ancient languages in Harvard College my health failed, and the fellers what hired me wanted me ter go ter Yoorup for an out, but I concluded ter come west ter look—hold upthar, yer infernal old flea-bitten ichthyosaurus," he bawled to an ox that was chewing a wagon cover.

I felt hot and feverish, and a long way from home.

"I got ready once ter go ter Rome—wanted ter complete my studies thar—but give it up," said the one called Dave.

"What fer?"

"They wanted me ter run fur guv'ner in Virginny."

"Yer beat 'em?"

"Thunder, yes."

"Why didn't yer stay thar?"

"Well, when my job as guv'ner give out they 'lected me 'Piscopal bishop an' I hurt my lungs preachin'. Come west for my lungs."

"Found 'em?"

"Well, I'm improvin'."

I did not rest well that night. As day came on, and the men began to turn over in their blankets and yawn, the tall one said:

"Hello, Bill. How yer makin' it?"

"O, I'm indigenous."

"An' Dave?"

"I'm endogenous."

"An' you, Lanky, yer son of a sculptor?"

"Exogenous."

150

"How do you feel, Jake?" inquired one of the three who had responded.

"Cryptogamous, sir, cryptogamous."

I walked out a few steps to a little stream, to get a drink. I felt thirsty, and I ached. Then I heard a voice from the blankets.

"Wonder if them durned ole dinother'ums of ourn are done grazin'?"

Then a reply.

"I guess they've got to the tertiary period."

I walked a little piece on the road, to breathe the morning air. I kept on.

# The Public Forum

THIRD HOUSE IN BLACK HAWK AND CENTRAL CITY

Black Hawk in Gilpin County was a prosperous hard-rock mining town situated below Central City in the front range of the Rockies. Gilpin County had the distinction of being the center of gold production during the 1860's in Colorado and the scene of the activities of the "Third House of Sovereigns." The Third House in the mining regions provided a popular forum for the expression of all kinds of political and social burlesque. The raillery of frontier wits struck at the open flanks of the political muftis of the day. The Third House of Carson City, Nevada, is the best known example of an institution that was named after the Third House of the political lobbyists and counted among its members the most distinguished wits in western Nevada. The enthusiasm in other areas for this type of diversion was more widespread than has been noted by historians.

(Meetings of the "Third House of Sovereigns" from the Black Hawk [Colorado] Daily Mining Journal, February 11, 18, and July 22, 1864.)

I

The Third House of Sovereigns in this place was organized last night, by the election of A. G. Langford, member from Brimstone, as Speaker. He was appointed a Committee to conduct himself to the Chair, according to usual custom, which he accomplished at the first trial and with the most irrepressible dignity. The Hall rang again with the cheers of his friends and the groans of his enemies. The House wished to elect the other officers, incident to legislative bodies, but the Speaker, who is a rigid parliamentarian, deciding with the most magnificent disregard for the rules of Jefferson, dispensed with it. The Sergeant-at-Arms was ordered to bring in the Fireman who was not present, but he came back after an hour's absence, speaking incoherently, and reported that he could not be found.

The election of Chaplain having been decided unnecessary, the Speaker directed the Clerk to read in lieu of any religious service the following ode to "Gimlet, Prints of Dunkirk":

"The fethered Quires
Hev diskontinered to wobble there musik
From the umbrajers shades iv the May—
Berin weeds. The limpin streams
Thet used to mutter along at the fut
Uv noles, elvashuns and smal hils
Hev koagerlated. The little Big Muddy hes friz.
The feels hev lost their variousgated hews
Uv red and orrange and yaller,
Showin there die-stuph tu be poor.
The erth hes roled up in a thin shete
For a long shiverin snuze,
The eyesickles hang penderent and glisnin
From ruffs, and straugh staks, rails and lims
And awl nachure luks as if like Nighoby it
Had petrified, weepin at the loss iv Ortum!
Awl annymate reashun looks as if stocks was
Fallin, and go about on the sqwekin
Sno in very medertative attytoods.
Turkeze and the web-futed tribe seam to se
Shadders iv kummlu evens cast abed—
Slay belz kum eckoin over the hills and vallies

153

With their meallojuis tinklin and ginglin,
And fellers go ridin about thair affi
Nancys bi their aides, rapt in each uthers
Arms and Buffylow skins and blankets,
And a warm brick under their fete.
Naybob a brase thru the streets with thair
Peedel extremightys poltised in furs,
And poor men go shiverin and dubbled up
As iph aphlikted with the newrology or roomy
Tism, or a krik in the smal of the bak.
Awl hale winter! How kould, pail, grand
Tremenzous and nice yu art!"

The Speaker then announced the Standing Committees, when a messenger arrived with Governor Dophunny's message. A mallet and chisel were brought into requisition to break the seal, and the Clerk proceeded to read it in the most melodious voice. It was an eloquent document, a fault which Governor Dophunny very naturally fell into, as not wishing to appear to copy from his colleague, Governor Evans. We have not space to notice it here, but as the House ordered 4 copies printed in plain English, 5000 in Spanish and 13 in Sioux, our readers will be treated to its perusal in due time. Reports from the Treasurer and School Superintendent were received and read, both of which exhibit the affairs of their departments in a serious light. The House fell into a meditative mood during their perusal by the Clerk from which it was hard to arouse it.

Mr. Peabody introduced a bill for the alteration of Mr. Swallow's name upon which a lively debate sprung up between the members from Spring Gulch and Arapahoe. As this was decidedly out of order the Speaker allowed it to proceed.

Com. French gave notice of a Bill for "The improvement of navigation in Spring Gulch."[1]

Mr. Lee gave notice of a Bill entitled, "How to do it."

[1] There are no navigable streams in the vicinity of Spring Gulch.

Mr. Keith gave notice of a Bill to amend an act entitled "An act repealing the Acts of the Apostles."

Mr. Mallory gave notice of a Bill "annexing the Washington Government to Colorado."

Mr. Fitzpatrick, (Page) gave notice of a Bill "making Clear Creek navigable as far as Golden City."[2]

Mr. Stanton, from Spring Gulch gave notice of a bill "to abolish Moral Evil."

Mr. Humphrey gave notice of a bill for "removing the business houses of Nevada and Central to Black Hawk, and providing in case of resistance, for the imprisonment of the inhabitants and confiscation of their property."[3]

Mr. Henderson, from the committee on Cap Rock and Crevices, asked leave to report, but was decided out of order by the Speaker.

An appropriation to pay for public printing was made by the House, under the gag rule. Thirty-two cubic feet of the currency of the Territorial Bank, to be established on Long's Peak, was set aside for that purpose.

Various petitions and memorials were received and referred to appropriate committees.

Business was lively, but on the whole, rather dry, as was the Hon. Speaker, for whom no refreshments had been provided. Motions to adjourn to some previous period of time were frequent, but were invariably ruled out of order by the Speaker. A large crowd was in attendance, and the proceedings, though dignified and orderly, were yet cheerful. The House finally adjourned, *sine die*, to meet at Lawrence Hall, Central, on Wednesday evening next at 7½ o'clock.

II

The Third House held its closing session, last evening in the Court House at Central. Besides the regular members, there was

2 Clear Creek is a roaring mountain stream.
3 There was at the time a strong spirit of civic competition between the adjoining mountain towns of Black Hawk and Central City.

a large concourse of log-rollers, lobby and floating members having axes of their own to grind, which they were ground. After preliminary organization of the House by the Speaker, it went into Committee of the Whole on Unfinished Business. A Bill for the Removal of the Seat of War was introduced, read once by sections and once by title, when under the rules of the last Session it was put upon its final passage. Passed, Ayes two; Noes, one. Division of the House called for but decided impracticable by the Speaker. House then resolved itself dry and adjourned to Billy Jones' to take a drink. Took it. Brought in some refreshments for the Hon. Speaker in an indescribable vessel more sinned against than sinning. It was intended as a compliment to the delegation from Black Hawk, but unfortunately, Speaker Langford had just called Mr. Hal Sayr to the Chair and the benevolent idea was nipped in the bud. Then arose a debate on the licensing of fancy horses and other amusements in which scintillations of wit and gems of eloquence were indulged with the prodigality of a Shakespeare. Mr. Faul was ordered to photograph the proceedings of the House in the best style of the art, which will be done. Numerous bills were introduced and referred to the Governor's private Secretary. The Governor's Message was printed and passed unanimously. People were prohibited in future from recording lode claims above 140 in any direction. This bill was vehemently opposed but the Speaker silenced all opposition by a vigorous use of his gavel and over-ruled all negative votes as treasonable. Bill finally passed with astonishing unanimity. The Bill for altering the Committee on county lines became a law, *de jure* if not de *facto*. Black Hawk was incorporated and its unique character ordered inscribed among the archives of Colorado. In the words of Webster, "There it stands." A company was incorporated to light the Main Street of Central, extending from Smith's toll-gate to the Prize Lode, with gas. The President of the company, Lum Nuckols, was ordered bored out for a gas pipe, but that gentleman objected on the ground that he was big enough bore already, in which decision the House finally coincided. Here our special Reporter, he became oblivious to all sublunary scenes, but upon coming to, this morning, he was told that after the Treasurer's Report and the appropriation from the U. S. Mint of a liberal sum to pay the members and the Executive, the Third House adjourned to *sine die*; much against the will of the people of Black Hawk and Central who having always treated the Government with distinguished consideration felt hurt at this summary removal of the Capital. Like our amiable President, the Hon. Speaker was reminded by all this of a story which he couldn't resist the inclination to tell. "One time," said he, "a fellow named Jones, bought a bobtailed coat, something on the style of those just coming into fashion now, too short to hang down. Meeting a friend, he says, 'Bob, how do you like my new coat?' 'Bully,' said Bob, 'only it's a little short.' 'Oh well,' Jones replied, 'it'll be long enough before I get another one.' Bob was tickled half to death at this innocent pun and came near off the handle onto the spur of the moment. Laughing all over, he hurried up town to tell the boys. Arrived at the store, he laughed. After several tremendous efforts he got his jaws within speaking distance, and said 'Oh boys, Jones said a fine thing down here, a real fine thing, best iv heard, ever, and then he laughed. What was it, Bob?' 'Oh, twas a nice thing, just as witty,' and then he laughed. 'Well, tell us, so that we can laugh too.' 'Well, you see,' said Bob, 'Jones is sporting one of them shorttailed coats made to wear in summer when fruit's plenty, and I met him down town and he asked me how I liked it.' Bob's mouth flew open like a desk knife and he laughed. 'I said, very well, only it was rather short. And he replied (haw! haw! haw!). I guess'll be a good while before I get another due.' No one laughed. Bob began to get sober. It didn't sound right. The auditors didn't see the point and were so regardless of Bob's feelings as to say so. Bob kept on sobering up. His plumes dropped. The muscles of his mouth gradually arrived at their usual state of rigidity. With a lost air which was inexpressibly comical, he soliloquized rather than answered, 'I declare I don't either, but I did.' And to this day Bob can't imagine how he lost the point of his story. Every-one has the right to premise that the Speaker's story is in its way applicable to the remarkable Session of the Third House, which was adjourned *sine die*, last evening, to meet again whenever a quorum shall be present.

III

The "Sovereigns" have postponed the further consideration of their constitution until July 4th, last. It is owing, we learn, to a disagreement with regard to offices. It was proposed to create an office for every man, woman and child, in the territory,— those who have never been inmates of a States Prison, excepted. Unfortunately the proposition prevailed without due considera-tion, being passed unanimously so that, there being no more timber for officers left among the "Sovereigns," and there being no one to move a reconsideration, and the "Sovereigns" being pervaded with a numerous antipathy against the bogus constitu-tion men, things came to a deadlock. A way out of the woods was at length descried by the keen eye of the "Gyasticutus," and the motion being made by Kurnet Say-all, the "Sovereigns" ad-journed the subject to the 4th inst., as above stated. Meanwhile it is designed to send to Sing-Sing for recruits, as it is considered certain that nothing but "constitutional" thieves can stand the State offices at the very economical figures which the "Sover-eigns" are compelled to attach to them. So that it will be seen the "Sovereigns" are not dead but sleepeth.

PUBLIC CENSOR

David Frakes Day, the editor and publisher of the Ouray, Colorado, *Solid Muldoon*, was a vigorous polemical writer whose newspaper evoked during the 1880's considerable public comment in Colorado. Mining ore was discovered in the vicinity of Ouray in 1875, and the town was incorporated in 1876. Day, a soldier in the Union army during the War of the Rebellion, commenced publication of the *Muldoon* on September 5, 1879, and declared publicly that his journal would be Democratic in party affiliation. The *Muldoon* stayed in Ouray until 1892, when Day moved it to Durango. (Editorial columns, *Solid Muldoon*, May-August 1883. Each selection is identified by issue in the text.)

The surface dude who squirts violent opinions into the columns of the Grand Junction *News* don't like our efforts in behalf of the *Queen Bee*; but, then, we are not running this *Muldoon* to please every pecan-headed intestine on the frontier. Revise your exchange list, Buddie. You don't have to read this *Muldoon*. (June 1, 1883.)

Whenever you see a railroad magnate, who carries enough religion to rupture the kidneys of an ordinary jackass, participating in a judical contest, you want to vote the other ticket.

No country is more picturesque and quaint than Silverton. There is something so novel in the long undulating rows of charcoal pits dotted here and there by innumerable "tin horns" foraging for time-checks. The buildings are mostly of the Gothic order, and the roads carefully adorned with empty peach cans, Budweiser bottles and other imported statuary. The population is about 400,000, 399,500 of whom have not yet arrived, and the remaining 500 are Chinamen and dancehouse rustlers. The principal industry is gall, large quantities of which are annually shipped to Durango, Oshkosh and Cheyenne. (June 8, 1883.)

Delta's Mayor wears a badge denoting the exalted position which he occupies. It is an excellent idea to label ignorance when it gets beyond its sphere.

The Pueblo *Chieftain* dude threatens to hold Governor Grant "personally responsible" for an extra session, if one is called. Governor Grant need have no fears, as about the only thing the *Chieftain* has ever been able to hold is the undivided and unanimous contempt of all who look upon honor and integrity as other than marketable commodities. The *Chieftain* is about the largest and most complete fraud south of the *Rocky Mountain News*. (June 15, 1883.)

The *Register-Call* congratulates Secretary Teller[1] upon the *Muldoon's* hatred. Wonder if it ever occurred to Mssrs. Laird and Marlow that an opposition possessing the merit of frankness and sincerity was far more preferable to a man of Secretary Teller's intelligence than the subsidized and sickening rot that daily surfeits the columns of that sheet. When the *Muldoon* alludes to Secretary Teller in terms complimentary or otherwise, he knows that we mean exactly what we say; but when the *Register-Call* indulges in flattery, the Secretary is in doubt as to the sincerity, but positive as to the actuating motive. He Pays For It!

Mr. York, who has undertaken the task of resurrecting the Weakly Somnabulist (Ouray Times), is getting along very nicely since he came over from Silverton. He now waltzes up to the bar like a grown man; eats pie with a fork; winks at the dining room girls; wipes his nose on the tablecloth, and exhibits other symptoms of civilization. Haller thinks that in another week he will be able to look thro' the window of a milliner shop without slobbering. (June 22, 1883.)

The Durango *Herald* is considerably exercised over a "strike in La Plata," but does not say whether a new hay ranch has been discovered or a grass widow downed another lumber merchant. Wonderful village for strikes, that Durango.

We understand that a petition is being circulated for the removal of Mills, Lake City's postmaster. Mills, it will be remembered, is the violent statesman who unloaded a set harangue in this village two years ago. (June 29, 1883.)

*The Breckinridge Leader* finds consolation in the idea that the "Lord knows who will be elected this fall." We had all along supposed that Senator Eddy[2] was running Summit County.

Senator Hill,[3] after eighteen years of research, has discovered

---

[1] Henry M. Teller was a lawyer and railroad promoter who served as Colorado's Republican U. S. Senator from 1877 to 1883 and as Secretary of the Interior in Arthur's administration.

[2] H. H. Eddy served in the State Senate of Colorado.

[3] Nathaniel P. Hill was a mining capitalist, who had taught chemistry at

that the conflict between "freedom and slavery is over." If the
Senator continues his explorations he may, ere many moons,
discover that the tussel between brains and wealth is gradually
depriving the latter of its grip. (August 17, 1883.)

If the Lord ever intends to stand in with this country, now is
the time. We are in elegant shape ourself, but the Denver and
Rio Grande is where salvation is needed.

We have heard at least fifty citizens express their disgust at
the action of Charley Haskins in lugging his maimed brother into
saloons for political purposes. If he had been in the habit of
visiting such places it would have been different; but to utilize
human misfortune for a political lever is just a little bit beyond
human edurance. Shame—shame—shame. (August 24, 1883.)

### EDITORIAL EXCHANGE

General James Allen, who had the last word in a written
exchange with the Red Bluff *Beacon,* was the editor of the *Washoe
Times,* a paper that commenced publication in October, 1862.
After the fatal killing of the publisher, G. W. Derickson, in a duel,
the General became the proprietor. A few months after his spirited
defense of the rights of old men he died while visiting Carson City.

I

("Has a Good Head," Unionville [Nevada] *Humboldt Register,*
June 20, 1863. Reprinted from the Red Bluff *Beacon.*)

General Allen, editor of the *Washoe Times,* a clever gentleman and a good editor, but getting along well in years, still loves
to talk about female beauty, and writes as flippantly about the
handsome girls in Washoe Valley as if he were a young man of
our age. He reminds us of an able statesman, (J. Q. Adams, we
believe it was) who, being twitted about his admiration of the
fair sex when he was eighty years old, said, that should he live

Brown University and who was chosen by a Republican legislature in 1879 to
represent Colorado in the United States Senate.

to be a hundred and eighty years of age, he would not cease to admire a handsome woman.

II

("A Thing of Beauty is a Joy Forever," Unionville [Nevada] *Humboldt Register*, June 27, 1863. Reprinted from the *Washoe Times*.)

So wrote Percy B. Shelly, the great hearted man and prince of philosophical poets. So thinks not, however, the editor of the Red Bluff *Beacon*. Because we happened to say, the other day, that Washoe Valley boasted more feminine loveliness than any other portion of our territory, this youthful youth of forty summers raps us over the knuckles, and dares to promulgate the abominable heresy that an elderly man has no right to think of, much less to speak of, young and beautiful women. The dolt! An elderly man, according to the wiseacres of *The Beacon*, must take his leave of aesthetics when he takes his leave of young manhood. He is not permitted to appreciate and love the beautiful, in nature and art, but must totter on to his grave, shrouded in gloomy selfishness, and as insensible to the joy inspiring things of beauty around him as though he had neither eyes or ears. To what a cheerless abnegation of the heart and intellect would the forty year old boy of *The Beacon* condemn old age! If an elderly man has not the privilege of admiring the forms of living beauty in his own race and lineage, by a parity of reasoning he has not the privilege of admiring beautiful landscapes, and still less the beautiful creations of the painter and sculptor, and the fascinating melodies of the musician. Marry, come up! None but ignorant and presumptuous boys—forty year old boys, with tastes and fancies as crude as Peavine copper ore—dare look on womanly beauty with eyes of admiration! Out upon such heinous heterodoxy.

Our assertion—that Washoe Valley stands pre-eminent over all other portions of our Territory, in the number and exquisiteness of its beautiful women—seems to have slightly stirred the bile of our excellent bachelor friend of the *Reese River Reveille.* He, however, puts himself into good humor by the consolatory anticipation that the Reese River country, though terribly destitute now in female loveliness, will some day have its full share of charming girls. To all which we must devoutly say—Amen!

# PART THREE

# Comstock Mining

# Washoe

## The Heyday of Virginia City

The history of Virginia City, Nevada, began in 1859 with the typical stampede rush for treasure. After the confusion created by the initial march on Washoe had lessened somewhat, the Comstock settled down to the business of mining, but its people never lost the inclination to shock, entertain, and match wits. The 1860's and the 1870's were abounding in vitality and a resident of the city during its heyday recalled scattered episodes which reflected the personality of the mining giant. (J. N. Flint, "The Comstock in the Early Days," San Francisco *Call*, July 28, 1889.)

The Comstock, for a number of years, was the most productive mining district that the world has ever known. Several years ago, from data furnished the writer by Superintendent Requa, a careful estimate was made of the dimensions of the pile, supposing all the bullion taken out of the mines up to that time had been concentrated in one solid block. I found it would make a cubicle brick twenty-six feet long, twenty-six feet wide, and twenty-six feet in height. I did not stop to figure out how many yolk of oxen it would take to haul the treasure. It was my fortune to reside in Virginia during the most interesting decade of mining prosperity, and I propose to record a few reminiscences of life and times in the famous mining camp.

In the palmiest days it was not an unusual circumstance for a million of dollars to be taken out of a single mine as a result of a month's labor. Those who lived directly over the mines at the time did not seem to have a full realizing sense of their wonderful richness or of the excitement the reports of the ore product was producing throughout the civilized world. One day I asked Superintendent Fair for a good piece of ore to send as a specimen to friends in the East. He picked up a piece of rock weighing five or six pounds which assayed 30,000 to the ton. The mass seemed to be almost solid silver and likewise carried about 40 per cent of gold.

The men who worked in the mines, the majority of them Cornishmen, were happy-go-easy set of fellows, fond of good living, and not particularly interested in religious affairs.

There were four church organizations in Virginia City—Catholic, Episcopal, Methodist and Presbyterian—but, with a single exception, the churches exercised but slight influence upon the male population of the town. A flourishing commandery of Knights Templar attended the Episcopal Church regularly once a year, on St. John's day, in full regalia. That duty performed, they felt that nothing further was required of them in the line of church-going. The miners who belonged to the Catholic denomination attended mass on Sabbath morning and participated in a target excursion during the afternoon. As regarded deportment, everyone was a law unto himself. Perhaps one reason for the laxity in the observance of the Sabbath was the fact that work in the mines went on uninterruptedly during the whole 365 days of the year. Another demoralizing circumstance was that most of the men employed in the mines were unmarried and enjoyed none of the refining, humanizing influences of home life. They boarded at a restaurant, slept in a lodging-house, and, as a general rule, spent their leisure time on the street or at the gambling-tables.

During the flush times as many as twenty-five faro games were in full blast night and day. When sporting men, as for example Joe Stewart, Cross and Bill Gibson, sat down of an evening to a friendly game of poker it was no uncommon occurrence for five or six thousand dollars to change hands at a single sitting. Some idea of the amount of money in circulation may be inferred from the fact that every working-man's wages amounted to at least 120 dollars per month. From what has already been written there is no desire to convey the impression that a low standard of morality was the rule in the Comstock mining district. Men quarreled at times and firearms were discharged with but slight provocation. Nevertheless they all had an acute instinct of right and wrong, a high sense of honor, and a chivalrous feeling of respect for the gentler sex. A woman unattended could pass along the streets of Virginia and Gold Hill without the slightest danger of insult or annoyance.

One of the most prominent traits of character as regarded the miners was their generous response to any worthy object. If a man of family lost his life in the mines thousands of dollars would be contributed to those dependent upon him. Each miner contributed regularly one or two days' wages for benevolent purposes. An annual fair given in aid of an orphan school under the charge of the Sisters of Charity, even in dull times, usually netted from 10,000 dollars to 12,000 dollars. Sister Fredrika, the Lady Superior in charge, a noble, liberal-minded woman, was greatly beloved by all classes.

When a man died he was given "a good send-off." A band of music headed the funeral procession, and if the officiating clergyman could not think of anything redeeming in the character of the deceased he carefully refrained from saying anything ill, in accordance with the precept ailde mortuis nisi bonum.

In the month of September, 1871, a fire starting in a lumberyard, near the Third Ward school-house on E street, baffled the efforts of the Fire Department and moved a wide swath through the central business portion of the town, which, however, soon recovered from its devastating effects.

Another startling episode was the dynamite explosion in the Bank of California Building, June, 1873, which shook the city from one end to the other and buried a number of hapless sufferers in the ruins. Conversation could be carried on with them although they could not be extricated from the mass of timbers and bricks that covered them for a time and formed a living tomb.

General Van Bokkelen who had rooms on the B-street side of the building, his sole companion being a monkey, had been experimenting for sometime with explosives, and is supposed to have been the unintentional author of the calamity. Van Bokkelen's body, blackened with powder but slightly disfigured otherwise, was taken out from under the sidewalk where it had been blown by the force of the explosion. The monkey was never found. The General, and one or two others, killed by the explosion, were Masons in high standing and were buried by the Knights with great pomp and impressive ceremonies.

By far the most notable event in the history of Virginia was the great conflagration occurring October 26, 1875, which consumed the greater portion of the town and destroyed 20,000,000 dollars worth of property. The fire, once started, swept over the town with the greatest rapidity. The heat from the burning buildings was intense and unendurable. So that pianos, baskets of silverware and other treasures on being carried out of a house had to be abandoned at the doorway. The very atmosphere itself seemed to be on fire and car-wheels melted down in the open air. For several days after the fire it was a difficult matter to find any sort of sleeping accommodations.

Many who were fortunate enough to get blankets camped in the sagebrush on the side of Mt. Davidson. The writer for several nights tried the hospitality of the Justice's courtroom, reclining on the soft side of a bench, with a law-book for a pillow. A snowstorm, which occurred shortly after the fire, complicated matters somewhat. The mines at that time were at the high-water mark of prosperity. New hoisting works were reared with amazing rapidity, and in a very short time the town itself was ready for rehabilitation. The Virginia and Truckee Railroad Company kept at work night and day rolling lumber and building material into the devastated camp. Twenty-dollar pieces were as plentiful at that time as halfs are now.

Gold Hill also had its full share of terrible catastrophes. The fires occurring at various times in the Yellow Jacket and other mines, the loss of life in the Imperial, the long imprisonment of workmen in the flooded Alta and their joyful release are still fresh in the memories of her citizens.

Nearly all of the notable people who visited the Pacific Coast took in the Comstock mines. It was something of an experience, and required considerable nerve, especially in the case of a delicately reared woman, to don a miner's suit and make the descent of 4,000 feet into the interior of the earth. A person's heart seemed to rise in his throat as he disappeared from the surface, gliding down noiselessly on the fast-going cage. The heat in the lowest levels was intolerable, and the miners at work in scanty attire could only stand it off by swallowing a large quantity of ice-water, which practice did not seem to interfere with the function of digestion as one would naturally suppose. The visitor, after a hasty exploration, was heartily rejoiced when the upcoming cage brought him or her to terra firma once more.

I remember well the grand ovation given to General Sheridan on the occasion of his visit to the Comstock, I think in 1878. Sam Jones and some other friends brought him over from Glenbrook to Virginia in a private conveyance. J. C. Carrie at the time was Mayor of the City and did everything in his power to welcome the distinguished visitor. Hundreds of school children in holiday attire, with their elders, were waiting on the Divide to catch a sight of the hero of Winchester.

General Grant and his family came a year later on their return from his voyage around the world. His arrival on the Comstock was the occasion of still greater rejoicing. He signed the roll of the Pioneers, was toasted and banqueted, shook hands with everyone and went his way.

General Sherman and President Hayes likewise were honored with every attention which a warm-hearted community could bestow, Sherman especially being greatly lionized.

When J. G. Fair, on his return from a trip around the world, decided on becoming a candidate for the United States Senate, a most vigorous campaign in his interest was begun, and continued without let-up until the Nevada Legislature declared him their choice for the high position. Towards the close of the canvass it was decided that a grand torch-light procession should take place in Virginia, the like of which never has been and never will be seen on the Comstock. The managers of the affair were given carte blanche as regards expense. Visitors from neighboring towns, seven or eight thousand miners—Democrats and Republicans—carried torches in the procession. There was a "Ship-of-State," while at intervals in the procession, on wagons loaded with combustibles, demons vomited forth Greek fire, Roman fire, aurora borealis, and every other kind of fire that the ingenuity of man could devise. Mount Davidson, from top to bottom, was ablaze with pyrotechnics. The pageant, taken all in all, was perhaps one of the finest ever witnessed on the Pacific Coast.

The only outlook from the Comstock is upon arid wastes and rugged mountain peaks. Far to the east lies the six-mile desert. At the north, on the Geiger grade, an immense bowlder looms up like a grim sentinel, keeping watch over the hidden treasures of the earth.

Those of us who had resided a long time on the lode often hungered for the companionship of forest trees, green fields and running brooks. At one time a bouquet of flowers commanded any price that might be asked for it. The writer once, in visiting the Gold Hill Cemetery, came across a child's grave whose sole ornaments were some pieces of quartz rock flanked with ocean shells, these being all the offerings the poor mother could bestow.

With the introduction of water from the Sierras all this condition of affairs was changed. Ornamental trees were planted and flowers thrived everywhere under the influence of the gracious water. It was an undertaking of considerable magnitude to bring the water down the mountain-side, across Washoe Valley, and up another mountain from which it could be flumed into Virginia and Gold Hill. . . .

### MEMORIES OF THE LODE

Arthur McEwen was associated for many years with the press of California and Nevada. A relentlessly outspoken man, he won respect for the many crusades he led in behalf of the public. In Nevada, he wielded the editorial column of the Virginia City *Evening Chronicle* to fight the rapacity of the railroads and aroused the people of the state to take a stand. As late as 1894 this born crusader wrote *Arthur McEwen's Letter* to have a free hand in slaying "the dragons of greed and dishonesty." He was nineteen years of age in 1870 when he began his journalistic career as a writer for newspapers in Oakland and San Francisco. At the beginning of 1879 he joined the staff of the *Evening Chronicle* and learned to know well the mood of the third decade of the Comstock's existence. (Arthur McEwen, "In the Heroic Days," San Francisco *Examiner*, January 22, 1893.)

The life of the Comstock in the old days never has been written so that those who did not share it can understand; it never can be so written, for to be like all would have to be set down, and that's a feat beyond mortal pen. Many have tried and all have failed. Mark Twain has come nearest the reality—not so much in what he has told, but in the spirit of his work. It was there that Mark got his point of view—that shrewd, graceless, good-humored, cynical way of looking at things as they in fact are—unbullied by authority and indifferent to traditions—which has made the world laugh.

You have heard a stranger telling a story to friends of his who were strangers to you of some drunken freak of a person known to them, and wondered why they roared. To you the story was simply that of a blackguard performance, eccentric perhaps, but shameful. But you see those strangers were in possession of knowledge of the drunkard's sober decorous life, and that served as a background against which the inebriate folly showed grotesquely and made mirth irresistible.

I think the illustration helps to explain why only a Comstocker can thoroughly understand and enjoy stories about the Comstock.

There was a deal of drinking in Virginia when the *Enterprise* and the town were new, but it wasn't all drinking. Some of the brightest men of the country were working as well as having fun there. Lawyers, I understand, admit that the bar was about the brainiest ever gathered together in one town in the size, or ten times the size. Adventurers, with keen wits and empty pockets, were drawn there as naturally as gamblers seek a faro-room. Rolling stones of every kind obeyed the moral law of gravitation by rolling up Mount Davidson. It was a city of men. If any of them were poor that troubled them not at all, for they expected to be rich next week, and had good grounds for their expectations. Those who were rich had so recently been poor that they had not forgotten it, and the circumstance was not so unusual as to be deemed a title to other's deference. Everybody was rated for what he was, not for what he had. There were no classes, only individuals. Pretensions were out of order.

Not to be a man of sense, frank, free-handed and without prejudices, was to find oneself a second or third-grader. The men most distinguished for ability were the best fellows, the heartiest roysters, the most democratic. Money was no object. There were oceans of it underground. Writing years later when a proportion of the lucky had set up their carriages and become respectable, Harry R. Mighels, that man of talent whose life was wasted on the frontier—said in his "Sagebrush Leaves":

"Somehow all of us are too well-known to one another—we fortune hunters and soldiers of fortune of the earlier days—to be safe in the assumption of any superior virtues. It is not so many years since we were strangers to all banks and bank accounts, all the pretentiousness and all the glamour of "society," all the assumptions and requirements of polished intercourse; it is only too well within the memory of your castaway when he was the open-handed Robin Goodfellow, and the now more fortunate Sir Kassimere Broadcloth served him his bacon and potatoes, and was not too high-spirited to render him the nimble obsequiousness of his very humble servant—though the sycophancy never was asked. We are all of the same household as it were, and are known to one another for what we are worth, and stand upon our merits and not our pretensions. Moreover, your 'flint-mill' is not without its value as a school. It has great virtue in that it shakes the snob out of a man and makes the manners of the parvenu sit awkwardly upon him."

But if anyone had the native disposition to be a snob while the Comstock was roaring in its fiery young vigor he took care not to show it. There was no time for airs; there was no one who could stand them, no one who wasn't as good as his neighbor and had his right acknowledged. It was a republic in which the ablest were the first. If a man lost his money he set about making more on the stock market. Between times he attended to whatever other business he might have, played poker and things and joined any other of the boys who were having a good time in their simple, sinful way.

Of this life audacious gaiety and gambling the *Enterprise* was the mirror, and participant. It was a Comstocker to the backbone. Money poured into its safe and the owners of that safe were gentlemen who knew how to spend its content for their own delectation and the good of the town.

# Speculation and Speculator

### A COMSTOCK FORTUNE

The winning of wealth on the Comstock was an experience shared by all kinds of people. Men of practical genius like John Mackay, the rival of William Sharon for the wealth of the Comstock mines, found the road to fortune by the systematic and patient execution of a grand plan. Another like "Sandy" Bowers had wealth thrust upon him and then lived carelessly and generously until the money was spent. The account of Lemuel L. Bowers' rise in the world of money and fashion was related in the *Territorial Enterprise* at the close of an epoch. ("Mushroom Wealth," Virginia City *Territorial Enterprise*, May 6, 1892.)

The sudden and great accumulation of wealth during the first fifteen years after the practical inauguration of the silver mining in Nevada has no parallel in the history of modern times. The fortunes made during the flush period in California were, to use a mild term, unimportant as compared with those acquired in Nevada in a day or night, simply by the fortunate stroke of a pick.

It was not business capacity nor shrewdness in any form that brought riches to the fortunate ones during that epoch of Nevada's greatest prosperity. It was sheer luck, as in the greatest number of instances those most ignorant of all the business

176

principles were more lavishly favored by fortune than their intellectual superiors.

The case of Lemuel L. Bowers, popularly known as "Sandy" Bowers, a superlatively illiterate but very generous man, is a fair substantiation of the above.

In 1859 he was earning a precarious livlihood by placer mining in Gold Canyon (now Gold Hill), and the latter part of that year, when the discovery of the silver in the Comstock was announced, he found that ten feet of his claim covered the portion of the lode; and the former, after being systematically prospected, gave promise of great value. The ten feet adjoining his belonged to a widow—Mrs. Cowan—his social and intellectual equal. Sandy and the widow had known each other a long time, and now, as a new and prosperous era seemed to dawn for them, they concluded to pool their respective wealth by getting married. The mining ground owned by this couple is what is known as Crown Point Ravine, Upper Gold Hill, and was called the Bowers Mine.

About the middle of 1860, while Sandy was taking out 2,000 dollars a day he was offered 500,000 dollars for his claim and refused to sell.

Neither he nor his wife had ever before been accustomed to any of the greater luxuries which are at the command of boundless wealth, and having a penchant for display of semicivilized grandeur, the reader can afford an idea of the regal doings of the Bowers' household. They were imitation of the "Racher" family, only that the Bowerses added a little more tinsel and red fire.

They believed themselves in possession of Aladdin's wonderful lamp, and they regulated their expenses accordingly. Their hospitality knew no bounds and they entertained everyone—but in such style as to cause considerable merriment for those who made their society debut before arriving on the Comstock.

The Bowerses were the wealthiest couple in Virginia City, and while innocently rendering themselves the subject of much ridicule when not present, their ready cash commanded for them much obsequiousness at other times. In 1862 Sandy conceived the idea of erecting a granite palace on a little ranch belonging to his wife in Washoe Valley. This so called ranch was then a howling wilderness. Mark Twain once spoke of this, and, to convey an idea of its perfect isolation, observed that the first architect sent to the ranch to select the most eligible site for the structure was killed by the savage Indians abounding in that locality. Specifications and plans were soon drawn on the most extravagant scale, but in full keeping with Sandy's crude conception of doing the "grand thing."

The Bowers mine continued to yield an enormous revenue, a large percentage of which was devoted to the completion of the palace in the wilderness.

Bowers' mansion, as the structure was named, was indeed a beautiful place, and good even at this age of a magnificent style of architecture to have been an ornament to Nob Hill. No expense was spared in its thorough equipment. Hot and cold water was conducted into the mansion from the hill in the rear of the grounds, which by that time had been cultivated in the most modern style of the landscape gardener's art.

To convey an idea to the reader of the extravagance indulged in the construction and fitting up of that establishment it is only necessary to say that every doorknob and stair rod was made of solid bullion, and all else about the premises was in strict conformity with that degree of lavishness.

The whole affair did not cost less than 250,000 dollars.

The matter of economy never entered their minds. In 1865 the revenue from the mine began diminishing from month to month, and in 1866 ceased altogether. The property soon became worthless, and the few dollars saved from the wreck soon followed the rest.

In 1867 Sandy Bowers died, having nothing to leave to his widow but the granite palace and what it contained. It can be easily imagined that Mrs. Bowers, after the extravagant career she had indulged in for six years, found it more than disagreeable to be unable to gratify every whim, as in the past, but to meet the expenses of her menage she was compelled to gradually dispose of the library, pictures, works of art, costly articles of virtu and silverware etc., until her friends scarcely recognized the interior of the castle.

For some years subsequent the mansion and grounds were used as a picnic resort for the people of Carson, Virginia and Reno, but now the place is a habitation for owls, bats and spooks. The widow is still a resident of Nevada and earns a living telling fortunes by means of Scotch "peepstones."

### A RED FLANNEL-SHIRTED SPECULATOR

The Comstock reveled in the grand exuberance, the cunning stratagems, and the incongruous exaggerations of men who envisioned ore in a cropping on the mountain side over the divide. These men were the forever hopefuls whether they were trading in the stock market or digging holes for silver ore in the streets of Bodie. The lively vein of conversation employed by a Comstocker of this type, who had found good prospects in Bodie, a mining town located in the high Sierra of California, was reported in a Virginia City newspaper. ("Major Jack Stratman," *Virginia City Evening Chronicle*, April 22, 1879.)

Major Jack Stratman, whom not to know is to confess yourself a tenderfoot, walked into the *Chronicle* office this afternoon. Walked? That isn't the word. His entrance was a landslide and his hearty but blasphemous greetings shook the plaster from the walls and produced a rumble of expostulation from the printers in the composing room. It was Jack, but how changed from the last time he was here. Then he was a lordly mining sharp in good clothing, casting a speculative eye on the Con. Virginia and a few other properties. The Bohemian carelessness of attire and *bonhommie* of manner which marked his old journalistic days in San Francisco were gone. Neither was he the living appurntenance of a diamond pin, as in the saloon-keeping period, nor yet the bustling business rattler of news-and-stationary stand era. Major Stratman was quiet, gentlemanly, shrewd, and rattled in his pockets what sounded like twenties.

To-day a fiery-flamed shirt, a battered slouch hat, topboots and a stained suit of shaggy gray cloth set off his manly figure. His wise beard covered his face like a light snow-fall, and a great drift hanging down on each shoulder made the fact prominent that in all his changes of character the Major boasts of the mastodon mustache of the coast. His face showed red through the snowy bristles and his keen gray eyes peered hard at one through a pair of elegant gold-rimmed eye-glasses. Major Stratman would have stood well for a statue of immortal Forty-nine.

"Tough, but hearty, boys!" roared the Major. "In from Bodie in twenty hours, and healthy as a blue-grass stallion!"

"Bodie is the boss," continued the Major, when the greetings were over. "You've been saying them placers was a fraud. You're dead off there. Why you kin jump down any hole you come to and fill up your pockets with dirt an' go an wash out two handsful and there you've got your two-bits. Bodie's just crawlin' with lucre, but the people there ain't got no energy—no git up, no rustle. Men get a claim an' dig a hole an' sit down by it an' stay there fur years an' grow thin. I'm goin' to send out some hand arasterers an' show the poor devils how to make their livin'. Take one o' them ere arasterers, go down in your hole, fill your hat an then come up an' grind out a decent livin' for yerself and yer family, if any woman's been sich a blasted fool as to marry you."

"How's the weather out there, Jack?" inquired the reporter.

"Weather?" said the Major. "Weather? Lord bless you, don't mention it. You see Bodie lies on the side of a hill—one of the hills that belongs to a detached range o' mountains that runs clear to the Serry Nevad, and there ain't no break in the way of valleys between the town an' the main range, an' every afternoon the wind comes tearin' over them hills chuck full of snow an' cold as hell. It comes down raw'r as blazes, an gives you pewmonis too

180

quick. It's the worst climate I ever see. Put a pot o' boilin' water outside your cabin door the warmest night in the year and it's a chunk of solid ice in the mornin'."

Here Major Stratman arose, and in a rather important but still off-hand manner observed:

"Well, so-long, boys. I'm goin' down to 'Frisco to-night. I'm takin' down three mines an' a tunnel. The tunnel's a big thing, an' will learn old Sutro a wrinkle or two. She starts at Cotton-wood Creek, where we've got water an' she'll strike under the Bodie at a depth of 2,500 feet. She'll be a mile an' a quarter when she's finished. We've got her in 125 feet already, and we've struck different stringers about as wide as your finger, but we haven't followed 'em to see what they're worth. Nothin' will stop us til we get to the end of that mile and a quarter. Your damned old Comstock ain't a marker to Bodie. You won't have twenty-five people living here inside of a year. Bodie 'll bust you. There goes Skae. Hey! Johnny!" bawled the Bodie capitalist, darting out, and he got the millionaire into a corner at the door of the Bank of California and whispered about the mile-and-quarter tunnel.

### FLUCTUATIONS OF FORTUNE

At the beginning of 1870, Mark Twain contributed an article to the *Territorial Enterprise* about the great changes in personal fortune that typified the flush period of Comstock mining. When he wrote the piece, he was editing the Buffalo *Express*, but the memories of Nevada were still fresh in his mind. He and his brother Orion had come to Nevada in 1861, and until 1864, when he departed for San Francisco, the life of the Lode was an open page to him. Much of his knowledge had been acquired as city editor of the *Enterprise*. Mark Twain, with his connections and enthusiasms, was an authentic part of the Lode's legend. (Mark Twain. " 'Early Days' in Nevada—Silverland Nabobs," Virginia City *Territorial Enterprise*, January 16, 1870. )

One of the curious features of Pacific Coast life is the startling uncertainty that marks a man's career in the mines. He may spring from poverty to wealth so suddenly as to turn his hair white, and then after a while he may become poor again so suddenly as to make all that white hair fall off and leave his beak as clean as a billiard ball. The great Nevada silver excitement of 1858–9 was prolific of this sort of vicissitudes.

Two brothers, teamsters, did some hauling for a man in Virginia City, and had to take a small segregated portion of a silver mine in lieu of $300 cash. They gave an outsider a third to open the mine, and they went on teaming. But not long. Ten months afterward the mine was out of debt and paying each owner $8,000 to $10,000 a month—say $100,000 a year. They had that handsome income for just about two years—and they dressed in the loudest costumes and wore mighty diamonds, and played poker for amusement, three men who had seldom seen $20 at one time in all their lives before. One of them is tending bar for wages now, and the other is serving his country as Commander-in-Chief of a street car in San Francisco at $75 a month, and he was very glad to get that employment, too.

One of the earliest nabobs that Nevada was delivered of wore $6,000 worth of diamonds in his bosom, and swore he was unhappy because he couldn't spend his money as fast as he made it. But let us learn from him that persistent effort is bound to achieve success at last. Within a year's time his happiness was secure; for he hadn't a cent to spend.

Another Nevada nabob boasted an income that often reached $16,000 a month; and he used to love to tell how he had worked in the very mine that yielded it, for $5 a day, when he first came to the country. Three years afterward he attained to the far more exceeding grandeur of working in it again, at $4 a day.

The silver and sage-brush state has knowledge of another of these pets of fortune—lifted from actual poverty to affluence almost in a single night—who was able to offer $100,000 for a position of high official distinction shortly afterward, and did offer it—and a little over a year ago a friend saw him shoveling snow on the Pacific Railroad for a living, away up on the summit of the Sierras some 7,000 feet above the level of comfort and the sea. The friend remarked that it must be pretty hard work, though, as the snow was twenty-five feet deep, it promised to be a steady job, at least. Yes, he said, he didn't mind it now, though a month or so ago when it was sixty-two feet deep and still snowing, he wasn't much attached to it. Such is life.

Then there was John Smith. That wasn't his name, but we will call him that. He was a good, honest, kind-hearted fellow, born and reared in the lower ranks of life, and miraculously ignorant. He drove a team, and the team belonged to another man. By and by he married an excellent woman, who owned a small ranch—a ranch that paid them a comfortable living, for although it yielded them but little hay, what little it did yield was worth from $250 to $500 in gold per ton in the market. Presently Smith traded a few acres of the ranch for a small undeveloped silver mine in Gold Hill. He opened the mine and opened a little Unpretending ten-stamp mill. Eighteen months afterward he quit raising hay, for his mining income had reached a most comfortable figure. Some people said it was $30,000 a month. Smith was very rich anyhow. He built a house out in the desert—right in the most forbidding and otherwise howling desert—and it was currently reported that that house cost him a quarter of a million. Possibly that was exaggerated somewhat, though it certainly was a fine house and a costly one. The bedsteads cost $400 or $500 apiece.

And then the Smiths went to Europe. And when they came back Smith was never tired of telling about the fine hogs he had seen in England, and the gorgeous sheep he had seen in Spain, and the fine cattle he had noticed in the vicinity of Rome. He was full of the wonder of the old world, and advised everybody to travel. He said a man never imagined what surprising things there were in the world till he had traveled.

One day, on board ship, the passengers made up a pool of $500, which was to be the property of the man who should come nearest to guessing the run of the vessel for the next twenty-four hours. Next day, toward noon, the figures were all in the purser's hands in sealed envelopes. Smith was serene and happy, for he had been bribing the engineer. But another party won the prize. Smith said:

"Here, that won't do! He guessed two miles wider of the mark than I did."

The purser said: "Mr. Smith, you missed it further than any man on board. We traveled 208 miles yesterday."

"Well, sir," said Smith, "that's just where I've got you, for I guessed 209. If you'll look at my figgers again you'll find a t and two oo, which stands for 200, don't it?—and after 'em you'll find a 9 (2009), which stands for 209. I reckon I'll take that money, if you please."

Well, Smith is dead. And when he died he wasn't worth a cent. The lesson of all this is, that one must learn how to do everything he does—one must have experience in being rich before he can remain rich. The history of California will prove this to your entire satisfaction. Sudden wealth is an awful misfortune to the average run of men. It is wasting breath to instruct the reader after this fashion, though, for no man was ever convinced of it yet till he tried it himself—and I am around now hunting for a man who is afraid to try it. I haven't had any luck so far.

All the early pioneers of California acquired more or less wealth, but an enormous majority of them have not got any now. Those who have, got it slowly and by patient toil.

The reader has heard of the great Gould and Curry silver mine of Nevada. I believe its shares are still quoted in the stock sales in the New York papers. The claim comprised 1,200 feet, if I remember rightly, or maybe it was 800—and I think it all belonged originally to two men whose name it bears. Mr. Curry owned two-thirds of it—and he said that he sold it out for $2,500 in cash, and an old plug horse that ate up its market value in hay and barley in 17 days by the watch. And Gould sold out for a pair of second-hand government blankets and a bottle of whiskey that killed nine men in three hours, and an unoffending stranger that smelt the cork was disabled for life. Four years afterward the mine thus disposed of was worth in the San Francisco market $7,600,000 in gold coin.

In the early days a poverty-stricken Mexican, who lived in a canyon right back of Virginia City, had a stream of water as large as a man's wrist trickling from the hillside on his premises. The Ophir Company segregated 100 feet of their mine and swapped it to him for the stream of water. The 100 feet proved to be the richest part of the entire mine; four years after the swap its market value (including its mill) was $1,500,060. I was down in it about that time, 600 feet under the ground, and about half of it caved in over my head, and yet, valuable as that property was, I would have given the entire mine to have been out of that. I do not wish to brag—but I can be liberal if you take me right.

An individual who owned 20 feet in the Ophir mine before its great riches were revealed to man, traded it for a horse, and a very sorry looking brute he was too. A year or so afterward, when the Ophir stock went up to $3,000 a foot, this man, who hadn't a cent, used to say he was the most startling example of magnificence and misery the world had ever seen—because he was able to ride a 60,000 dollar horse and yet had to ride him bareback because he couldn't scare up cash enough to buy a saddle. He said if fortune were to give him another 60,000 dollar horse it would ruin him.

The shiftless people I have been talking about have settled sedimentally down to their proper place on the bottom, but the solid mining prosperity of California and Nevada continues—the two together producing some $40,000,000 annually in gold and silver. White Pine is giving birth to the usual number of suddenly created nabobs, but three years hence nearly every one of them will be scratching for wages again. Petroleum bred a few of these butterflies for the eastern market. They don't live long in Nevada. I was worth half a million dollars myself, once, for ten days—and now I am prowling around the lecture field and the field of journalism, instructing the public for a subsistence. I was just as happy as the other butterflies, and no wiser—except that I am sincerely glad that my supernatural stupidity lost me my great windfall before I had a chance to make a more inspired ass of me than I was before. I am satisfied that I do not know enough to be wealthy and live to survive it. I had two partners in this brilliant stroke of fortune. The sensible one is still worth a hundred thousand dollars or so—he never lost his wits—but the other one (and by far the best and worthiest of our trio) can't pay his board.

I was personally acquainted with the several nabobs mentioned in this letter, and so, for old acquaintance sake, I have swapped their occupations and experiences around in such a way as to keep the Pacific public from recognizing these once notorious men. I have no desire to drag them out of their retirement and make them uncomfortable by exhibiting them without mask or disguise—I merely wish to use their fortunes and misfortunes for a moment for the adornment of this newspaper article.

# Toilers of the Comstock

## AFTERMATH OF A MINING ACCIDENT

The hard rock miner on the Comstock worked for a minimum wage of $4.05½ a day, the price of labor power established by the Miners' Union. Each day for this amount of money the miner went down the shaft knowing that there was a possibility of not coming up. There were dangers arising from excessive heat, impure air, cave-ins, premature blasts, falling timbers, broken cables of the lift cages, and innumerable other difficulties, but the most dreaded occurrence was fire. An eyewitness account of the toll exacted by a fire in the Bullion mine was recorded in a local newspaper. ("Recovering the Dead," Virginia City *Evening Chronicle*, July 5, 1879.)

Yesterday morning the bodies of the three men suffocated in the Bullion mine on Tuesday night were found by Superintendent Schultz and his party. It was four days from the time the fire alarm sounded to the time when the bodies and the dead were reached. During this period Superintendent Schultz had been indefatigable in his work of subduing the fire and looking for the dead.

Four bulkheads had been put in, as previously described in the *Chronicle*, and on Thursday Mr. Schultz, with a gang of men, went down the Imperial shaft to reach the Bullion incline and put in the last bulkhead. A *Chronicle* reporter accompanied the party. The route from the Imperial to the Bullion incline lay along the 1840 drift of the Bullion, a distance of 2700 feet. The drift for a long time had only been used for ventilation, and was in a bad state of repair.

When the men started they knew full well what their errand was, and calculated the chances of their never coming back alive. They took with them several pails of water, and about one hundred pounds of ice. In addition to this, each man was provided with a small bottle of ammonia and a sponge. The sponges are used to tie over the mouth when the wearer is in proximity to foul gases, and are saturated with ice water. If a miner feels faint from inhaling the gases, the ammonia revives him. A sudden cave was looked upon as liable to spread the gas. In putting in the bulkhead in the Bullion mine Mr. Schultz proposed to shut off the gases coming from the winze, and then the current of the air from the 1840 level, entering the incline above the bulkhead, would free it of bad air and enable him to explore the incline above that point. The journey through the 1840 drift was something fearful. The mud and water were knee deep in many places, and the bottom of the drift was strewn with loose rock, old pipes, broken timbers and dismantled bulkheads. Above the weight of the rocks had forced the timbers out of place, and their jagged edges came down nearly half way to the floor. The sides were crushed in in a similar manner, and as the men advanced they stumbled over the obstructions, floundered through the mud, and crawled on their hands and knees.

The incline was finally reached. At the station was an air compressor run by steam, but of course the engine had been abandoned. By leaning over the platform the smell of the gas was plainly discoverable, and a faint trace of smoke swept up by the draft. The men placed sponges over their faces and lowered themselves down. Instantly their candles were extinguished by the foul air; again and again the lanterns were lowered and went out instantly. The next thing done was to order the men back on the platform and disconnect the air pipes. Two

188

pipes passed that point, and after considerable labor they were disconnected, and this gave a fresh supply of air. While this was being done the men worked with the same sponges over their mouths, and these were kept saturated with ice water. Some placed pieces of ice the size of their fists in the hollows of the sponges and sucked them. Part of the time they were in the incline, the sponges becoming impregnated with the gases had to be wrung out every five minutes. The men drank two gallons of ice water in half an hour.

After about an hour's work the gas in the incline seemed to be increasing and the heat was frightful. Orders were finally given to leave the place and go back to the Imperial cooling station. The men availed themselves of the order at once, and returning to the Imperial remained there an hour, and after recuperating returned again to the station with timbers and canvas for the bulkhead. This bulkhead was constructed only with great labor and was finished at 1 o'clock yesterday morning. Two compartments had to be bulkheaded. Timbers were laid closely together, just below the floor of the station. They were covered with canvas and clay thrown over the canvas. The heat was so intense that the clay had to be kept wet with a hose. After everything was secured tight about the bulkhead the gas still escaped, and a spray hose was put down through the bulkhead. The shower of water from this kept back the gas, and in half an hour the atmosphere was comparatively pure. This took until nearly 3 o'clock in the morning, and when the incline was considered safe two men were sent up to the 1600 station.

At this point, as was expected, a body was found. When the men held their lanterns in this section a horrible sight presented itself. The naked body of a man was seen crouched down under the end of an air pipe. It was swollen to twice its natural size and discolored here and there from decomposition. It was the body of young Donahue. In his right hand was the flat plug which is placed in the end of the air pipes when they are not in use. His dinner bucket was by his side. This indicated that he was in the

189

station cooling off when the deadly rush of gas came from below, otherwise he would have left his bucket at some point lower down the incline had he been fleeing for his life. He had taken off his overalls, as men sometimes do in a cooling station, to wring them out. It had been supposed that anyone in the cooling station at the time of the first rush of the gas could have lived there at least twenty four hours on the air from the pipe. His death was easily explained. Either from neglect or inability he had not turned the damper in the pipe. It was just beyond his hand, and the supposition is that he was so suddenly overcome that he could not reach it. A piece of canvas was at once sent up from the 1840 and the body was sewn up in it and left at the station until a car could be sent down the incline.

A gang of the men were next sent down the Bullion shaft at 7 o'clock in the morning. On reaching the first station of the incline, on the 800 level, they found the body of Perry. It was lying on the last sill, and within seven feet of a cooling station. He was evidently trying to reach the station when he was over- taken by the gas. His lantern was found about one hundred feet below in the incline. The body was much swollen and discolored. It was sewed up in a canvas sack and taken to the cooling station.

Search was next made for the body of Crocker. It was found thirty-five feet below the 1200 level. The dead man's back was supported by a center-post and his legs were resting on one of the sills. He appeared as if he had been struck and fallen as found. Like the others, the body was swollen and discolored. The face was so much so that it had a ludicrous expression. The body was placed in a canvas sack, and soon afterwards an improvised car was sent down from the head of the incline and the bodies of Donahue and Crocker taken up and laid alongside that of Perry.

## A Mean Mine Superintendent

At the helm of every deep mining operation was the mine superintendent. Some of them like James G. Fair, a principal

190

owner of the Consolidated Virginia and the California mines, knew thoroughly the details relating to the mines and mills which they directed, a knowledge which won them the respect of the rank and file. At the opposite pole was the boss pilloried in a parody written for a Comstock newspaper. ("Saving Transportation," Fairplay [Colorado] *Flume*, February 24, 1881. Reprinted from the Virginia City *Territorial Enterprise*.)

"Talk about your mean men," said old Pioneer Shinderson, at Phil McGovern's saloon, the other night, "the very tightest, closest, far-seeing, calculating old skinflint I ever seed, was old Klamskatter, the mine superintendent, who died up at Gold Hill the other day."

"Was, eh?" encouragingly remarked a customer, who was feeding Phil's dog with petrified sandwiches from the lunch table.

"Yes, sir; he was just pizen, he was; closer than the bark to a tree. When he was running the Hornet mine up at Virginia he used to skulk around the levels, disguised as a mule tender, just to pipe off the men who didn't keep hard at it, so as to dock 'em the next Saturday."

"Why, the dern cuss!"

"But wait. He actually encouraged a drill-runner to tell a long story one day while waiting for some machinery to be repaired, and afterward docked the man half a day, and all the men who heard it four bits apiece for stopping to laugh. He charged one man 10 cents for a single grin."

"Great gosh!"

"That's nuthin. Juns Briggs, who was up on the lode when old Klamskatter handed in his checks, said that about an hour before the old miser died, he sent for the doctor and says he: "Doc, give us the straight business. Is there any show for me?"

"Nary show," says the doctor; "you'll strike bed rock afore night."

"Then," says old Klamskatter, "I want some of you boys to

carry me up to the top of Mt. Davidson, right off. If I can light out from there it will save my soul a clear mile of transportation."

"And did they do it?" asked a man who had waked up over by the stove.

"Well, no," replied the narrator, simply. "The boys took him over, put him on the cage and let him down to the lowest level of the Hornet, instead. They said they guessed he had made a little mistake about the direction, somehow. To the best of their judgment, his soul was going the other way."

# Comstockers

## PIUTES IN TOWN

Captain Charley, a chief of the "Pah-Utes," was in the habit of visiting the editorial sanctum of the local newspaper when he came to town. On one of his visits to Gold Hill in February, 1869, he stopped at the office of the *News*, informing the staff that he had been on a three or four month tour of the Piute nation and was planning a visit to White Pine the following summer. Among other things he reported that he had lost both of his horses in the vicinity of Austin after striking a brother Piute who had beaten him at poker. Several months after his visit he returned to relate his experiences with earthquakes and this interview is reprinted here. The Piutes subsisted upon pine nuts and grass seed, and those living around Virginia City were peaceable. ("Piute Earthquake Ideas," Gold Hill *News*, December 30, 1869.)

Captain Charley, the well known Piute Sachem, paid us an official visit yesterday, as is his usual custom when he comes to town. He was rigged out in full regimentals of bobtailed coat and red stripes, plug hat trimmed with brass buttons, and numerous chunks of brass and clamshells dangling in his long dark tresses. Commanding his staff to await him on the porch, he entered our sanctum and gave us important official information of the late earthquake and its general effect upon the Piute Nation. He was just in from camp near Washoe Lake, and

193

the following were his answers to our eager and interested questionings:

"Did you feel that earthquake pretty strong—the shakum up of the ground, you know?"

"Oh! yes; heap catchum shake; ground git pooty sick; heap scarum squaw."

"What do the Injuns talkee about it?"

"Piutee no says nottin."

"But what does Piutee think about this big shake up that scare all the white folks—the pale faces, you know?"

"Piutee no tink nottin."

"Didn't any of 'em get down—like this—and pray?"

"No sabe."

"What Piutee 'spose make the ground shakum?"

"Piutee don't 'spose nottin; he don't know. Some white mans tell 'em, heap fire way down in ground, and devil he gone stir 'em up. Me tink its pooty good. Devil heap likum fire. Don't 'fraid of it."

"Didn't you never hear about these earth shakums before?"

"Yes, 'bout two years ago."

"Yes, yes, that's so, but before that time didn't you never sabe earth-shakum?"

"Oh, heap long time way back, comes big shakum; ground gittum heap sick—he-e-eap shakum."

"How long ago was that?"

"Me no sabe—me little boy, all same so high."

"How old are you, Charley?"

"Don't know."

"You must be about 30 years old."

"Yes, guess so. Me little boy. Heap hear old mans tell 'bout it."

"Well, what old mans say?"

"Oh, heap tellum 'bout big ground shakum. Alee Piutes go catchum pine nut, jackass rabbit. Bime by come from Walker ribber, Carson, Truckee. All Injuns come Sink Carson pishin—heap catchum pish. Ground heap gittum big sick; knock down

Injuns, wooh! All 'long ribber brakum banks, fall down. Ground heap break off. You sabe Stillwater Station, on ribber? Well, banks heap fall down all 'long ribber; ground heap brakum, so ribber run 'nudder way, all same now. 'Spose it's all right; pish don't likum pooty good, I tink. Well, good bye, now; me go Virginia. Bime by me come again. Good bye."

### MELICAN MARRIAGE CEREMONY

Of the non-Caucasian races, the Chinese showed the most willingness to accept the customs of the Americans. They were peaceably inclined, and one Comstock editor could not recall a Chinaman ever being a highwayman, rioter, drunkard, bully, or an election bummer. Their industry poured ninety-six thousand dollars into the treasury of Calaveras County. They were much discriminated against and were often forced to pay extralegal road and poll taxes. ("The 'Coming Man' Marries the 'Coming Woman,'" Elko [Nevada] *Independent*, November 26, 1870. Reprinted from the Virginia City *Territorial Enterprise*.)

The *Territorial Enterprise* gives the following account of a marriage ceremony in that city, uniting two Celestials, who desired to be married in true American style. The knot was effectually tied in the "Pigeon English" dialect.

Yesterday forenoon a gallus-looking Celestial, with well oiled tail, hanging down to his heels, followed by a robust specimen of the Flowery Kingdom, with her hair dressed a la fan-tailed pigeon, came to Justice Ellis' courtroom to be married "Melican" style.

"You have got license, John?" asked the Judge.

"Yes, me hab got," answered John, "me go one cote housee, one law man, me heap catchee license."

"Well, you likee me marry you Melican fashion?"

"Yes, likee all same one Melican man."

"You got any wife now, John?"

John, astonished—"No, me no hab got one wifee; me likee

195

catchee one wifee; me likee catchee him," pointing to the almond-eyed female at his side.

"Are you married?" asked the Judge of the Celestial; "you got no man?"

"No, me no got one man; me one man China country—he come die one time."

"Well, all right. What's your name, John?"

"Me name Su-u-ng Fung."

"What? Some Fun?"

"No, me namee So-u-o-ng Fu-o-ng."

"Oh! Sing Fung! Well, what's her name—the woman's?"

"Who, him" Him namee Ho-ye Go."

"Hoy Goy! All right, you stand up here. Take her by the hand, John. No, stand this way. Not that hand; this hand. Now, John, what's your name?"

"Me namee Su-u-ung Fung."

"Now, John—Sung Fung, you takee him woman—what you callee him name, John?"

"Callee him Ho-ye Go-ye."

"You takee him, Hoy Goy, to be your wife, and promise to keep her heap good; heap plenty ricee give her eatee; no kick her; be good man all time, hey?"

John—"You bet, me belly good man, Judge. Me no kick him plentee."

Judge—"Now, you hear, Hog Eye, or whatever your other name is—you takee him to be your man; be belly good wifee to him all time; no run away; cook him ricee all time—bet your life?"

Hoy Goy—"Me one belly good woman; cookee um ricee; no run away all the time; stay housee allee time—bully wifee me."

Judge—"All rightee. Me plentee power; me big mandarin—two swordee man—me tellee you all one piecee—one piecee man—one piecee wifee. Plentee fix, all done. John, cash. John, money—sabe?"

John paid up, but was determined (so pleased to find himself married "Melican" fashion) to have a blow-out. He sent out for

196

wine and glasses, and treated all hands. After this was over the pair struck out for Chinatown, remarking, "Hi yang chin powe, sung te pin chin tow-ee hug!" as they went, which shows that they were highly delighted with the "Melican" marriage ceremony.

### NIGHT SIGHTS

Alcoholic beverages were consumed in quantities in Virginia City, often suborning the morals of the great and small. The "Speckled Bird" of this newspaper item, whose real name the *Enterprise* writer avoided mentioning for politic reasons, was identified only as highly placed in the religious movement of the town. ("Rambles of a 'Speckled Bird,'" Virginia City *Territorial Enterprise*, July 9, 1868.)

The night of the late "glorious Fourth" we beat our weary and virtuous footsteps homeward just at that hour when the sheeted dead and the "three sheeted" living are most abroad. We came to the stairs at the corner of C and Taylor Streets, and were about ascending, on our way to B Street, when we saw before us some half dozen steps up the stairs in the deep shadow of the California Bank (an institution that often does cast a very black shadow, as many who have been under it can testify), the figure of a man. He was seated, and resting his head and right shoulder against the wall of the building in whose shadow he was reposing. His black slouched hat was pushed from his head by its contact with the wall and rested in a style of graceful bravado over his left ear. We felt that we stood in the presence of some ardent but considerate patriot, and thus saluted the recumbent figure: "What, ho! stranger, why halt you here?" The head of the figure was slowly raised and turned toward us; the slouched hat was pushed back, and we saw the dim outlines of a face standing out from a mop of disordered hair. We could distinguish no single feature in the darkness, yet we felt that a pair of inflamed eyes were staring stupidly at us. "Who are you, old fellow?" asked we, "and what is the matter with you?" Slowly the head turned toward us, and a voice that we with some difficulty recognized as that of Gideon Groanwell, one of the pillars of the church, a powerful exhorter and a mighty disburser of psalmody before the Lord, said: "I'm the speckled bird of the mountain of Gillus; stay me with flagons, comfort me with apples, for I am sick of love." "Bah!" cried we, "get up and go home; why, you are tight as a brick." "My love," cried he, gesticulating ponderously with his left hand, "my love, sir, is like a young hart on the m-mountains. Bether, Rejoish, O daughter of Zion; saout, O daughter of Sherusalem, behold thy King cometh unto thee!" and he tried to get up and "go forth," as he would have said. "Get home, Gideon—get home!" cried we, "you are fearfully and wonderfully drunk." "Home? no, sir—no sir! Live while you live; life is short, sir; we are like flowers of the field, sir, like lilies of er valley—lilies of the valley. Let us not be proud or puffed up, sir; for we are all lilies of er valley. I'm not puffed up, sir—nozur. I've been among the daughters of the Teuton, sir; even among the cunning dancers whose feet are beautiful on the moundains—whose white feet twinkle as alabaster in the waters of the Jordan—also have I been among the women of Jubal, even such as handle the harp, the organ and the psaltery. I have danced even as David danced and drank wine even as Noah when he began to be a husbandman, sir; but tell it not in Gath, publish it not in the columns of the *Enterprise*! I've looked on the faces of the Philistines, even as Samson looked on the face of Delilah. Now, sir, I'm ready to carry off er gates of Gaza. Springing to his feet he cried: "The gates of Gaza, sir—show me the gates of Gaza; I'm on it!" We now felt it our duty to speak quite plainly to Gideon of the impropriety of a man of his standing becoming clamorous to tackle the gates of Gaza at such an hour of the night and hinted that the doors of the station-house would be the first hinged obstacle he would be likely to encounter, and a policeman his first Philistine—the "sons of Belfal" he pronounced them. At once his tune was changed. "Woe is me" cried he, "how could I dare to burn incense unto Baal and walk after strange gods. Silver spread into plates is brought from Tarshish and gold from Upars, but who shall be able to keep shekels of silver or wedges of gold, or rings of jasper, or sardonyx, or topas, or jacinth, or beryl, or chrysolites, or amethyst from these greedy Delilahs. For the moundains I will rise up a weeping and wailing and for er habitations of er wilderness a lamendation! Take the speckled bird from the cellars and from the secret places of the daughters of the Teuton—I flee from them; they are black as the tents of Kedar! Tell it not in Utah, sir, publish it not in the streets of Reno, neither in the pages of the *Mazepper*! How can I face that good woman, Hanner—bone of my bones and flesh of my flesh—for in the day that I see her face will there come, that self-same day, a blowing of trumpets, a breaking of seals, and a pouring out of vials! No, sir, don't talk to me, sir, or wrestle with me sir, all night long, sir, even as the angel wrestled with Jacob at the ford of Jabbok; whither thou goest I cannot go; whither thou lodgest I cannot lodge! I'm er speckled bird over er mountains of Gilboa, sir, and thither I flee to lift up my voice against the woman of scarlet, sir, even the daughter of the Teuton, like a hungery pelican in the wilderness, sir!" With these words the speckled bird spread its wings and took an unsteady and zigzag flight, and doubtless soon had some of its fine feathers picked out by the good Hannah, that mighty blower of trumpets, breaker of seals, and outpourer of vials before the Lord.

### An Apparition

A second instance of muddled reasoning, contrasting pleasantly in its fustian manner with the grand oratory of the "Speckled Bird," is here presented. Both this piece and the preceding one represent individuals who were Comstockers to the core. ("A Man with a Tail," Virginia City *Territorial Enterprise*, June 19, 1879.)

Yesterday afternoon a man who had taken aboard so much tangle-foot whisky that he found it a very difficult matter to maintain his equilibrium came to a halt at the corner of Union and D street. He seemed to be considering whether to go on down Union street or to turn back.

"No use to go down to Ole Joe's," said he, "Ole Joe's cross whenever he looks at me. He wouldn't give me a drink if I was perf'ly sober."

"As the fellow thus stood soliloquizing and swaying to and fro, a sixty-pound dog, with a milk pan attached to its tail, came down the steep slope of Union street as though fired from a howitzer. His eyes were shut and his ears laid back on a level with his neck, and so swiftly was he flying that he seemed a long, dim streak of dog. Blindly he ran and squarely between the legs of the drunken dreamer he darted before the fellow had time to see what was coming, if he even, in his oblivious condition, noted the clatter behind him.

"The pan striking fairly upon the calves of the fellow's legs, something had to give and something did give. The man was on his back in an instant. The jolt seemed to startle some little sense into him, and he was upon his feet in an astonishingly short space of time, his condition being taken into consideration. Rubbing himself vigorously in the rear, he began to gaze upon the spot from which he had just risen in a bewildered way. The dog had disappeared around the corner, but there on the ground where the collision had occurred lay the tin pan, and near it about four inches of the dog's tail, which had been cut off at the joint at which the twine fastening the can was tied.

The motion of the piece of tail—which was squirming like the half of an angle worm attracted his attention, and stooping to pick it up he eyed it in a drunken wonder.

Rubbing himself behind he held the tail up on a level with his eyes and gazed at it with all his might and all the sight of his half closed eyes.

"This," said he, "this is (hic) unfortunate! Never before knowed

200

or even suspected I had sich a thing as a tail till I go an' fall down an' break it off. Might made a (hic) fortune 'zibitin' myself as man with tail. There'd bin millions in it—millions (hic) in it! Jis my dam luck. Whenever I git a good thing it's always gone before I (hic) find it out."

Rubbing his hurt, and still gazing at the tail, he said: "Must a bin mine—must a bin mine! Fresh blood! An' I kin feel place where it (hic) broke off from. Devilish unfortunate I fell an (hic) broke't off. However, I'll make best of it; I'll (hic) take it down to Ole Joe's an' get a drink on't."

## OUTFLANKED

George Birdsall, a prominent Virginia City citizen, was involved in a number of extravagant hoaxes during his long residence in the town. While serving as City Marshall in 1866 he had joined with several others to celebrate Mark Twain's return to the Comstock by holding him up on the divide, a prank that did not set too well with Mark. On another occasion he had tried to outwit the lads of the turf, but was outflanked in the attempt. Wells Drury in *An Editor on the Comstock* gives an independent version of the affair. ("Birdsall's Soft Thing," Virginia City *Evening Chronicle*, June 10, 1879.)

"Speakin' of horse racin'," said Jailer Birdsall last evening to a select coterie in the City Jail, the tricks of the turf being under discussion, "I had my dose an' I'm a horsethief if I haven't kept it dark for eighteen years. I was keepin' a big stable on B street in '60, and there was a sight o' racin' goin' on in them times and I wanted my fin in everything o' that kind. I was younger and fresher than I am now. Two horses, a black and gray, were brung up from Genoa to run for a thousand a side at the track near Long Valley. The race was to come off on Saturday, and there was some heavy betting on the thing. I was holdin' back for points before puttin' up any coin. Bill Harness comes to me a-Thursday an' put up the prettiest job I ever hear tell of. You

don't remember Bill, I s'pose? Well, he was lynched over to
Pioche in '71, poor feller. We took Rough Hardy in an' was
agreed that the swag was to be divided equal. It was a pretty
job, an' the chief beauty of it was that it was so almighty easy
and simple. It was just for Hardy an' me to take the horses out
the night afore the race an' speed 'em around the track until we
found their pace. It wouldn't be no trick, then, at all, for us to
haul in all the pool and clean up handsome. The nags were in my
stable, which made the business just too easy. Friday night me
an' Hardy set to work an' got the jockeys blind, stavin' drunk, an'
by midnight they was as limp an' as senseless as a pair o' lines.
Hardy an' me, when we'd got 'em so they couldn't tell a stirrup
from a distance pole, laid 'em out in the straw in an empty stall,
an' took the black an' the gray out for practice. It was a pretty
moon-light night, clear as day, an' everythin' worked slick. I
rode the black, an' it beat the gray easy, although they was both
powerful good goers. Then I took the gray and Hardy took the
black, so there couldn't be no suspicion of roots agin one another,
and still the black a'most distanced the gray. We just laughed til
the tears rolled down our jaws, when we led them horses back
to their stalls, to think of the soft thing we had on the boys, an'
Hardy an' me was quite willin' to put in about two hours rubbin'
down them flyers, so as to remove all the signs o' the work they'd
been through. The race was mile heats, best two in three, an' me
an' Hardy was on the track good an' early next day takin' everythin' that was offered agin' the black. We both had scads in them
times an' when the start was made we'd about five thousand on
the black between us. We let up bettin' jest out of pity for the
poor devils that took us up so innocent and eager. Every now an'
then Harness and Hardy an' me would meet an' go take a drink
an' roar out laughin' so you could hear us a mile. When the horses
started Hardy an' me felt bigger'n old Grant. It kind o' surprised
us to see the way the gray lifted his feet though, an' when he
come in a length ahead o' the black it kind o' made us feel uneasy
about the gills. Of course we knowed it was the darn jockey's

fault, an' I managed to git to him an' slip five twenties into his fin. "Let her out this time," I sez. "If the black wins you'll get two hundred more." He give a wink an' nodded. Boys, you kin roast me if that damn gray didn't *distance* the black in the second heat! In ten minutes I was blind drunk an' knowed no more until mornin'. Then I oiled up my shooter and started out to find Hardy. If I'd found him he wouldn't a been water-tight long. I was sure he'd put the job up on me on the track Friday night. We didn't happen to meet. Friends looked out for that, I know now. Harness wasn't nowhere around, an' I found he'd gone to the Bay. It wasn't forty-eight hours afore the whole town was howling with delight at the way Hardy an' me'd been eat up. It was that cussed Harness an' his gang. They'd loaded the shoes o' the gray with lead an' then put Hardy an' me up to our little game. "It was," said Mr. Birdsall, with tears in his eyes at the mere memory, "the lowest down shennanigen that ever was played on two honest men. Only think what would have happened if Hardy an' me had met. He was huntin' for me just the same as I was after him. The game was blowed before we did come together, an' then after minutes talk we started for the Bay to see Harness. He skipped before we got there, an' although we followed him for more'n a month, he kept ahead of us. They give him his dose over to Pioche, though," added Mr. Birdsall cheerfully, and then he sighed and relapsed into tobacco smoke and silence.

### Burlesque in a Comstock Courtroom

The self-reliant Comstocker was often brash in the use of radical expedients. The ludicruous fate in a court of law of an overconfident Virginia City lawyer, formerly a constable of that city, was recalled by a Comstock journalist. ("Curiosities of Law," Virginia City *Evening Chronicle*, June 27, 1879.)

The Comstocker who does not remember Tom Harkin has a very bad memory indeed. When his name was mentioned in

Judge Knox's court-room last evening every one of the old pioneers present cocked up his ears at once and inquired: "What-
inell's become of him, anyhow?" Harkin had been Constable at
Gold Hill, and during his service in that capacity picked up such
an extensive knowledge of roguery that upon the expiration of
his term he felt justified in hanging out a tin sign and becoming
a police court lawyer. He rigidly confined his practice to Judge
Wright's Court. The name of Harkin moved a lawyer in Knox's
court-room last evening to tell how two Portuguese were arrested
in Gold Hill for a breach of the peace, in loudly abusing two
Frenchmen. Harkin was retained by the vengeful Gauls to prose-
cute the gentlemen from Portugal, and Major Foote (he, poor
fellow, like Judge Wright, has gone to his grave) represented
the defendants. Harkin soared aloft in his opening speech, and
painted with all his well-known eloquence the terrible outrage
to which his clients had been subjected.

Then Major Foote got up gravely, and, winking slightly to the
Judge, took the astounding ground that this being an English-
speaking country it was impossible to shatter its peace with any
amount of the Portuguese language. The Court stared, but
another sly wink from the Major explained things. Harkin was
evidently in a panic, and was breaking out into a cold sweat of
apprehension, when lawyer Kelton, who had caught the Major's
wink, leaned over and whispered to Harkin:

"Send to Foote's office and get Viduc's 'Curiosities of Law,'
and on page 653 you'll find a decision in your favor on this very
point."

Harkin whispered to a friend, who at once bolted for the
Major's library to look for the impossible work mentioned by
Kelton, and when Foote sat down the ex-Constable began an
oratorical charge against time. While he was in the midst of a
tremendous howl of indignant eloquence the messenger who had
gone for the book returned and whispered that the book wasn't
to be found. Then Harkin announced to the Judge that he
desired to go out for a moment. It was his wish to bring and lay

before the Court the well-known standard authority, Viduc, who in his celebrated volume, "The Curiosities of Law," on page 653, had a decision with which all lawyers who had a right to call themselves lawyers should be familiar. The time, in spite of a vehement protest from Foote, was granted, and Harkin rushed over to the Major's library and eagerly ran his eye over the volumes. No such work on Viduc's "Curiosities of Law" could be found, but on the top shelf there was a vacant space from which a volume had been taken, and Harkin, in a boiling rage, returned to the court-room. He informed the Court and all assembled that up to this time he had regarded Major Foote as a gentleman, but now he could no longer dignify him by that title. "For," cried Harkin, shaking his finger at the Major, who by this time was on the verge of hysterics, "for, sir, you, well knowing Viduc's unanswerable decision on this here p'int, have gone and hid away that there book of his! You, sir, knowing how damaging it would be to your case, and so important to mine, have stole an' secreted Viduc's 'Curiosities of Law.' Such conduct, may it please the Court, is a disgrace to any member of the profession who calls himself a gentleman."

To Harkin's no small astonishment and delight, the Court, rapping down the shrieks of laughter in which all the lawyers save the puzzled Harkin were relieving their feelings, decided that the peace could not only be broken in Portuguese, but that to its mind Portuguese was a tongue peculiarly fitted for that sort of illegal exercise.

Up to the time that Harkin left the town he had never learned why a lawyer always went into convulsions when he inquired if he happened to have Viduc's "Curiosities of Law" in his library.

# Comstock Entertainment

## MULE SENSE

The tall tale was as popular on the Comstock as standing up
to the bar. A Comstock miner, who had seen exciting days in
Pioche, a camp located in southeastern Nevada, explained his reasons for appreciating the temper and wickedness of mules. ("The
Master Mule," Virginia City *Evening Chronicle*, April 17, 1879.)

This morning a couple of miners were seated on a
boulder alongside the road to Sutro, discussing the
kicking powers of the mule. One had just returned from Sutro
and the other was on the way there, and having met near the
rock they sat down for a talk.

"Have you quit over there?" said the one who was eastward
bound.

"Yes."

"Why?"

"Mules."

" 'Fraid of 'em?"

"You bet. I saw one yesterday alongside an old boiler kickin'
off the rivet-heads one by one. Never missed one. I was just goin'
on shift, and when I saw the mule and heard there was more of
'em inside, I weakened and threw up my job. I've got a wife and
three children dependin' on me, and I don't take no chances."

"The worse mule I ever saw," said the other, "was in Pioche

some years ago. It was one I owned. One day it rubbed against some nails sticking out of a post and it turned square round and drove those nails in one by one, using a single blow of the hoof with the iron shoe on for each nail. It never missed its lick and always drove 'em just into the head. Then he saw a few tacks on the post a little lower down which were only half driven in, and he drove them in too with light taps of the hoof, just as gentle and easy as could be. One day a man came along and set out a can of nitroglycerine and giant powder. He wanted to get the mule to kick it and get killed. I saw him about the corral with the can and knew what was up. At first I was going to stop him, but then I thought if my mule was any kind of a mule at all he could take care of himself. So I just watched. Well, the mule saw the can and walking up smelt of it, and then squared himself for the kick. The man was sneaking off, and just as the mule was going to kick the can he caught sight of the feller and changed his position so that his tail was towards the man. He lifted his tail just like he was takin' aim and let fly his right hoof. The can went flyin' through the air and hit the man square in the rear just as he was gettin' over the fence about a hundred feet away. The thing exploded, and I never saw the man again. But next morning Pat Holland came out in the *Record* and said that the town had been visited by a shower of blood.

"Mules are immense when they git roused."

"You bet."

### A Bostonian in Virginia City

The frontier press lost no opportunity to lampoon the airs of the proper Bostonians when the question of local pride was at issue. A Comstock newspaper with a display of considerable fooling made fun of the innocence and credulity of a journalist newly arrived from Boston who was making a whirlwind visit to the mines. ("A Bonanza of Fact," Virginia City *Evening Chronicle*, June 6, 1879.)

An influx of Eastern correspondents to the Comstock had already begun. One comes along nearly every day and they have orders from their various papers to find out everything that is going on here, even if they have to remain in the city a week. One who arrived in the city yesterday was met by a *Chronicle* reporter on C street this morning.

The correspondent talked very freely about his mission and was confident that the country was a big thing.

"Have you been down in the mines?" asked the reporter.

"Oh, yes; one, and learned much which I never knew before. I came here yesterday morning an absolute ignoramus, so to speak, on the subject of mining, and now I have it on my fingers' ends. The Superintendent, Mr. Taylor, was very kind and showed me everything about the place. We went down the California shaft."

"The California has no shaft."

"I mean we visited the double C mine, and went through all the north and south crosscuts. I don't suppose there was a foot of the mine I didn't inspect thoroughly. It's wonderful."

"You will have excellent material for a course of lectures when you return East."

"Ah, yes; I intend to lecture. I shall lay the Comstock bare when I get to New York. I am satisfied that the Comstock has never been thoroughly understood, but with my explanations and diagrams I shall make all these wonderful things as simple as A, B, C."

"Have you seen the South Lady Bryan?"

"Ah, indeed, I recollect visiting a man named Kelly, the Captain of the Sarsfield Guard. He informed me that he had a shaft in the South Lady Bryan which could not be burned. I think it a fine idea to make shafts fire-proof. Such a plan insures safety. I shall purchase some of the stock before I return. My proprietor, the owner of the Boston *Adverb*, told me if I could invest a few thousands advantageously to do so. As the South Lady Bryan is fire-proof I think money put in there is safer than if it were invested in some mine liable to be destroyed by an unexpected and perhaps unavoidable conflagration. You see, we Eastern investors give these things a good deal of thought, and do not invest in the wild haphazard style so characteristic of Nevada."

(Note.—The South Lady Bryan has no shaft, and it is a favorite joke of Captain Kelly to say that his shaft can never burn, being absolutely fire-proof.—Rep.)

"Do you think," continued the Bostonian, "that Mr. Kelly would allow an Eastern man and a non-resident in any considerable extent in his mining property?"

"It is just possible, if the man came well recommended from some good Eastern men and had the ready cash to invest, that he would let him in for a few thousand shares. There are plenty of men here who, like Mr. Kelly, own outside mining properties which they do not care to cast into the filthy pool of Pacific coast speculation, but would prefer to have the securities held by good, substantial Eastern men, or, like yourself, the representative of some reliable and influential newspaper."

"I like to see men of that type. I also saw Mr. Canavan and secured a good deal of interesting matter about his big ballroom in the New York mine. He tells me his ballroom is capable of accommodating two hundred couples a thousand feet underground."

"Quite likely; and it is the resort of the wealth and fashion of the ledge. The cages are fitted up with plush velvet and mirrors like those in the Palace Hotel. The wine-cellar is the finest on the coast and they sink two thousand feet below the ground to get a cool place."

"I thought the lower they got the hotter it became?"

"Such is the case only in the north end mines. At the south end it gets cooler until at a depth of two thousand feet the men wear ulster overcoats, and there is a stove in every drift."

"How astonishing, and is it not curious that not one of the Eastern correspondents ever mentioned the fact?"

"It was studiously kept from them, because a knowledge of

the fact would cause such a rush for the stock that the mines at that end would pass beyond the control of the Comstockers. A good many shares are out and they propose to get them in before the deal. This odd atmosphere indicates rich deposits of horn silver. For heaven's sake don't mention this in the Boston papers. I would be assassinated if it got out through me."

"Ah, my dear boy, I can't help that, I must report all I know and hide nothing. The great drawback to this country has been the lamentable disposition on the part of the correspondents to hide the facts. I will never be a party to anything of such a nature." Here the Boston man rushed off to write up the bottom facts.

### Acclimating to Western Freedom

To mention Bodie and Boston in the same breath brought dissimilar visions. In the frontier mind the Bostonian was far removed from the quick tempered ways of the men inhabiting the wild little mining camps of the Sierra, but a reporter from the Comstock discovered a Bostonian who had become rapidly acclimated to western freedom in the manner of the swaggerers of Bodie. ("A Bad Man Turns Loose," Virginia City *Evening Chronicle*, June 16, 1879.)

A Virginia gentleman just up from San Francisco, confided some of his experiences to a *Chronicle* reporter yesterday. While at the Bay he stopped at the Palace Hotel and made a practice of dropping into the bar-room of that establishment of an evening, it being a retired and rather high-toned place. On Wednesday evening last the Comstocker lounged into the bar-room and was pleased to behold there as the only occupants Senator Sharon, Seth Cook, Tom Sunderland and a few other historic capitalists, sitting at a large round table, in the center of which stood sundry bottles bearing the mystical word "Roederer." Presently a middle-aged man, soberly dressed in black broadcloth and wearing a plug hat, staggered in from the hallway and lurching up to the bar yelled for everybody to come up and have something to drink. The Sharon-Cook party paid no attention to the boisterious new arrival, but quietly went on with their gossip and Roederer. Giving a furious whoop and smashing his tile down on his head the stranger performed a war-dance to the middle of the room and declared himself. He was a bad man, he said, and always made it a practice to strew upon the floor the bowels of any person who declined to drink upon his invitation. To point his remarks the stranger wound up by drawing an eighteen-inch Arkansaw toothpick from the back of his collar and advanced upon the table. There was a stampede. When the Virginian peeped up from behind the bar, to which position he had quietly and calmly walked at the beginning of the trouble, he perceived that Sharon and his friends had gone out and that a policeman was lugging the warlike stranger out of the place.

"Who is he?" asked the Virginia man of the bar-keeper.

"Oh, he's a good enough man when he isn't in liquor," replied the man of drinks, nervously polishing the rosewood bar with a towel. "He was one of the quietest men I ever saw when he first came here about two days ago, but he's bad when he's full."

"From Bodie, I suppose?" suggested the Virginian.

"Bodie? Hell, no. He's from Boston. He belongs to that Sunday-school excursion party."

## THE THEATRE

Wells Drury wrote a spirited memoir recalling the Comstock of the 1870's and the 1880's. His early life had been one of adventure and tragedy. At the age of one he had lost his parents from Asiatic cholera while the family was crossing the Plains; at eleven he was an Indian interpreter; while attending the University of California he worked as a compositor for the *Alta California*, but the lure of the Comstock cut short his stay in Berkeley. He arrived in Virginia City in 1874 and was hired by Alf Doten to do a reporter's job for the Gold Hill *News*. He stayed on the Lode for fourteen

years and knew intimately its social and cultural life. (Wells
Drury. *An Editor on the Comstock Lode*. Foreword by Ella
Bishop Drury. [New York and Toronto, Farrar & Rinehart, Inc.,
1936], 54–59.)

The Comstock had a fine sense of the dramatic. Of its
several theatres, foremost by far was Piper's Opera House, in
Virginia City. Really, there were three theatres upon its site, for
Piper lost his opera house twice by fire. This temple of the arts
welcomed the most brilliant stars of the era. For some years, the
companies which played in Maguire's Theatre in San Francisco
also appeared at John Piper's opera house.

Shakespeare had no lack of avid admirers on the Lode, and his
plays were staged by a succession of repertory companies, all of
them good and several outstanding. *Hamlet* was most often
presented. Edwin Booth, Lawrence Barrett, John McCullough
and Tom Keene were Hamlets who trod Piper's ample boards,
besides several others of magnificent talent, though not so well-
remembered. When he explained to the stage-manager his requirements for the fifth act, Edwin Booth was assured that he
should have a practicable grave. He was astounded at the
thoroughness in executing this promise. A section was sawed out
of the stage-floor, a couple of Cornish miners did valiant pick-
work, and that night the yokel gravediggers shoveled some
interesting specimens of ore onto the stage and were able to hand
up Yorick's skull from the profound depths of a real grave. When
Booth cried out, "This is I, Hamlet the Dane!" and leaped into
Ophelia's grave to tussle with Laertes, he had the experience,
unique in his long stage career, of landing on bed-rock....

The dramatic offerings were most varied. In the '70s and '80s,
when I was on the Comstock, we were entertained by presenta-
tions such as *Camille, Lucretia Borgia, Ten Nights in a Bar-
Room, London Assurance, Ticket-of-Leave Man* (again and
again), *Rosedale, The Forger's Daughter, Monte Cristo, The
Two Orphans, Galatea, The Octoroon, Under the Gas-Light,*

*Led Astray, Mexican Tigress, Leah the Forsaken,* and a series of Drury Lane melodramas. *East Lynne* and other tear jerkers had a poignant appeal. *The Lady of Lyons, or Love and Pride* was a prime favorite; I essayed the part of Claude Melnotte myself in an amateur production—"Dost thou like the picture?" . . .

Tremendous excitement was created, of course, when *The Black Crook* came, with its sumptuous ballet. Then, the troupe of Red Stocking Blondes, who filled the house as well as their hose. That other rollicking contingent, the Victoria Loftus' British Blondes, could not complain of their welcome to Virginia City, either, unless indeed they objected to being gazed at by the curious. When their train puffed in, at least five hundred males, mostly white-haired, bald-pated or red-headed, assembled around the depot, and a cheer broke from the throng as the blonde beauties passed up Union Street to Piper's Opera House, where a much better view was gained that night. . . .

All kinds of political and social meetings were held in Piper's Opera House. With its dress-circle, parquet and gallery, it seated more than a thousand people. Lectures were far more popular in those days than they are now, and Henry Ward Beecher, Colonel Robert Ingersoll, Henry George and other nationally known personages were heard, sharing attention with Hermann, the Wizard, and Professor O. S. Fowler, the famous phrenologist who so captivated me that I paid good money for a course in the then-budding science which somehow has failed to come to fruition in half a century.

SOLD

Dan De Quille (William Wright), the Comstock satirist and humorist, deceived readers and journalists alike with his tall tales and "sells." He came from an old Quaker family that had immigrated to Pennsylvania in 1681. Though much of his early work appeared in the *Golden Era,* the bulk of it was written while he ran the local column of the *Territorial Enterprise.* Mark Twain's style was probably influenced by the one man in Virginia City who could outdo him at perpetrating a hoax. Among his more modest contributions for 1869 were the "April Fool sells." Though inordinately successful with his hoaxes, he had competitors who tried to trick him at his own game.

I

(Virginia City *Territorial Enterprise*, April 1, 1869.)

### A Great Curiosity

At Perry and Irwin's saloon, North C street, is to be seen a great curiosity in the shape of a piece of chloride ore, from White Pine, in which is firmly imbedded the tooth of some large animal of the mastodon species. The lump of ore weighs about 10 pounds, and the tooth, which is a grinder, measures nearly two inches across its face. This very curious specimen was captured by Jack Perry, who is now in White Pine, and was by him sent to this city to enrich the very fine cabinet which adorns his saloon here. What will the savans do with this wonder?

### The Irish Giant

The famous Irish Giant arrived in this city last night, and took rooms at the International. He is eight feet one and a quarter inches in height and very well proportioned. He will appear at the Opera House to-night, at the conclusion of the play, when he will perform several feats of strength, such as tying a half-inch bar of iron about his waist, etc. Owing to the fact that his arrival was quite unexpected, Mr. Piper was unable to make mention of him in the programmes for this evening. His name is Patrick O' Baldwin, and he is now just 29 years of age, to-day being his birthday.

### Strange

Officer Downey last night picked up the head of a Chinaman at the corner of E and Union streets. The head had been severed from the trunk as though at one stroke with an axe or cleaver.

The head was found about 11 o'clock, and though strict search was made throughout Chinatown, no body could be found. The head was taken to Justice Ellis' court-room, where it is to be seen hanging—a ghastly sight. Coroner Symons is undecided about holding an inquest on the head; he thinks that the strict letter of the law requires him to have the "body."

## A Baby Camel

A baby camel arrived at Cooper & Baldwin's hay-yard last night, where it may be seen for a day or two by the curious. It was born on the Carson, near Fort Churchill, and, as Artemus Ward would say, in case he was alive to see it, is a funny looking little cuss.

II

("A Daniel Comes to Judgment," Gold Hill *News*, April 2, 1869.)

Mr. Daniel De Quille, the ancient and venerable local of the *Enterprise*, waxeth exceedingly merry, and in this morning's issue of that paper cackleth with exceeding hilarity and great glee over the success of various ingenious items in the way of "April Fool sells" which he published yesterday morning. That "baby camel," the "mastodon tooth," "Chinaman's head," and the "Irish Giant," were all capital sells, and took well; but after all, the worst sold man of the crowd was the wicked Daniel himself. We had a little item in yesterday's *News* to the effect that a huge blast of about a dozen kegs of powder was prepared to be let off that day at 2:00 P.M. in the surface ore workings of the Sierra Nevada mine, whereby some hundreds of tons of ore were expected to be thrown out. Now it never struck our Dan that there could be any sell about this matter, being too intent on selling others in the guileless innocence of his heart to guard against being himself sold; therefore he took it for granted, and consequently his local mining report in this morning's *Enterprise* contains the following stunning piece of information:

Large Blast.—A blast of 15 kegs of powder was yesterday let off in the Sierra Nevada Works. A drift had been run into the bank to the depth of 60 feet, and tremendous execution was done. Although the quantity of powder used was so great, the report was not heard in the city; in fact, there was scarcely any report—just a dull heavy rumble, and a shaking and quivering of the ground as from the shock of an earthquake. Hundreds of tons of ore were loosened by the blast.

Now the fact of it is that no blast whatever was let off at the Sierra Nevada mine yesterday. A blast of that magnitude would have about the effect he describes—but yesterday was "April Fool Day," Old Smarty.

MONOMANIA

When Nevada was still a Territory, Mark Twain was showered with gifts and attentions by office-seekers. As a reporter he covered the legislature for the *Territorial Enterprise*, and as the friend of Governor Nye he seemed to have that dignitary's ear. A splendid opportunity eventually offered itself to make known his contempt of these self-seekers after the legislature passed a law to curb the appointment of notaries by Governor Nye. The position was highly prized for the lucrative fees that were paid to have notarized the daily sale of thousands of shares of stock. In a piece written for the *Enterprise*, Mark singled out the notarial office-seeker for his satiric barbs, and he paraded a monomania that applied equally on the Comstock to every endeavor. Mark Twain's distinctive style, with its broad humor and derisive wit, is readily apparent. (Mark Twain. "Washoe Wit," *Golden Era*, February 28, 1864. Reprinted from the Virginia City *Territorial Enterprise*.)

Mark Twain, the wild humorist of the Sage Brush Hills, writes from Carson City to the *Territorial Enterprise*, telling all about the Legislature, Governor Nye, and the rest of mankind at Nevada's Capital. He says:

A strange, strange thing occurred here yesterday, to wit: *A Man Applied for a Notary's Commission.*

Think of it. Ponder over it. He wanted a notarial commission— he said so himself. He was from Storey county. He brought his little petition along with him. He brought it on two stages. It is voluminous. The County Surveyor is chaining it off. Three shifts of clerks will be employed night and day on it, decyphering the signatures and testing their genuineness. They began unrolling the petition at noon and people of strong mining proclivities at once commenced locating claims on it. We are too late, you know. But then they say the extensions are just as good as the original. I believe you.

Since writing the above, I have discovered the foregoing does not amount to much as a sensation item after all. The reason is, because there are seventeen hundred and forty two applications for notaryships already on file in the Governor's office. I was not aware of it, you know. There are also as much as eleven cords of petition stacked up in his back yard. A watchman stands guard over this combustible material—the back yard is not insured.

Since writing the above, strange events have happened. I started down town, and have not gone far, when I met a seedy, ornery, ratty, hang-dog-looking stranger, who approached me in the most insinuating manner, and said he was glad to see me. He said he had often sighed for an opportunity to becoming acquainted with me—that he had read my effusions (he called them "effusions,") with solemn delight, and had yearned to meet the author face to face. He said he was Billson—Billson of Lander—I might have heard of him. I told him I had—many a time—which was an infamous falsehood. He said "D——n it, old quill-driver, you must come and take a drink with me:" and says I, "D——n it, old Vermin-ranch, I'll do it." (I had him there.) We took a drink, and he told the bar-keeper to charge it. After which, he opened a well-filled carpet-sack and took out a shirt-collar and a petition. He then threw the empty carpet-sack aside and unrolled several yards of the petition—"just for a starter," he said. "Now," says he, "Mark, have you got a good deal of influence with Governor Nye?" "Unbounded," says I, with honest pride; "when I go and use my influence with Governor Nye, and tell him it will be a great personal favor to me if he will do so and so, he always says it will be a real pleasure to him—that if it were any other man— any other man in the world—but seeing it's me, he wont." Mr. Billson then remarked that I was the very man; he wanted a little notarial appointment, and he would like me to mention it to the Governor. I said I would, and turned away, resolved to damn young Billson's official aspirations with a mild dose of my influence.

I walked about ten steps, and met a cordial man, with the dust of travel upon his garments. He mashed my hands in his, and as I stood straightening the joints back into their places again, says he, "Why, darn it, Mark, how well you're looking! Thunder! it's been an age since I saw you. Turn around and let's look at you good. 'Gad, it's the same old Mark! Well, how've you been—and what have you been doing with yourself lately. Why don't you ever never come down to see a fellow? Every time I come to town, the old woman's sure to get after me for not bringing you out, as soon as I get back. Why she takes them articles of yourn, and slathers 'em into her old scrap-book, along with deaths, and marriages, and receipts for the itch, and the small-pox, and hell knows what all, and if it warn't that you talk too slow to ever make love, dang my cats if I wouldn't be jealous of you. I would, by the eternal. But what's the use fooling away time here?—let's go and gobble a cock-tail." This was old Boreas, from Washoe. I went and gobbled a cock-tail with him. He mentioned incidentally, that he wanted a notaryship, and showed me a good deal of his petition. I said I would use my influence in his behalf, and requested him to call at the Governor's office in the morning, and get his commission. He thanked me most heartily, and said he would. (I think I see him doing of it.)

I met another stranger before I got to the corner—a pompous

little man with a crooked-handled cane and sorrel moustache. Says he, "How do you do, Mr. Twain—how do you do, sir? I am happy to see you, sir—very happy indeed, sir. My name is ——. Pardon me, sir, but I perceive you do not entirely recollect me— I am J. Bidlecome Dusenberry, of Esmeralda, formerly of the city of New York, sir." "Well," says I, "I'm glad to meet you, Dysintery, and—" "No, no—Dusenberry, sir, Dusenberry!—you—" "Oh, I beg your pardon," says I; "Dusenberry—yes. I understand, now; but it's all the same, you know—Dusenberry, by any other name would—however, I see you have a bale of dry goods—for me, perhaps." He said it was only a little petition, and proceeded to show me a few acres of it, observing casually that he was a candidate in the notorial line—that he had read my lucumbrations (he called it all that) with absorbing interest, and he would like me to use my influence with the Governor in his behalf. I assured him his commission would be ready for him as soon as it was signed. He appeared overcome with gratitude, and insisted, and insisted, until at last I went and took a drink with him.

On the next corner I met Chief Justice Turner, on his way to the Governor's office with a petition. He said, "God bless you, my dear fellow—I'm delighted to see you—" and hurried on, after receiving my solemn promise that he should be a Notary Public if I could secure his appointment. Next I met William Stewart, grinning in his engaging way, and stroking his prodigious whiskers from his nose to his stomach. Sandy Baldwin was with him, and they both had measureless petitions on a dray, with the names all signed in their own hand writing. I knew those fellows pretty well, and I didn't promise them my influence. I knew if the Governor refused to appoint them, they would have an injunction on him in less than twenty-four hours, and stop the issue of any more Notary commissions. I met John B. Winters, next, and Judge North, and Mayor Arick, and Washoe Jim, and John O. Earle, and Ah Foo, and John H. Atchinson, and Hong Wo, and Wells Fargo, and Charley Strong, and Bob Morrow, and Gen. Williams, and seventy-two other prominent citizens of Storey county, with a long packtrain laden with their several petitions. I examined their documents and promised to use my influence toward procuring notaryships for the whole tribe. I also drank with them.

I wandered down the street, conversing with every man I met, examining his petition. It became a sort of monomania with me, and I kept it up for two hours with unflagging interest. Finally, I stumbled upon a pensive, travel-worn stranger, leaning against an awning-post. I went up and looked at him. He looked at me. I looked at him again, and again he looked at me. I bent my gaze upon him once more, and says I "Well?" He looked at me very hard, and says he "Well—well what?" Says I, "Well—I would like to examine your petition, if you please." He looked very much astonished—I may say amazed. When he had recovered his presence of mind, he says "what the devil do you mean?" I explained to him that I only wanted to glance over his petition for a notaryship. He said he believed I was a lunatic—he didn't like the unhealthy light in my eye, and he didn't want me to come any closer to him. I asked him if he had escaped the epidemic, and he shuddered and said he didn't know of any epidemic. I pointed to the large placard on the wall: "Coaches will leave the Ormsby House punctually every fifteen minutes, for the Governor's mansion, for the accommodation of notarial aspirants, etc, etc.—Schemerhorn, Agent"—and I asked him if he didn't know enough to understand what that meant? I also pointed to the long procession of petition-laden citizens filing up the street toward the Governor's house, and asked him if he was not aware that all those fellows were going after notarial commissions—that the balance of the people had already gone, and that he and I had the whole town to ourselves? He was astonished again. Then he placed his hand upon his heart, and swore a frightful oath that he had just arrived from over the mountains, and had no petition, and didn't want a notaryship. I gazed upon him a moment in silent rapture, and then clasped him to my breast.

After which, I told him it was my turn to treat, by thunder. Whereupon we entered a deserted saloon, and drank up the contents. We lay upon a billard table in a torpid condition for many minutes. but at last my exile rose up and muttered in a sepulchral voice, "I feel it—O Heavans, I feel it in my veins!" "Feel what?" says I alarmed. Says he, "I feel—O me sainted mother!—I feel—feel—a hankering to be a Notary Public!" And he tore down several yards of wall-paper, and fell to writing a petition on it. Poor devil—he had got it at last, and got it bad. I was seized with the fatal distemper a moment afterward. I wrote a petition with frantic haste, appended a copy of the Directory of Nevada Territory to it, and we fled down the deserted streets to the Governor's office.

But I must draw the curtain upon these harrowing scenes—the very memory of them scorches my brain. Ah, this Legislature has much to answer for in cutting down the number of Notaries Public in this Territory, with their infernal new law.

A FAREWELL

(C. C. Goodwin. "The Prospector," Eureka [Nevada] *Sentinel*, November 27, 1872. Reprinted from the Hamilton [Nevada] *Inland Empire*.)

How strangely to-night our memory flings
From the face of the past the shadowy wings,
And we see far back through the mist and tears,
Which make the record of twenty years;
From the beautiful days in the Golden State,
When Life seemed taking a lease of Fate;
From the wondrous visions of "long ago"
To the naked shade that we call "now."
Those halcyon days; there were four of us then—
Ernest and Ned, wild Tom and Ben.
Now all are gone; Tom was first to die;

We held his hands, closed his glazed eyes,
And many a tear o'er his grave we shed,
As we tenderly pillowed his curly head,
In the shadows deep of the pines that stand
Forever solemn, forever fanned
By the winds that steal through the Golden Gate
And spread their balm o'er the Golden State.
And the others, too, they all are dead!
By the turbid Gila perished Ned;
Brave, noble Ernest, he was lost
Amid Montana's ice and frost:
And Bennie's life went out in gloom
Deep in the Comstock's vaults of doom
And we are left, the last of all,
And as to-night the cold snows fall,
And barbarous winds around us roar,
We think the long past o'er and o'er:
What we have hoped and suffered, all,
From the twenty years rolls back the pall,
From the dusty, thorny, weary track,
As the tortuous path we follow back.
In our childhood's home they think us, there,
A failure, or lost, till our name in the prayer
At eve is forgot. Well, they cannot know
That our toil through heat, through tempest and snow,
While it seemed for naught but a portion of pelf
Was more for them, far more, than ourself.
Well, well, as our hair turns slowly to snow,
The places of childhood more distantly grow.
And our dreams are changing; 'tis home no more.
But shadowy hands from the other shore
Stretch nightly down, and it seems as when
We lived with Tom, Ned, Ernest and Ben.
And the mountains of earth seem dwindling down
And the hills of Eden, with golden crown,

Rise up, and we think, in the last great day
Will our claims above bear a fire assay?
From the slag of earth and the baser stains
Will death's crucible show of precious grains
Enough to give us a standing above
In the mansions of Peace, in the cradle of Love?
And thus do we dream while the tempests beat
While fall on our casement the ice and sleet,
And the fierce winds moan as they sweep the nights
Of these desolate hills, through these desolate nights;
So changed in life since the bright days when
We lived with Tom, Ned, Ernest and Ben.

# Index

*The Mining Frontier* has been cast on the Linotype machine in Caledonia, a face partly inspired by Scotch Modern, which, though popular from the nineteenth century, had grown too wooden and mechanical for twentieth-century taste. By combining some elements from an English design by William Martin, of about 1790, and adding a restrained calligraphic stroke, the late W. A. Dwiggins created Caledonia for present-day book use.

The paper on which this book is printed bears the watermark of the University of Oklahoma Press and is designed for an effective life of at least three hundred years.